The New Tycoons

Since 1996, Bloomberg Press has published books for financial professionals, as well as books of general interest in investing, economics, current affairs, and policy affecting investors and business people. Titles are written by well-known practitioners, BLOOMBERG NEWS® reporters and columnists, and other leading authorities and journalists. Bloomberg Press books have been translated into more than 20 languages.

For a list of available titles, please visit our Web site at www.wiley.com/go/bloombergpress.

The New Tycoons

*Inside the Trillion Dollar
Private Equity Industry
That Owns Everything*

Jason Kelly

BLOOMBERG PRESS
An Imprint of
WILEY

Published by John Wiley & Sons, Inc., Hoboken, New Jersey.
Published simultaneously in Canada.

For general information on our other products and services or for technical support, please contact our Customer Care Department within the United States at (800) 762-2974, outside the United States at (317) 572-3993 or fax (317) 572-4002.

Wiley also publishes its books in a variety of electronic formats. Some content that appears in print may not be available in electronic books. For more information about Wiley products, visit our web site at www.wiley.com.

Library of Congress Cataloging-in-Publication Data:

Kelly, Jason, 1973-
    The new tycoons : inside the trillion dollar private equity industry that owns everything/Jason Kelly.
        p. cm. — (Bloomberg Press series)
    Includes bibliographical references and index.
    ISBN 978-1-118-20546-4 (cloth); ISBN 978-1-118-22851-7(ebk);
    ISBN 978-1-118-24081-6 (ebk); ISBN 978-1-118-26567-3 (ebk)
        1. Private equity.   I. Title.
    HG4751.K45 2012
    332.6—dc23

                                                                    2012017193

Printed in the United States of America
SKY10050259_063023

For Jen, Owen, William, and Henry

"We accept and welcome . . . as conditions to which we must accommodate ourselves, great inequality of environment; the concentration of business, industrial and commercial, in the hands of a few; and the law of competition between these, as being not only beneficial, but essential for the future progress of the race."
—Andrew Carnegie

"There's a certain part of the contented majority who love anybody who is worth a billion dollars."
—John Kenneth Galbraith

Contents

A Visual Tour of Private Equity   xi

Deciphering Private Equity   xv

Prologue   xix

Chapter 1 Find the Money   1

Chapter 2 All the Money in the World   19

Chapter 3 The L Word   43

Chapter 4 "When Was the Last Time
               You Bought a Toilet Seat?"   55

Chapter 5 Modern Art   73

Chapter 6 Put on Your Boots   95

Chapter 7 Aura of Cool   111

Chapter 8 Hundreds and Billions   123

Chapter 9 Take This Exit   141

Chapter 10 The Taxman Cometh   155

Chapter 11 It's a Steve, Steve, Steve World   165

Chapter 12 Not-So-Private Equity   187

Afterword   199
Notes   203
Acknowledgments   211
About the Author   215
Index   217

A Visual Tour
of Private Equity

FOLLOWING THE MONEY

CalPERS,
ADIA,
Harvard

Limited Partners
80%

KKR,
Carlyle, TPG
and
Blackstone

General Partners
20%

FIND

PROFIT IT

Take This Exit

Through dividends, IPOs or sale of
the entire company to another investor
or large corporation, private equity gets
its money back, with a profit.

SELL IT

The Rise of Ops

Jobs may be gained or lost, facilities
opened or closed as the new owners spend
several years reworking the company.

OWN

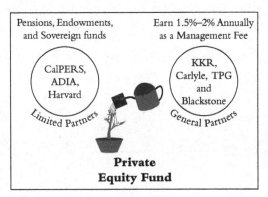

Pensions, Endowments, and Sovereign funds

Earn 1.5%–2% Annually as a Management Fee

CalPERS, ADIA, Harvard

KKR, Carlyle, TPG and Blackstone

Limited Partners

General Partners

Private Equity Fund

GROW IT

The L Word

Wall Street banks provide loans and bonds for deals they help arrange. Leverage gooses returns for private equity, just like a homeowner with a mortgage.

BUY IT

Dealmaking

Buying the company involves wooing existing owners or public shareholders. Internal groups at private equity firms may spend years studying a target before making an offer.

Deciphering
Private Equity

You or someone you know almost certainly works for a company connected to private equity or is invested in a buyout fund through a pension or retirement account. Getting smart about the way these things work means getting comfortable with the alphabet soup of acronyms and abbreviations they use. Some are meant for pure shorthand, but others feel like they're meant to give it a sheen of importance and others to obfuscate what's actually going on. For example: "TPG and KKR aren't likely to exit the TXU LBO through an IPO. There was no way they could do a recap, and the LPs will be lucky to get their money back. The GPs can probably forget about carry and it's going to make a huge dent in the funds' IRRs."

If you're in the business, feel free to skip ahead, but for anyone who's curious about the lingo, here's what you need to sound conversant, with explanations in plain English.

Firms and Players

Bain Capital: The private-equity firm founded by Mitt Romney. Distinct from Bain & Co., the consulting firm, where Romney and others at Bain Capital once worked, and that provided Bain Capital with its start.

Blackstone Group: Founded by Peter G. Peterson and Stephen Schwarzman in 1985 and headquartered in New York. Stock symbol: BX, on the New York Stock Exchange.

Carlyle Group: Founded by William Conway, Daniel D'Aniello, and David Rubenstein in 1987 and headquartered in Washington. Stock symbol: CG on the Nasdaq.

General partner: Abbreviated as GP, it's another term for a private-equity manager. Blackstone, Bain, Carlyle, KKR, and TPG are GPs.

ILPA: The Institutional Limited Partners Association. A group of investors in private-equity funds who conceived a set of guidelines to encourage more transparency and lower fees. Usually pronounced as "ILL-puh," it began as a supper club in the early 1990s and evolved into an influential trade association.

KKR: The firm founded by Jerome Kohlberg, Henry Kravis, and George Roberts in 1976. Headquartered in New York. Trades as KKR on the New York Stock Exchange.

Limited partner: Abbreviated as LP, these are the pensions, endowments, and sovereign wealth funds that commit the money that comprises private-equity funds. Public pensions in California and Washington are examples of LPs.

9 West: The iconic sloping building on West 57th Street in Manhattan that houses KKR, among other private-equity firms, and offers sweeping views of Central Park.

TPG: Created by David Bonderman, James Coulter, and William Price in 1992 and originally called Texas Pacific Group. Headquartered in Fort Worth, Texas, though most of its senior executives work in San Francisco. Not publicly traded.

Industry Terms

AUM: Assets under management. Refers to the value of funds overseen by a private-equity manager plus the value of the companies it owns through those funds.

Carried interest: Also known as "carry," this is the portion of profits a private-equity manager keeps from a successful investment. Unlike salaries earned in other professions, carry is taxed at the lower capital gains rate instead of the tax rate for ordinary income. Some have argued that it should be treated as ordinary income, which would roughly double the taxes paid on this income by managers. Managers argue that carry is investment income akin to the "sweat equity" in an entrepreneurial venture and should be treated like a profit from selling a public stock or bond. The fight boiled over into a mainstream issue amid the Occupy Wall Street protests and the 2012 presidential election.

Dividend recap: Short for dividend recapitalization, this involves a payout to the private-equity manager, usually through additional borrowing against the company's assets. Called recapitalization because it's a way of returning the manager's initial capital investment, it's sparked controversy around how and when private-equity firms get paid.

Exit: Shorthand for how a private-equity firm gains a profit for itself and its investors when it sells the company it originally bought. Firms can "exit" their investment by doing an initial public offering, a sale to another private-equity firm, or a sale to a corporation.

Financial engineering: A term, usually used derisively, for the practice of buying a company with lots of debt, doing very little to the company itself, and selling it quickly for a profit. Private-equity firms increasingly tout their ability to make changes to the underlying business and its operations to prove they aren't simply financial engineers.

Fund: Private-equity firms collect discrete funds to make investments in a variety of companies. A firm typically manages a number of funds. Carlyle alone has 89 active funds around the world.

IPO: Initial public offering. A sale of shares of a company to shareholders who can then buy or sell the stock on an exchange like the New York Stock Exchange or Nasdaq. Private-equity firms including Blackstone, Apollo, and Carlyle have pursued IPOs for their own firms, as well as companies they control.

IRR: Internal rate of return. A common way to measure a fund's performance, this takes into account the amount the manager generates as well as the amount of time the money was invested.

MOIC: Multiple of invested capital. Another performance measure, this calculates how much actual money was generated during the investment period. Investors usually use both IRR and MOIC to judge a fund and its manager's success.

Portfolio: Such as a stock portfolio; private-equity managers use this term to describe the slate of companies they own through their funds.

SWF: Sovereign wealth fund. Refers broadly to pools of capital tied to governments. China, Singapore, and a number of Middle Eastern countries have funds worth hundreds of billions of dollars. These funds are increasingly important limited partners in private-equity funds as well as co-investors.

Vintage: Similar to the term for wine, the year a specific private-equity fund officially started. Since the broader market has an effect on a fund's performance, investors often compare funds of the same vintage.

Prologue

S tanding in Legoland in Carlsbad, California in 2011, fulfilling a
promise to my then eight-year-old son William, it hit me. I was
strolling around a Blackstone-owned property. We'd woken up
in a Homewood Suites, owned by Blackstone-backed Hilton. We'd
driven to the park in a rental car from Hertz, owned by private-equity
firms Carlyle and Clayton, Dubilier & Rice. Practically every time I'd
opened my wallet that day, it had been to a company owned by private
equity. Even on vacation, I couldn't escape.

A few months later, I had dinner with Greg Brenneman, who'd
held top positions at Continental, Burger King, and Quizno's, all
private-equity-owned at the time he was involved. Brenneman is now
the chairman of CCMP Capital, whose investments have included
1-800-Flowers.com and Vitamin Shoppe. We talked at length about the
ubiquity of PE ownership—my J. Crew sweater, the Dollar General
store in my wife's hometown in the Catskills. I started a running list on
my BlackBerry that quickly grew to dozens of examples. Brand names
piled up, from Toys "R" Us to Petco. The more I looked, the more
I found it.

The numbers are staggering. Private-equity firms globally and collectively had almost $3 trillion in assets at the end of 2011.[1] The companies they own account for about 8 percent of the U.S. gross domestic product by one estimate.[2]

Contemplating how they got all that money in the first place triggered another thought, a memory of a colleague mentioning that her mother was a teacher in suburban Toronto and had her retirement account in the hands of the Ontario Teachers' Pension Plan. I'd profiled that pension for *Bloomberg Businessweek* in early 2010—they were pursuing a strategy of buying companies directly, like vitamin retailer GNC. Thousands of other pensions, endowments, and government funds, from California to Singapore, were committing hundreds of billions to the likes of Blackstone and KKR. I thought of my in-laws, each with a pension. They, and millions of folks like them were, usually unknowingly, owners of dozens of companies on my ever-growing BlackBerry list.

While the business of buying and selling companies is far from new, the emergence of these players was relatively sudden. What began as a cottage industry known as bootstrapping and leveraged buyouts in the 1970s and 1980s, had blossomed in the 1990s as a handful of small players started to grow rapidly and others, eyeing a huge opportunity, hung out their own shingles. Somewhere toward the turn of the twenty-first century, the more genteel "private equity" became the chosen descriptor. The name may have changed, but the basic business model was the same: collect money, pair it with debt, and buy a company with the intent of selling it down the line for a profit.

The period from 2000 to the present changed everything. Small private partnerships accustomed to rounding up a few hundred million dollars suddenly were raising funds well in excess of $10 billion, accepting huge sums of money from pensions and endowments eager for investment returns topping 20 or 30 percent a year. Wall Street became an eager lender, developing new ways to provide the debt financing in order to get the associated fees. Big investment banks took to investing alongside their clients.

All that money meant that almost nothing was out of bounds for private equity, and 2005 to 2007 saw a spate of deals for companies deeply entrenched in the infrastructure of our everyday lives, from hospital giant HCA to credit card processor First Data to hotelier Hilton. My own introduction was a baptism by fire; I began covering the industry in February 2007. During my first week, news leaked of the biggest-ever takeover, the leveraged buyout of power producer TXU.

What happened next was a different sort of education. Deal making came to a screeching halt with the credit freeze of 2007 and 2008 that triggered the broader global financial crisis. The private-equity managers generally hunkered down, and tried to soothe their own anxious investors pummeled by the public markets—investors who also were worried about what they owned through their buyout funds. Unlike hedge funds, where a bad trade can mean huge losses, an ill-conceived private-equity deal can linger. When the dust settled, private-equity firms still owned all of the companies they'd bought in the boom.

Emerging from the crisis, existential questions abounded. My Legoland epiphany demonstrated just how embedded private equity was in our everyday lives. What seemed like an arcane corner of finance when I arrived was actually central to all of us and very few people actually knew who they were or what they did.

Reporting and writing about business, especially finance and especially in New York, can sometimes feel like a demented sports beat, simply keeping score and tracking rich people getting richer or marginally less rich. But in this case, that's just scratching the surface. What these guys are doing matters to all of us in some form or fashion.

Private equity by its nature and design, is secretive, a breathtakingly wealthy corner of the world where the names only occasionally escape the business pages, names like Stephen Schwarzman, David Bonderman, and David Rubenstein. The relatively small firms they've created, by virtue of what they were able to buy with those ever-growing pools gave them outsized influence as owners and employers. Blackstone, Schwarzman's firm, alone counts almost a million employees through companies it controls. They are modern day Wizards of Oz—the men behind the private-equity curtain.

The best way to understand these men is to look at what they've created, and it's startling how much each of the largest private-equity firms are mirrors of the founders themselves. There's an egotism at the center of the whole exercise. After all, each of these men, some more willingly than others, ditched successful careers because they deeply believed they saw something that only a handful of others did. And then they went a step further. They decided to build what have become massively influential institutions meant to outlast them.

To understand what they created and what it means to have them so entrenched in our lives, I decided to follow the money to reveal through their words and actions the implications of their activities to fix actions. The trail begins in the sanitized meeting rooms of public pensions, moves to palatial suites in skyscrapers with top-of-the-world views, and on to discount stores and pizza chains and hotels, before it comes all the way back to those same vanilla pension offices and eventually to the retirement checks of teachers and firefighters and, in one of several twists, even some workers of the companies owned by private-equity firms.

Along the way, that money finds itself augmented by debt and pushed into companies that may thrive, implode, maintain, or simply fade away. The money befuddles Washington lawmakers and regulators, in a debate sharpened by the presidential candidacy of Mitt Romney. His private-equity career has brought the industry into the public consciousness in a never-before-seen way, prompting its largest players to explain themselves with at times surprising candor.

Their contemplation stems not only from a bright spotlight but from their own personal situations. Having created unbelievable amounts of wealth for themselves, they're mulling their own legacies, in terms of the empires they've built and what they'll ultimately do with their riches.

With all the talk of retirement, it's easy to forget the relative youth of the industry. I've come to think of private equity as a teenager with a lot of potential, but still struggling with adolescent tendencies—at times unresponsive, rash, selfish, and fluctuating between arrogance and self-doubt. By virtue of some hard work and a lot of luck, it's ended up in a position to potentially be an upstanding member of society. To ignore it or wish it away is foolhardy. It's here and the influence is growing. And whether it's the price of your morning cup of coffee, your bed sheets on a business trip, or the size of your retirement check in the mailbox, you're involved.

Chapter 1

Find the Money

Oregon to Abu Dhabi

From Steve Schwarzman's corner office 44 stories above Park Avenue, the northern landscape of New York City unfurls before you, Manhattan melting into the Bronx. It calls to mind the old cartoon, "The New Yorker's View of the World," where the details of the city quickly give way to everything else beyond. On a clear day, Schwarzman can see both the George Washington and Tappan Zee bridges as the Hudson River snakes northward. Looking west, he can peer deep into New Jersey. In both views he can also pick out a couple of his fiercest competitors and sometime collaborators. Henry Kravis's office is perched on the 42nd floor of a building on 57th Street, a 10-minute walk from Schwarzman. A five-minute stroll to the west is the Carlyle Group's New York office, its biggest outpost despite its Washington headquarters. When Carlyle co-founder David Rubenstein is in town, he sits on the 41st floor. A couple more avenues toward the Hudson, TPG's David

Bonderman and Jim Coulter decamp 37 stories up when they're visiting from San Francisco.

This dozen square blocks in the middle of Manhattan is the undisputed home of the private-equity industry. Walk into just about any skyscraper along Park Avenue and the building's directory is bound to feature a handful of firms practicing leveraged buyouts or some variation thereof. This is where the moneymen ply their trade. At first glance, they are indistinguishable from the rest of the always-in-a-hurry New Yorkers of a certain stature, ferried about in black sedans, catching up and cutting deals over expense-account lunches at restaurants tucked into the towers.

The story of how the money flows really begins on the opposite side of the country, along U.S. Interstate 5. Dotted along the country's western-most north-south highway, the only road to touch both Canada and Mexico, sits a handful of nondescript offices that have played a crucial role in the formation and the history of private equity. It's there where the journey begins, and what happens from there has profound consequences on the global economy and our individual livelihoods.

Any serious exploration of private equity has to start with the simple question: Where does the money come from? Money doesn't magically appear in private equity funds. Someone has to give it to them, and what buyout managers discovered over the past 30 to 40 years is that there are a lot of someones—pensions needing to pay their retirees, universities looking to grow their endowments, rich people looking to get richer, and foreign governments looking to diversify their state-run funds—willing to listen to their promise to turn money into more money. Lots more than they could get simply by plunking it in stocks or bonds. These are the so-called limited partners in private equity.

■ ■ ■

Tigard, Oregon, is a suburb of Portland, about a 20-minute drive from downtown. The low-slung building that houses the offices of the state pension fund's investment division sits a couple of blocks from a sandwich shop called Big Town Hero, a local chain.

It was in a small conference room at the Oregon Treasurer's office in suite 190 that Hamilton "Tony" James, the president of the Blackstone

Group, found himself in July 2010 with a group of Oregonians seated in a semicircle around him, peppering him with questions about his funds' performance, the types of fees he was charging, and the state of his current investments.

James arrived confident that he could win a commitment, which would be the state fund's first investment with Blackstone after decades of trying. Oregon's staff had already vetted Blackstone's proposal and met or talked with fund-raisers who worked for James numerous times. The investment board, wary about the damage the global financial crisis had inflicted on their investments across the board, wanted to ask James several questions to his face.

For an hour, he fielded mostly friendly, but occasionally pointed, questions. "That all sounds really great, and you probably raised money at the right time so you could go out and get deals," board member Katherine Durant said to James during the meeting. "That said, why does Fund V look so bad?" James said the firm's fifth buyout fund was valued at a loss of 2 percent, compared with a 7 percent loss in the Standard & Poor's 500 Index during a specific period.[1] Another board member pressed James to promise that they wouldn't throw fancy investor meetings that the pension would have to pay to attend. James smoothly assured him that instead of a resort, they held their meetings in New York, at the Waldorf-Astoria hotel, which had the benefit of being Blackstone-owned through its control of the Hilton hotel chain.

James eventually emerged victorious, with a $200 million commitment for Blackstone Capital Partners VI, a fund that eventually would total in excess of $16 billion when James and his colleagues finished collecting commitments the following year. To secure Oregon's money, Blackstone agreed to reduce some fees, a deal it then extended to all of its investors. The firm already had told potential investors it would lower the management fee to 1 percent a year, from 1.5 percent, for those who committed $1 billion or more.

Less than a year later, the same group of Oregonians entertained a visit from KKR co-founder and co-CEO George Roberts and committed $525 million to KKR's latest fund.[2] While that was smaller than previous investments (Oregon invested $1.3 billion in KKR's 2006 fund), the new pool was targeted at $8 billion, about half the size of the previous fund. Roberts may have edged out James in the fund sweepstakes by dint of familiarity. He was making a pitch to a group he had sold on KKR for the first time three decades previous.

Roberts made his first meaningful contacts with Oregon's pension fund in the early 1980s, a series of meetings that helped create the modern private equity, industry. Oregon is widely credited with being among the first U.S. pension funds to commit meaningful sums to private-equity funds and then keep re-upping. Oregon was quickly followed by the state pension up the road in Washington State. By 1990, the California Public Employees' Retirement System, known as CalPERS, would create a program for so-called alternative investments like private equity that would become the nation's biggest such effort.

Soon pensions across the country got into the act and, in addition to going to the likes of Tigard and Olympia, private-equity managers trekked to Austin, Texas, and Harrisburg, Pennsylvania, to make their case.

The motivation for the pensions was simple: investment returns that weren't available anywhere else, money they needed to pay their retirees what they'd promised. KKR, and later its competitors, proved they could take a small slice of a pension and double it, or better. Oregon's early investments in KKR funds yielded more than three times what the pension gave Roberts and co-founder Henry Kravis, an annual average return in some cases of close to 40 percent a year.

University endowments also are influential LPs, and schools like Yale and Harvard have benefited from long associations with some of the most successful buyout managers. Endowments are attractive to private-equity managers in part because schools tend to be comfortable locking some of their money up for long periods of time, a key element of private equity's business model. Funds tend to have lifespans of 10 years, giving the managers the ability to spend the first handful of years investing the money, and the latter part of the fund selling those investments to reap profits for themselves and for their backers. Unlike hedge funds, where the best managers can reap profits in seconds or minutes, private-equity managers' pitch involves buying companies that will take in most cases years to fix, expand, or grow but will eventually generate huge gains when they're sold. Pensions are arguably the most interesting way to explore the limited partner world because they ultimately invest money for hundreds of thousands of retirees. They also have seen fit to release some of their data to the public, making it easier to analyze their strategies and those of the managers they choose.

Without these institutions, without the people sitting in that conference room in Oregon and their counterparts in state and national capitals around the country and around the world, Tony James wouldn't have his job.

And so that day in Oregon, James cut the sort of deal that makes it all possible. Oregon agreed to give Blackstone the responsibility for $200 million for the next 10 years. The pension agreed to pay the firm $3 million each year (1.5 percent of the total commitment) as a management fee, a levy meant to help Blackstone pay for salaries and rent. Blackstone would spend roughly five years using Oregon's money to buy companies and roughly the next five selling what it bought, hopefully at a profit.

Blackstone agreed that as those profits came back, 80 percent of them would go back to Oregon, with 20 percent staying at Blackstone. This is the fundamental partnership that defines private equity, between the investors (referred to as limited partners, "limiteds," or simply "LPs") and the managers (known as general partners, or "GPs").

James, Schwarzman, and a handful of other Blackstone executives would replicate this process dozens of times during a two-year period, piecing together promises of money like Oregon's until they were satisfied they had an ample war chest. In mid-2011, they would "close" the fund, shutting it off from new commitments. At about $16 billion, it was the biggest pool for leveraged buyouts raised since the end of the global credit crisis. While less than Blackstone's record-setting $21.7 billion fund that closed in 2007, here was proof that money was still available despite the still-visible scars of the financial crisis.

■ ■ ■

The terms, though, had changed. Big investors, especially those outside the U.S. public pension system, have long weighed how to recapture some of the fees they pay to managers like Blackstone, KKR, and Carlyle. The most aggressive in this regard have been, interestingly, a handful of Canadian pension plans that have built large in-house investment teams to effectively work around the big private-equity firms.

One of the most powerful investors in Toronto, Canada's financial capital, sits not along Bay Street in the downtown banking district but in a squat suburban office building a 20-minute subway ride away.

The Ontario Teachers' Pension Plan during the past two decades has helped raise some existential questions about the private equity industry and pressed some of the most important economic issues around the business. Teachers' has effectively voted with its feet, limiting its traditional third-party investments to a small group of managers, building an in-house staff to make direct deals, most of the time skirting the private-equity barons altogether.

The strategy was born largely of necessity. In the early 1990s, Teachers' saw what most every pension that was paying attention did—that leveraged buyout firms were delivering amazing returns to their small clutch of existing investors, far outstripping what those investors could get from public equities and fixed income. With a bias toward domestic managers, they looked around Canada for private-equity funds and found not very many. So they started their own effort.

It barely survived its infancy because the first deal was a disaster. In 1991, Teachers' paid $15.75 million for White Rose Crafts & Nursery Sales, a company that promptly went bankrupt within a year. The wipeout stands as a testament to the Canadians' fortitude and a reminder of how deals can fail—it's engraved right alongside the fund's best deals in the Teachers' boardroom at headquarters, dubbed the "Wall of Fame and Shame."

Teachers' has gone on to invest in the likes of vitamin seller GNC, which it bought with Ares and later took public, as well as Canada's Yellow Pages Group and luggage maker Samsonite. The fund also at one point owned several local sports franchises, including the Toronto Maple Leafs hockey club, the Raptors pro basketball team, and the city's professional soccer outfit; it agreed to sell the company that controlled those teams in 2011. Its total assets under management were C$117.1 billion ($115 billion) at the end of that year.

During the LBO boom and bust, Teachers' arguably became most famous for a deal it ended up not doing. The fund was part of a consortium that had won a fierce auction to buy BCE, Canada's biggest phone company. The $42.3 billion purchase price would have made it the second-biggest leveraged buyout ever announced, just behind KKR and TPG's $43.2 billion TXU deal, according to data compiled by Bloomberg.

When the credit markets seized in mid-2007, almost everyone involved in the deal got nervous, especially the banks who'd agreed to finance the deal, including Citigroup, Deutsche Bank, and Toronto-Dominion. Were the deal to happen, the banks would be stuck with billions of dollars worth of debt tied to BCE on their balance sheets. The debt would be valued at less than face value and no one would want to buy it, and estimates at the time pegged the immediate losses to the banks if the deal went through at C$10 billion.[3]

Teachers', along with Providence Equity and Madison Dearborn and the buyout arm of Merrill Lynch, were similarly worried. The deal had been conceived in an economic environment defined by confident consumers and heady growth prospects. Now the would-be owners were staring at owning a huge corporation going into a nasty recession. All the parties scrambled through 2008 to recut the deal or get out of it. In December of that year, they got a much needed reprieve—an auditor judged that the company would be insolvent if the deal went forward, which allowed the buyers to walk away, and the banks to breathe a huge sigh of relief. A year after the deal collapsed, Teachers' Chief Executive Officer Jim Leech was understated, saying, "It was the product of a euphoric time."[4]

The BCE near-miss didn't dissuade Leech from his strategy, which blends direct investing and commitments to firms like Ares and Providence, where Leech and his team have determined the firm has a specific expertise they can't easily replicate.

Leech has become a strong and vocal advocate for the pension players in the equation, publicly questioning fee structures that he sees as unfair to the limited partners. "Private-equity firms are first and foremost in business for themselves," Leech told me when I called to talk to him about the state of the business in late 2011. "They are perfectly misaligned on the fee side. I believe that's because a lot of investment bankers got into the business and perverted the model."

It's harder to stray, Leech said, when your investors are stopping by your office all the time. Most days, a handful of retired teachers show up at Teachers' to deal with some sort of question. "The reason we can keep focused is we know who we work for," he said. "In many asset management firms, the people who make the investments never even see their clients."

The Teachers' hybrid model has been adopted selectively elsewhere. The Canada Pension Plan Investment Board, its Toronto neighbor, hired Mark Wiseman, Leech's former lieutenant at Teachers', in part to pursue a direct strategy. CPP has emerged as a significant direct investor and frequent co-investor in deals like Dollar General, Nielsen, and Univision. CPP has a larger number of investments than Teachers' into traditional private-equity funds, with commitments to Blackstone, KKR, and TPG.

Like Teachers', Wiseman's group is an active investor and engages heartily with the managers it backs. While limited partners in general are asking for more information, CPP is among the few who will actually show up at a manager's office for more information, and to soak up the knowledge and expertise of the GP.

Public pensions in the United States quietly grumble that even if they wanted to pursue a Teachers' or CPP-like strategy of direct investment, they couldn't. U.S. pensions have neither the government permission, the political will to seek it, or the staff to execute a strategy like Leech's or Wiseman's. Part of the secret sauce for the Canadians is an ability to pay something closer to market rate for their staff, or at least far in excess of what a comparable staffer at a U.S. plan would make.

Leech earned C$4.38 million ($4.39 million) total compensation in 2010 and Teacher's head of investments, Neil Petroff, earned C$3.5 million, according to Teachers' annual report that year. That's almost six times more than Joseph Dear, the chief investment officer at CalPERS, who earned $552,052 in 2010, the most recent data available.[5] While Leech may not be bidding against tycoons like Steve Schwarzman and Henry Kravis for a house, the paychecks far outstrip his U.S. peers.

Where the Americans and Canadians have found the most fertile common ground is an effort that also has its roots in Toronto. The Institutional Limited Partners Association began as an informal supper club in Canada in the early 1990s, around the time Teachers' was beginning its grand experiment. In the wake of the financial crisis, it's become a much-needed megaphone for the institutional investor community to voice their concerns about the excesses embedded in the private equity industry.

To get a private-equity manager's attention in 2010 and 2011, especially if you had a pot of money to invest, you just had to utter the word "ILPA" (most people pronounce it as "ILL-puh"). That's because, in 2009, ILPA released a set of investing "principles" that rattled the world of private equity for a simple reason: The industry's biggest backers had never gotten together before and spoken with anything resembling a common voice.

The story of the ILPA Private Equity Principles, as they're officially called, goes back to the financial crisis, when the biggest pensions were scratching their heads about what had just happened to them and their portfolios. The question was more than academic—all of their investments had been crushed in the crisis as stocks plunged. Even the best hedge funds posted losses (though less than the broader indices), and private equity for its part was essentially frozen. The global meltdown had another real impact on pensions especially—they realized their own underfunding woes had become a full-blown crisis. Public pensions in the United States as of 2010 were facing $3.6 trillion in unfunded liabilities, according to a study by Joshua Rauh of Northwestern University and Robert Novy-Marx of the University of Rochester.[6]

That left pensions in a pickle with private equity. Clearly, they needed the returns that buyout managers had delivered over the years. In a time of effectively zero interest rates, the siren song of double-digit annual returns was more than compelling. And yet the pension managers ranged from befuddled to furious at the behavior they'd witnessed over the previous decade, especially the high fees they'd paid in return for what was feeling like middling performance.

Having poured money into funds raised during the first years of the new century, they watched as deals crept in size to never-before-seen heights in 2006 and 2007. Private-equity firms outmaneuvered each other on some deals, then pooled money with other firms—a practice known as "clubbing"—to buy bigger companies. The net effect was extraordinary exposure to giant deals, especially for big investors with commitments to multiple managers. Take Freescale, the semiconductor firm taken private in 2006 by Blackstone, TPG, Carlyle, and Permira. CalPERS had commitments to every one of the firms involved in the deal, according to data posted on its website, a bet made all the more painful as that deal ran into a buzz saw of a bad economy and the failure of its biggest customer.

Private equity had long been touted as uncorrelated to the broader markets, its illiquidity—a technical way of saying you couldn't get your money out anytime you wanted—seen as a safe haven of sorts. When the financial markets cratered around the world in 2008, private equity was far from immune. While they weren't forced to sell what they owned, the companies they owned were struggling. And the buyout firms' investors were worried. And mad.

The stars aligned in 2009 to rally investors. That January, a group of roughly a dozen U.S. and Canadian pension managers—together they represented more than $1 trillion—met in a conference room at the Denver airport with the express purpose of talking about private-equity managers and whether they could grab control of the discussion around the industry's economics. What became informally known as "the Denver Group" decided while snacking on peanuts to come up with a wish list they could bring to private-equity managers.

The meeting was the brainchild of a Texan named Steven LeBlanc, a senior managing director at the Teacher Retirement System of Texas, a $110 billion pension fund run from Austin that has 1.3 million members. LeBlanc had responsibility for about $35 billion, the slug that's been designated for private capital, which encompasses private equity and real estate.

LeBlanc, whose mother was a teacher's aide, took the Texas Teachers job after a career spent on the other side of the table, raising money for, and investing, real estate funds. His last job in the private sector was as the CEO of Summit Properties, a real estate investment trust (REIT), where he earned shareholders a 144 percent return during his tenure. He took a job teaching real estate at the University of Texas, a formalized way to do the mentoring he'd always enjoyed while he plotted his next move. Then Britt Harris called.

Harris was the chief investment officer of Texas Teachers and worked to convince LeBlanc to join the pension. LeBlanc pressed back—the teachers at the time were organized to treat private equity and real estate separately and he wanted them both. Harris put them together and LeBlanc took the job in 2008, at a 75 percent pay cut from his last corporate gig.

LeBlanc relished the fox-in-the-henhouse situation he'd created for himself and immediately started asking questions inside and outside the organization. As the broader economic situation worsened and he watched scores of private equity and real estate funds stumble through the post-crisis world, his voice only got louder. He found like-minded LPs who wanted to take action, which is how he found himself in Denver that January.

The small clutch in Denver wasn't the only group talking about pulling private-equity back into alignment. That March, in Atlanta, ILPA held an annual meeting where the group's executive director, Kathy Jeramaz-Larson, held a working session with attendees about the same issues of transparency (what exactly are you doing with my money), and fees (what am I paying you, when and why). During the subsequent months, the Denver group and ILPA initiatives melded and refined the principles.

The first version, released in September 2009, was strident in terms of public statements by pensions. Citing the complexity and length of agreements between private-equity managers and their investors, the principles read in part that "it has become increasingly difficult to focus on what aligns the interests of the limited partner with the general partner."[7] What it boiled down to was pretty simple: Tell us exactly what you're doing and make tons of money only when we do. Private equity's biggest investors were for the first time singing from the same songbook, and most buyout managers didn't like the tune. ILPA's intent was to get both sides of the equation—LPs and GPs— to publicly endorse the principles. Most private-equity firms balked. Despite ILPA's explanation to the contrary, buyout firms viewed the principles as an all-or-nothing proposition and were worried they'd be blessing a set of rules they couldn't, or wouldn't, ultimately comply with.

LeBlanc didn't like that. He and his staff sent out a detailed survey to Texas Teachers' own limited partners to drill down into the document and find out what individual firms did and didn't like in the principles. He and a handful of other ILPA board members spent much of 2010 working the managers personally, figuring out how to revise the principles to get a larger number on board. In early 2011, more than a year after the initial volley, version 2.0 of the principles was released.

The language was less aggressive ("This release retains the key tenets of the first Principles release while increasing their focus, clarity, and practicality"[8]) and ILPA made it clear that this was not an all-or-nothing document. Within weeks, KKR, arguably the best-known brand name in private equity, publicly endorsed the new version. Blackstone, Carlyle, and TPG followed.

The ILPA principles are seen as a boon, especially to institutions with smaller staffs who don't have the time or resources for extensive due diligence on a manager. The principles can serve as a cheat sheet, or at least a starting point for every fund-raising discussion. Understaffed pensions feel emboldened to press for better terms, knowing that their brethren were making similar demands. "It's a game-changer," said Joncarlo Mark, a former senior portfolio manager at CalPERS who served as chairman of ILPA from 2007 to 2010.[9]

LeBlanc has another set of principles specifically for his pension, a PowerPoint manifesto of sorts called The Texas Way that takes the principles a step further, his way of hitting the reset button with the private-equity firms.

I first met LeBlanc in October 2011, as he was finishing a dinner at Brasserie 8½, a French restaurant that sits just below 57th Street in midtown Manhattan. The name of the place is a nod to the famous-in-finance address of the building, 9 West 57th Street, known colloquially in private-equity and investment circles simply as "9 West." It's the longtime home of KKR, and fans of the book *Barbarians at the Gate* will recall many scenes set there. The building also houses private-equity firms Apollo, Providence, and Silver Lake.

He was finishing dinner with Scott Nuttall of KKR. As the firm's global head of capital and one of Roberts's and Kravis's chief lieutenants, Nuttall has broad responsibility within the firm, including fund-raising and investor relations. During the past several years, he's overseen a rapid expansion of those efforts at KKR, growing the staff from about half a dozen to more than 40 employees around the world. The biggest investors like LeBlanc get a lot of special attention.

How big and how special LeBlanc was would become publicly apparent several weeks later. The next morning, LeBlanc was back at 9 West for a separate meeting with Apollo's top executives. At the two meetings, he was wrapping up a deal to commit a total of

$6 billion to KKR and Apollo. The sweeping mandate of $3 billion to each firm was an unprecedented agreement in its scope.

Because of the size of the commitment, KKR and Apollo agreed to lower management fees than they'd usually charge, a major victory for LeBlanc, who had pushed, through the ILPA principles and The Texas Way, to lower those levies and put the bulk of the economic benefit for the private-equity firms on the back end. In other words, don't let them get rich getting the money; let them get rich when they make money for the investors.

KKR and Apollo got their respective money on different terms, too. Instead of committing money to a single discrete strategy, Teachers told KKR and Apollo to use the money across a variety of investments, from traditional buyouts to energy to debt. In addition, the agreement had a "recycle" provision that gave each firm the ability to plow some of the pension's profits right back into investments instead of returning the cash and going through the time-consuming and costly process of asking for it again. The biggest investors, like Texas Teachers, CalPERS, and sovereign wealth funds, are hamstrung to some extent by their size and the need to put large amounts of money to work in big slugs. The theory is that with fewer firms to oversee, pensions can do a better job with that oversight. They're more likely to see a manager straying from his stated investment strategy if their attention is focused. LeBlanc's desire to put more money with fewer managers is a key tenet of The Texas Way.

His particular approach is to create a "Premier List," an intense screening process to assess managers up front and then actively manage them once they do win a commitment. The best performers get more and more money, the worst get thrown out of the program, either through attrition (not re-upping on the next fund) or by being sold on the secondary market, where a handful of specialty funds shop for unwanted stakes in private-equity funds.

What's interesting is the confidence, and at times ferocity, with which pensions and other investors in private equity are evaluating their managers. The new approach is being driven largely by pension executives like LeBlanc, who've been in the room all along, just in a different seat. They know all the tricks of the trade and are blending their experience with the leverage provided by efforts like ILPA. (LeBlanc ultimately decided to leave that seat, after fulfilling what he and Harris described as a five-year plan. He stepped down to rejoin the private sector in mid-2012).

Other former private-equity executives have taken on top roles at pensions. In New York City, Lawrence Schloss in 2011 undertook an ambitious plan to coordinate the investments of the numerous employee plans for city workers.

Schloss also set about cutting the number of managers the city worked with, aiming to reduce it to 70 from more than 100 when he arrived at the start of 2010. The reason wasn't just the large number of relationships, but poor performance. For the 12 years before he arrived, the average annual rate of return was 6.8 percent, which he characterized as "not very good," especially in light of the pension's desired 8 percent a year return for its entire portfolio. Yet the good managers stood to get more money under Schloss. He said in 2011 he was raising the percentage of the fund allocated for private equity to 6.5 percent from 4 percent.[10]

Across the Hudson River in New Jersey, Robert Grady is the chairman of the New Jersey Investment Council. He's a former managing director at Carlyle who at one time was responsible for the firm's venture capital activities. He left Carlyle in 2009 and joined a small private-equity company in Wyoming called Cheyenne Capital. Grady's pursuing a similar strategy of more money to fewer managers. At the New Jersey Division of Investment's monthly meeting in December 2011, Grady unveiled a deal with Blackstone that was similar in scope and tone to the tie-up between KKR, Apollo, and the Texas teachers. New Jersey approved a plan to give Blackstone $1.8 billion, $1.5 billion of which would be divided into so-called separate accounts, pools that contain only New Jersey money instead of commingling with other investors' commitments. Those allow Blackstone and New Jersey to invest together on individual investments, in this case a pool each for traditional buyouts, credit investments, and energy deals. New Jersey committed another $300 million into funds that included other Blackstone clients designed for natural resources, credit, and the firm's flagship buyout fund.

With the deal, Blackstone brought its total New Jersey commitments pledged in a 12-month period to $2.5 billion, the most it had attracted from a single investor during one year in its history. What did

New Jersey get? In addition to the promise of future profits, Blackstone agreed to cut its fees to the tune of $122 million over the life of the agreement, according to New Jersey's calculations.[11] Blackstone cut a similar deal in May 2012 with CalPERS, agreeing to manage $500 million in a separate account for the giant pension. The clear message to Tony James and his cohorts was that the money is there, in some cases more than was available even at the height of the private-equity frenzy in 2006 and 2007. But from Oregon to New Jersey, the money's a lot harder to get and you've got to assure your backers that they'll get paid before you do. The relationships are different once you get on a plane bound for points overseas.

■ ■ ■

The Abu Dhabi Investment Authority occupies a soaring tower along the Corniche, the beachside road in the capital of the United Arab Emirates. Abu Dhabi is lesser known than its fellow emirate Dubai, about an hour's drive through the desert, the long stretches broken only by what appear to be gates to Gulf-front palaces. Dubai gained international prominence in the first decade of this century for its unbelievable growth and shows of wealth, and the real estate crash that followed in 2009. It still boasts the tallest building in the world, the Burj Al Khalifa, its name an honorific to the president of the UAE and ruler of Abu Dhabi.

Abu Dhabi, which sits on a massive oil reserve, bailed out its ultimately poorer, and oil-bereft, cousin Dubai after the collapse, leaving clusters of see-through buildings and sprawling half-finished developments like Dubai World. ADIA remains one of the most influential investors in the world, by virtue of its size and tentacles into money managers around the world. The government won't disclose how big ADIA actually is, but studies have pegged ADIA's assets at around $750 billion and have called it the largest sovereign wealth fund.[12] With ADIA and its brethren funds in the Gulf Cooperation Council enjoying a rise in oil prices through the early 2000s, the region became an increasingly important subsector of potential limited partners. While Dubai favors glitz and spectacle and made a name for itself by pushing for superlatives, I found Abu Dhabi to be much more understated, the opulence less prominent. And yet it's clear that money is abundant, much more so than at the public pension funds back in the United States. After showing ID and saying who I was there to visit, I was escorted to a small table and offered a menu with various coffee and tea beverages served by a waiter. Once upstairs, I took in panoramic views of the emirate, which sits on the Arabian Gulf. It felt much more KKR than CalPERS.

ADIA was among the investors who went a step further than investing in funds, seeking a tighter relationship with some private-equity managers. The Abu Dhabi fund bought a stake in Apollo itself, paying to own a slice of the manager, not just participating in the funds. Carlyle cut a similar deal with Abu Dhabi-based Mubadala Development Company, another arm of the government whose specific charge was buying stakes in and backing companies that could benefit the emirate directly.

The Middle East was an alluring and seemingly untapped part of the world for the private-equity barons, both as a proven source of capital and potentially as a source of deals. After a speed bump around the financial crisis, when a number of funds in that region made bad bets on U.S. and European financial institutions, the latter theory about a source of capital has continued to be true. However, the notion that the Middle East could be a lucrative emerging market for deals has thus far not played out.

The confluence of capital-raising and deal-making came into the open in 2007, when the well-regarded Super Return conference series decided to put on a regional version in Dubai. This was the time when Dubai had burst onto the international financial scene, with gleaming skyscrapers, an archipelago of manmade islands meant to mimic a world atlas with "countries" for sale to be developed as private getaways, and a nightlife whose thinly veiled excesses evoked Las Vegas.

The collective private equity industry was salivating (mostly over the investment opportunities). Here was a dream combination—resident capital that appeared to lack the infrastructure and experience found in New York and London but wanted it; local companies eager to grow to meet the crushing demand of a fast-growing regional economy; and a market that was bending traditional financial and business rules tied to Islamic mores in order to accommodate outside investment to help fuel the growth.

Carlyle co-founder Rubenstein and TPG co-founder Bonderman, two of the industry's best-known and successful practitioners, headlined

Super Return Middle East, each man using it as an excuse to make his pitch publicly and then meet with existing and would-be investors around the GCC. Ten months later, and only weeks after Lehman Brothers filed for bankruptcy, throwing the U.S. and global markets into turmoil, Blackstone's Schwarzman showed up at the second-annual event, along with Kravis. Schwarzman—wrongly—declared the end of the credit crisis that had taken deep root with the collapse of Bear Stearns earlier in the year, praising U.S. regulators for their swift action. And at that moment, Dubai and its neighbors in the Gulf were at least removed from the troubles back in the U.S., and potentially a safe haven of real growth as the West stumbled.

Carlyle, given its penchant for covering the world through a combination of Rubenstein visits and local executives, in 2007 opened an outpost in the Dubai International Financial Centre, becoming the first large U.S. firm to set up an office there. The DIFC, built around a signature squared arch known as The Gate, became an expat banker hub, where French-cuffed Europeans and Americans mixed with Emiratis and other Arabs in dishdasha, the traditional dress. In the food court below the Gate still stands an outlet that's an emblem to U.S./Gulf private-equity cooperation. Caribou Coffee, a Starbucks rival started in Minnesota, was eventually bought by Arcapita, a private-equity firm in Bahrain funded by Arab investors whose North American offices are located in Atlanta.* KKR eventually followed Carlyle to Dubai with a small office, as did Blackstone. All of them heralded the region as a fast-growing land of opportunity, with potential deals aplenty. They conceded that it wouldn't be like the United States or Europe, with traditional leveraged buyouts, take-privates, and transactions that gave the U.S. GPs controlling stakes in their targets. Instead, they would more likely be partners with local investors, or buy minority stakes in high-growth companies.

The opportunity, of course, turned out to be a mirage, at least immediately, and especially in and around Dubai. By late 2009, the emirate was enveloped in a real estate and credit crisis of its own, requiring the bailout from Abu Dhabi. It became a symbol of excess in its own right, shorthand for bubble.

---

*Arcapita filed for Chapter 11 bankruptcy protection in 2012.

Yet Dubai's troubles and the so-far missed, or elusive, opportunities in terms of investments can't overshadow the enormous role the sovereign wealth funds continue to play in the world of private equity. By most accounts, they will become the biggest source of capital for private-equity funds within the next decade, a shift that stands to have profound implications on the form and strategy of the industry. The sovereign wealth landscape is increasingly influenced by Asia, and especially China. As in many other aspects of the global economy, China has emerged as both an ally and potential threat to private equity. China Investment Corp., a sovereign wealth fund, bought a stake in Blackstone around the time of its IPO in 2007. Schwarzman and his biggest competitors have pursued deals in China. At the same time, China has feverishly developed its own private equity industry to rival their U.S. counterparts. All of this serves to add another element of competition to the mix.

Carlyle's Rubenstein believes that the big investors will continue to press for lower fees and in some cases ask for co-investment vehicles that give them more discretion over where their money goes. Meanwhile some SWFs will follow the Ontario Teachers' model and nurture staffs that can invest money directly and avoid third-party managers for at least some of their private-equity strategy. "The economic model is evolving a little bit," Rubenstein said.

He maintains that ultimately people like him—professional private-equity investors—will win the lion's share of money to be invested in leveraged buyouts and related businesses. It's an admittedly self-interested opinion. But the tens of billions he raised across the world during the past two decades give his take a little more credence.

Chapter 2

All the Money in the World

Inside Carlyle

D avid Rubenstein begins most every speech he gives with a survey of the audience, polling to see what type of crowd he's speaking to. "How many of you are LPs? GPs? Consultants?" Depending on what's happening in the world, he might ask whether Greece is going to default or whether the Democrats will keep control of the U.S. House of Representatives. Usually he'll throw a funny question in, like, "How many of you think my taxes are going up?"—a reference to a long-standing effort in Washington to change how buyout managers' profits are taxed.

To many in and around the industry, he is the most recognizable private-equity manager, thanks to the sheer volume of his appearances. He is ubiquitous, giving dozens of speeches a year around the world and visiting investors. He would, as the saying goes, turn up for the opening of an envelope.

Rubenstein told me several years ago he subscribed to Woody Allen's axiom that 80 percent of success is simply showing up. He is an indefatigable fund-raiser and is almost singlehandedly responsible for the firm's growth by assets under management through his near-constant visits, some to places where no private-equity manager had been before, especially in the Middle East. "Because of David, the amount of money Carlyle can raise is essentially infinite," one rival manager said, with a mix of admiration and envy.

His approach to an audience of hundreds, a dozen, or one is disarmingly understated. His sense of humor is sneaky and dry. On the sidelines of a speech in Dubai in 2007, I asked him what had changed about the Middle East. Without missing a beat, he said, "More reporters from New York."

His own travels are reflected in Carlyle's myriad funds, which in sheer numbers (89 as of May 2012, the vast majority of which were private equity) dwarf any of its competitors. In private equity, Blackstone has one large global fund and a handful of smaller regional funds, including one in China; KKR has a similarly small number. The ability to raise money and recruit local teams to manage them is fundamental to the firm's business model and its biggest competitive advantage over its peers. The basic structure allows a manager in say, Brazil, to hang out a Carlyle shingle and receive fund-raising help from Rubenstein and the fund-raising team numbering in the dozens. In exchange, Carlyle gets a generous slice of the partnership and a proportion of the carried interest once the fund has made investments and reaped profits.

Competitors dismiss Carlyle's approach as a franchise model—the private-equity equivalent of opening up restaurants around the globe, with a familiar name but sometimes uneven quality, usually the further away from the headquarters you are. The f-word is not popular with Rubenstein or other Carlyle executives, who insist that programs like "One Carlyle," spearheaded by chairman Daniel D'Aniello, along with financial incentives to encourage cooperation, keep everyone singing from a single Carlyle songbook and financially rewarded to do so.

Rubenstein's mien is nerd-charming. His Woody Allen approach puts him on the road upwards of 250 days a year, demanding that he subsist on little sleep. He eschews caffeine and meat. His white hair contrasts with his chosen uniform of blue pin-striped suits and white shirts. He speaks quietly, rarely raising his voice or getting overly animated about much of anything, and eye contact in one-on-one conversation is often elusive. On stage, he undergoes a mild transformation, leveraging his aloofness into an eccentric, dryly humorous persona. During one appearance in 2012, he noted that his mother encouraged him to be a dentist instead of the lawyer he became.

By the design of the founders, Rubenstein is the face of the firm, to both investors and to the press. He concedes it's a role that didn't come naturally, but he has overcome whatever latent shyness he has through sheer force of will. He consumes media nonstop, reading several books a week along with a complement of daily newspapers and magazines, and seems to enjoy parrying with reporters, professors or colleagues. Watching him chat people up, it's as if he has an overstuffed file cabinet in his head where he's constantly pulling out folders, stuffing notes into them, and moving on to the next topic to do the same thing. His wonky nature was honed in his early career, as a domestic policy adviser in the Carter White House, which he speaks of both as a formative time and uses as a punch line in speeches and interviews, especially when asked about inflation. "In the Carter White House, I got it to 19 percent—very difficult to do. I've often said to people in the Federal Reserve, 'If you're worried about deflation, bring me back, because I can cure that problem.' "[1]

He grew up in a blue-collar Jewish neighborhood in Baltimore, where his father was a postal worker and his mother worked in a dress shop. He won scholarships to Duke University and the University of Chicago Law School, and began to go down a well-trod Washington path, winning a job at law firm Shaw Pittman after leaving the White House after Carter lost to Ronald Reagan.

As he navigated through his thirties, he found himself bored with practicing law and, he said, not especially good at it. He read an article that said entrepreneurs start their companies by the time they are 37. He took note of a leveraged buyout deal for Gibson Greetings, led by a New York firm called WesRay, which had delivered a $200 million return on a $1 million investment. WesRay was an investment firm created by the late former U.S. Treasury Secretary William E. Simon and Raymond Chambers (the firm's name was derived from Chambers's first name and Simon's initials). WesRay also led leveraged buyouts for Avis Rent A Car and Wilson Sporting Goods.

Rubenstein convinced his former colleague from the Carter years, another former Treasury secretary, Bill Miller, to start a firm in Washington to pursue similar deals. Rubenstein soon found that he and Miller didn't have the same vision.[2] Miller was focused on advisory work; Rubenstein, who'd kept his law job while he helped out Miller, wanted to make investments. So he called Ed Mathias.

Mathias first met Rubenstein in 1977, at a dinner hosted in Washington by the late Bob Brimberg, a relentless networker who'd earned the nickname "Scarsdale Fats." Then working for Carter, Rubenstein had been identified as an up-and-comer in Washington circles. His Herculean work ethic—the first to arrive, the last to leave, he often bought meals from the vending machine—helped the myth. Mathias, who then and now had a knack for collecting interesting people and staying in touch with them, was intrigued by the 20-something Rubenstein. His impression of the future Carlyle co-founder: "He was purposeful. He is totally serious about what he undertakes and there's not a lot of emotion. He doesn't internalize the risk of failure. That has not changed in 35 years."

Mathias occupies an angular interior office at Carlyle that looks out into the cross-shaped lobby dominated by a massive, four-sided clock (the building that houses the firm was used as a set in the movie "Broadcast News"). Today, he's involved in Carlyle's efforts around growth capital, investments that aren't classic leveraged buyouts and have some similarities to venture capital. As a long-standing member of the firm, he also has the ear and trust of the founders. In the run-up to Carlyle's 2012 IPO, he was named to the firm's board of directors. He spoke of Carlyle like a proud parent, and indeed, he helped birth it.

Back at T. Rowe Price, Mathias and his bosses saw what was going on in venture capital in the nascent leveraged buyout business where a handful of players like KKR were making extraordinary returns. They wanted to test-drive this business. Mathias pulled together a syndicate of investors that included his firm, as well as Baltimore investment bank Alex. Brown & Sons. First Interstate Bank of Los Angeles, and the Mellon family, one of Mathias's clients.

Mathias put together a total of $5 million, $2 million for working capital, and $3 million for investments. Then he and Rubenstein set about rounding out the group.

Rubenstein got in touch with Steven Norris, a Marriott executive he knew through legal work at Shaw Pittman. Norris recommended a colleague, Daniel D'Aniello. Another contact of Mathias turned him on to Conway, who had risen to become chief financial officer of MCI and, Mathias was told, was restless. Rubenstein cold-called Conway. Mathias interviewed Conway at Gary's Steak House, a now-defunct restaurant in downtown Washington. He agreed to join.

For his part, D'Aniello was a relatively happy guy. He was working amid a veritable dream team of finance whizzes within Marriott. His colleague Steve Bollenbach would go on to run Hilton Hotels; one of his bosses, John Dasburg, would go on to be CEO of Burger King.*

A week into his tenure at Marriott, D'Aniello got a call from Bill Marriott, Sr., asking him to come up and translate a bevy of financial instruments that at the time were transforming the hotel business. D'Aniello became the senior Marriott's go-to guy on matters financial

Bill Marriott Jr. was in charge when D'Aniello was contemplating joining Rubenstein. It was a conversation at the younger Marriott's office that sealed D'Aniello's decision to leave and help form Carlyle. Summoned to discuss his potential new job, D'Aniello arrived to explain himself to Marriott. He invoked the senior Mariott's own story. "I'm only emulating your father's example of following his dreams. I'd like to have your blessing to pursue an opportunity like that." Years later, when they ran into each other at a business event, Marriott said, "I don't know why you ever left us. You're only paying more taxes." While D'Aniello's father-in-law worried that he might be taking a grass-is-greener approach, he realized he didn't want to risk regret. "I didn't want to be 70, sitting in my rocking chair saying, 'Why didn't you give yourself a shot?' "

He did and the four original partners—the three who remain today, plus Norris—went to work. They named their company after the famed

---

*In a private-equity twist, both Hilton and Burger King were eventually acquired by private-equity firms—Hilton by Blackstone, Burger King by TPG—and in both cases the new owners replaced the CEOs.

hotel in New York after reading a biography of Lazard banker Andre
Meyer who'd lived in Carlyle on Manhattan's Upper East Side.[3] Soon,
several of their backers realized that having a stake in a firm like Carlyle
posed conflicts, mainly because anything Carlyle bought would be off the
table as a potential customer for banking services. The founders pooled
their money and bought out Alex. Brown, T. Rowe Price, and First
Interstate Bank. Mellon stayed in for a number of years more. The
founders' stake went from 52 percent to 90 percent. "One of our most
profitable investments ever," D'Aniello said, "was the one in ourselves."

One holdover of the earliest days was Mathias, who called Conway
and Rubenstein in 1993 and said he was thinking about leaving T. Rowe.
They asked him to join Carlyle. "It wasn't a big deal with job interviews
and catharsis," Mathias said. "We had an affinity for each other."

■ ■ ■

As with the other big firms, there was a deal that helped define Carlyle:
the $130 million purchase of BDM International from Loral in 1990.
The defense industry was a natural place for the Carlyle founders to look
for deals for a variety of reasons. First, its epicenter was in the neighborhood, giving them a built-in advantage. They'd also managed to link
up with former U.S. Defense Secretary Frank Carlucci and signed
him up as an adviser, the notion being that he could provide intro-
ductions and ideas. BDM was the first case.

In the late 1980s and early 1990s, the fall of the Berlin Wall reor-
iented the global landscape. Defense-related companies were cheap,
largely because the larger companies who'd earlier swallowed them up
didn't see a bright future for Cold War-geared units. As part of a deal
where Loral bought Ford Aerospace, Carlyle bought the BDM subsidiary from Loral. Carlyle and its investors made 14 times their money
by the time they fully exited BDM seven years later, but D'Aniello and
Conway both said BDM was as significant for what it taught Carlyle
about the broader opportunity in defense and other government-related
firms as well as the private sector

"BDM changed everything," Conway said. Beyond being financially rewarding for Carlyle and its investors, "it showed we understood
businesses that do business with the government."

The company also helped bolster the nascent Carlyle network; as the firm looked at similar deals, it regularly consulted former BDM executives. It would also provide a template for future nondefense deals, where Carlyle would use seasoned executives to source deals, conduct due diligence, and serve on boards of directors. "In the beginning, this business was all about financial capital," Conway said. "It became apparent to us that intellectual capital was really what was in short supply."

The results of the first fund, totaling $100 million, showed how much understanding the businesses you bought mattered. About 42 percent ended up in aerospace and defense deals and that $42 million became more than $372 million. The remaining $58 million of the fund invested outside of those areas ended up worth $30 million, Conway said.

■ ■ ■

The firm's roots in Washington and its founders' disparate backgrounds inform how it evolved, and despite its large Manhattan presence, Carlyle is distinctly Washington-conservative in its demeanor. The nerve center remains a nondescript warren of halls on the second floor of a building on Pennsylvania Avenue. There's no on-site kitchen beyond a break room with Dunkin' Donuts coffee. Showing up in anything other than a suit and tie is frowned upon. "There's an initial premise that all of our competitors are smarter than us," Carlye's chief operating officer Glenn Youngkin said. "Maybe it's because we grew up in DC and not New York."

Location also proved useful in pursuing deals that no one else was interested in, in a town where finance is far from the most important line of work. "If we'd been in New York, we'd have been slogging it out with everyone else," said Allan Holt, the co-head of U.S. buyouts who joined the firm in 1992. "Washington is a company town, but it's politics, not finance. I still go to social functions and people hear Carlyle and say, 'Now what is it exactly that you guys do?'"

The interplay among the founders is by most accounts, including their own, integral to what Carlyle has become. Each founder claims they've never raised their voices to each other, and yet there are checks and balances inherent in the triumvirate. People internally and externally are well aware of the breakdown.

Rubenstein is the front man and fund-raiser, Conway is the deal-maker and de facto chief investment officer, and D'Aniello is charged with much of the firm's administration, personnel matters, and firm-wide initiatives like the One Carlyle effort meant to keep everyone across the firm's 33 offices in sync; he also has responsibility for the real estate investments. For years, the three men, who rarely socialize outside of work, met each weekend for breakfast or coffee at the Hilton in McLean, Virginia to, hash out whatever company matters needed their collective attention.

The division of labor was in part a product of circumstance and background. Both Conway and D'Aniello had business backgrounds and therefore could evaluate potential deals and figure out the firm. Rubenstein, the lawyer, was left to raise the money. "It was clear to me the other guys knew finance," Rubenstein said. "I figured I would add value by raising the money."

During a wide-ranging conversation at Carlyle's office on a Sunday afternoon, he laid out his philosophy for fund-raising, noting at the start that of all the courses of study in business curricula, from marketing to finance to operations, there isn't one on how to raise money. "And yet it's very unlikely that someone could live a week without asking for, or being asked for money," he said. On this particular nonofficial work day, he wore what passes for casual Rubenstein, a blazer and slacks, with a tie firmly tied.

He started his fund-raising self-education by asking his family and friends, then went to people in the area, then the rest of the country, and so on. There was virtually nowhere he wouldn't go in person. His ferocious curiosity overwhelmed his discomfort so he enjoyed meeting and talking to people. Rubenstein found he had two built-in advantages. First, people like hearing about working in the White House, even in an administration short on public admiration. He also realized being a founder of the firm, even a tiny one, gave his visit a patina of credibility in the eyes of those he was meeting.

His secret seemed to be his willingness to show up, again and again, even though he rarely verbalized "the ask," especially in the later years, figuring they knew why he was there. "I almost never actually ask people for money," he said.

Rubenstein envisioned the scope that Carlyle could achieve early on. Pete Clare, now the co-head of Carlyle's U.S. buyout business, was relatively new to the firm in 1994 and working on a deal to buy Fresh Fields, a regional chain of organically oriented grocery stores based in Maryland. The deal was small by modern standards; the total equity check was about $36 million. But days ahead of the closing, Carlyle was short by about $3 million.

Clare was in the office the Saturday before the Wednesday closing, nailing the final details, and sweating the multimillion-dollar shortfall. Finally, he walked down the hall to talk to Rubenstein. He found his boss hunched over a yellow legal pad, sketching out a fantastical vision of the future Carlyle. Lines emanated from a circle in the center, denoting Carlyle Europe and Carlyle Asia. Rubenstein pushed the pad toward Clare and walked him through it in detail. Clare listened as patiently as he could before finally blurting out, "David, that's great, but I really need $3 million right now!" Rubenstein waved him off. That part was easy. Seventy-two hours later, Rubenstein had filled the gap for the Fresh Fields deal.

Rubenstein told me that while he didn't recall the exact incident, it sounded right. "Clearly it made more of an impression on Pete than it did me," he said, but he admitted to plotting a global empire nearly from the beginning.

■ ■ ■

The wealth generated by realizing that vision has turned Rubenstein into one of the more prominent philanthropists during the past decade. He's a signee of the Giving Pledge, the movement founded in 2010 to get wealthy people to commit to giving away at least half their money. Created by billionaires led by Warren Buffett and Bill Gates, the Pledge has drawn the support of families and individuals including investors Carl Icahn, Julian Robertson, and Ronald Perelman. Peter G. Peterson, the co-founder of Blackstone, is the only other founder of a big private-equity firm to sign the pledge.

Rubenstein wrote a 1,400-word letter explaining his decision. In describing his path to philanthropy, Rubenstein wrote about realizing at age 54 that the average white male lived to be 81, meaning he was, statistically speaking, two-thirds through his life. "I did not want to live the other third, get to my deathbed, and then ask someone to give away my accumulated resources as they saw fit," Rubenstein wrote. He noted that he hoped to fulfill the pledge, that is give away more than half his wealth, while he was still alive.

Rubenstein has brought the ubiquity approach honed in his fund-raising and Carlyle lives to non-profit boards; he serves on more than two dozen, a number he is winnowing down in order to focus on what he calls transformative gifts. In early 2012, he donated half the cost to repair the Washington Monument after it was damaged in a 2011 earthquake.

(By way of personal disclosure, Rubenstein is a Regent of the Smithsonian Institution, one of only a handful of private citizens in that position. His donations to the Smithsonian included a 2011 gift to the National Zoological Association, where my father serves as the director).

He's also the chairman of the Kennedy Center for the Performing Arts, one of the most prestigious philanthropic posts. Much to Rubenstein's private chagrin, Schwarzman managed to wrangle the job first and served an eight-year term, but now that he has it, Rubenstein is reveling in the role. The gig has helped raise his profile, and brings him into contact with high-octane celebrities. In the fall of 2011, his duties paired him with comedian Will Ferrell, the recipient of the Mark Twain Prize for American Humor. As part of the ceremony, Rubenstein presented Ferrell with the actual award and, in a well-rehearsed bit, handed the "priceless" prize to Ferrell only to have him drop and shatter it.

That made-for-YouTube moment followed a private visit by Rubenstein and Ferrell to the White House, where they met with President Obama. It was there, unscripted, that Ferrell actually left the prize in the Oval Office, prompting the leader of the free world to chase him down through the halls of the White House.

■ ■ ■

Conway and Rubenstein are the pair most likely to be at odds, with Conway counseling patience and Rubenstein pushing for more expansion, more funds, more lines of business. One former executive says it this way: "David has his foot on the gas, Bill has his on the brake."

Conway pressed his foot hard on the brake in 2007. Even as other firms were continuing to do deals, he sent out a strongly worded letter to Carlyle's employees imploring them not to get swept up in the euphoria of the deal heat surrounding them. He warned his colleagues that cheap debt was driving Carlyle's peers to do bigger and bigger deals. To drive his point home, he hit the all-caps button: "OUR STRATEGY SHOULD EVOLVE TO TAKE LOWER RISK DEALS AND EARN LOWER RETURNS, RATHER THAN HIGHER RISK DEALS AT ONLY SMALL INCREMENTALLY HIGHER RETURNS."[4]

Looking back at the time, he said he simply put in to words what was plainly happening. "It was like the emperor's new clothes," he told me. "Everybody knew we were in a market that was radically overheating. I just said, 'It just looks to me that this party is near the end.'"

Carlyle called on its companies to draw down their revolving lines of credit in anticipation of tough times ahead.

The data show the extent to which Conway, who knows each of Carlyle's deals in excruciating detail, got cautious that year in terms of new transactions. In 2006, Carlyle announced about $75 billion worth of takeovers, including three deals worth $10 billion or more. In 2007, the total dropped about 40 percent, to $44 billion. The largest deal was the $8.5 billion purchase of HD Supply, the contractor-oriented arm of Home Depot, according to data compiled by Bloomberg. Perhaps to underscore Conway's own point, that deal turned into one of the more troubled of the boom era, struggling mightily in the teeth of the U.S. housing crisis.

Conway is, at his core, a deal guy, and widely regarded as one of the smartest investors in private equity. He is affable and physically imposing, and while charming and self-effacing, he is arguably the most feared person inside the firm. A practicing Catholic who attends Mass most days, he grew up in New Hampshire and earned his undergraduate degree at Dartmouth. He went on to earn an MBA from the University of Chicago at night while working for a bank there. After joining MCI, one of his clients, he rose to become chief financial officer. Working at one of the area's biggest companies made him known to most everyone in finance around Washington.

"Bill is the moral compass of the firm," said Youngkin, noting that as the consulting firm McKinsey & Co. grew, people there tested ideas by asking what its founder, Marvin Bower, would do in a particular situation. "The question everyone at Carlyle should ask is 'What would Bill do?'" Every new employee gets a framed list of those rules when they join the firm. "We want to have Bill be in the room with everybody," Youngkin said.

With Rubenstein gathering the money and giving speeches and Conway garnering a dealmaker's rep, D'Aniello is the least publicly known of the founding trio. He hails from western Pennsylvania from modest means. He graduated from Syracuse University and among the small number of mementos in his office is a signed basketball commemorating the 2003 Syracuse national championship men's basketball team.

He's a formal person, almost never removing his suit jacket through the entire work day. His manner is calm, his voice almost soothing. He and Conway, he conceded, gladly eschewed the spotlight, letting Rubenstein be the front man. Conway was totally focused on deals, Rubenstein on raising money, and raising Carlyle's profile. D'Aniello was happy to be left to running the firm and figuring out how to build a lasting culture. Ed Mathias jokingly summed it up this way: "Bill has been totally focused on investments. If I called him and said the third floor of the building was on fire, his first response would be, 'Call Dan.'"

Among D'Aniello's key efforts is One Carlyle, which he was careful to point out was not just a culture, but a business strategy. These sorts of projects are often well-intentioned, but a skeptical outsider just as often views them as something fluffy and easily dismissed, just a bunch of business school mumbo jumbo. Yet there are actual financial systems in place to "encourage" cooperation. Funds are encouraged to invest in other funds' deals. That means a team in Brazil can enlist New York colleagues specializing in consumer products on a specific deal and if everyone works together, some of the carry goes to New York, and the U.S. buyout fund has a chance to co-invest.

"This is about taking the Rubik's cube of industry expertise, product, and geography and turning it so its face best projects our strengths against an opportunity," D'Aniello said. "Winning in this business is a game of inches. This collaborative approach empowers our firm's business model, and our strong One Carlyle culture lubricates its successful execution."

■ ■ ■

As Carlyle prepared for the public markets, where institutional investors also care deeply about the future management of companies whose shares they own, a more-than lingering question was how the founders, now all in their 60s, would hand off the firm to the next generation. As a public company, Rubenstein and Conway are co-chief executive officers, with D'Aniello as the chairman of the firm.

The founders in 2009 created an eight-person operating committee that's responsible for the day-to-day operations of Carlyle and the seeds of succession are sprouting there. Through the process of pitching the IPO, Youngkin was the most consistently present executive other than the founders and chief financial officer Adena Friedman. The public offering was effectively Youngkin's deal to run. At Carlyle since 1995 (he worked at McKinsey and CS First Boston before that), he ran Carlyle's operations in the United Kingdom for five years before running Carlyle's industrial investments group in Washington. He also served as the interim finance chief for a five-month period at the end of 2010 and the beginning of 2011.

People who know the firm said Youngkin has internalized the culture of Carlyle as well as anyone, and his appeal to the founders comes from his ability to represent each of their perspectives, a key attribute if carrying on DBD's legacy is important, which it appears to be. One person familiar with Carlyle's personnel told me that if the three founders had a baby, it would be Glenn Youngkin.

Youngkin rose to be first among equals because of those qualities, a personal evolution that reflects his long tenure at the firm relative to his peers on the operating committee. For many of the functions that weren't deal-related, Carlyle looked to its extended family and sometimes beyond. David Marchick, responsible for all of the firm's external and governmental affairs, was an outside lawyer working for Carlyle and member of the Clinton administration; he joined in 2007. Friedman arrived at Carlyle from Nasdaq in 2011, as the firm was preparing its public filing. Mitch Petrick, responsible for the trading businesses, got to the firm in 2010 after a 21-year career at Morgan Stanley.

Youngkin also serves on the much smaller management committee, whose membership is limited to him, the founders, and Friedman. That group is charged with making the strategic, firm-wide decisions DBD used to make at their weekend breakfasts.

His baptism by fire came in 2008, when the founders asked him to step out of day-to-day deal-making and think about existential issues related to the firm. What started as a real-world business school exercise of re-imagining the firm organizationally quickly became an exercise in preparing the firm to survive a global financial crisis. "We ran the 'world falls apart' scenario," Youngkin said. "We went through an exercise of deconstructing the firm."

The recommendation to the founders, which they took, was to get liquid, in part because the firm needed to be able to meet capital calls if limited partners defaulted. Conway, D'Aniello, and Rubenstein took no bonuses for the year. Every partner pitched in to buy $200 million worth of assets off the firm's balance sheet and the firm took out $100 million in costs to get Carlyle to a more comfortable position in terms of cash flow. Looking around the world at what was either too new, or too fragile, to withstand the coming storm, the firm shuttered its Eastern Europe office and gave responsibility for deals there to other European outposts. It similarly disbanded a South American real estate group, moving responsibility to the U.S. Asian credit was abandoned altogether for the time being. By that September, when Lehman Brothers' bankruptcy and other events brought the world to the brink of financial Armageddon, Carlyle had battened down the hatches.

But within roughly six months, Conway's pessimism had been transformed. Poring over data gleaned from its roughly 200 portfolio companies, Conway zeroed in on the financial results that showed container shipments were heading upward month after month. "Things were better on the shop floor," Youngkin said. "We decided to lean forward on the investment side. Bill's the one who waves the flag."

Life resumed some semblance of normalcy by mid-2009 and Youngkin and the founders revisited his original assignment of thinking about Carlyle as an organization. That process, which involved Youngkin polling executives inside and outside of the firm, ultimately led to the formation of the operating committee that oversees all the non-deal activities of the firm.

A key player in professionalizing Carlyle was Daniel Akerson, who left the firm in 2011 to become the CEO of General Motors. His departure was felt deeply throughout the top ranks of the firm, largely because he was Conway's closest confidant and a key barometer for measuring how something would play with the chief dealmaker. That closeness and Akerson's background running General Instrument among other executive positions gave him a stature almost no one else had in the firm. He could tell the founders what they should do, without hesitation. Louis Gerstner, who had run IBM before becoming Carlyle's chairman, held similar sway.

"They could go to them and say, 'It's not a small firm anymore, it's an institution,'" Marchick said. "They convinced the founders they had to foster the next generation."

The operating committee is meant to formalize the transition of some responsibilities of the founders into new hands. Marchick and Michael Arpey, who leads the investor services group, act as mini-Rubensteins. Youngkin and Friedman have taken on much of the administrative burden once shouldered by D'Aniello. Clare and Holt, who co-head the U.S. buyout efforts, are Conway's chief lieutenants.

Ironically, that shift makes the founders even less likely to leave because each man has been able to keep only the parts of the job he really likes. As for how long the founders will stay, they haven't said. One person familiar with their thinking said the conventional wisdom has Rubenstein staying as long as humanly possible. Through his extraordinary stamina, he's found a way to satisfy his philanthropic desires while working full-time, so why would he leave?

Rubenstein, this person said, is like the last speck in the frying pan after everything else has been burned off. Conway, too, has made no decision about reducing his role. D'Aniello, the oldest of the trio at 65, may consider an emeritus role around the time he hits 70.

I pressed Rubenstein on the point of retirement, or leaving Carlyle in some fashion, and it's clearly something he thinks about constantly, echoing a sentiment from every one of the 60-something private-equity founders. He made an interesting point about the difficulty of letting go. "When you're the founder of a company, an entrepreneur, you recognize the people you work with may not have the same entrepreneurial bent," he said. "They may actually enjoy working for a larger company or one where they did not have to take the risk of getting it off the ground."

This argument serves to underscore a crucial point about all of these firms, and one that was a common theme throughout almost every conversation I had with people inside and outside the big firms. Because the firms are so much created in the image of their founders, succession isn't just about who will do the next couple of decades worth of deals. With their names literally or figuratively on the door, the founders are thinking beyond who is willing and able to run the firm. They need to find someone they trust to nurture the legacy of the men themselves. Most companies with similar scope and stature dealt with these issues long ago, and the fact that private-equity firms are dealing with it for the first time underscores the relative immaturity of the industry. They are far from the tiny private partnerships they began as. If Rubenstein's vision is to become permanent beyond his stewardship, he and the other founders have to figure out the best ways to let go.

■ ■ ■

If KKR are the barbarians, Carlyle is the spooky, government-connected group in the public imagination. Roots in defense deals are largely responsible. Carlyle's is one part Wall Street technology (the LBO) mixed with its hometown's most pervasive business (the government and defense). Its first chairman was Carlucci, who cemented the perception that Carlyle was a key institution in the military-industrial complex. Former Secretary of State James Baker III was an adviser. Former U.S. President George H. W. Bush also advised the firm, specifically on doing business in Asia. Former U.K. Prime Minister John Major also served as an adviser. The founders stressed that none of the politicians advised on deals and were there simply to lend credibility to potential and current investors.

The associations clearly helped Carlyle in the early days establish a name for itself. As the years wore on, it found the darker interpretations of those relationships hard to shake. What was a cottage conspiracy theory during the 1990s, when the former government officials were kicking around Carlyle, blossomed into much broader, darker rep after the terrorist attacks of September 11, 2001.

Aside from public pension funds, who are in many cases by law compelled to reveal where they've invested money, the identities of other limited partners are a well-guarded secret. Rubenstein's success in raising money, especially in the Middle East, where networks of families have accrued astonishing wealth from natural resources like oil and natural gas, had brought a number of investors who prized that sort of secrecy and discretion. One secret revealed in the wake of the 2001 terrorist attacks was that one such wealthy Middle East family was the bin Ladens of Saudi Arabia.

On the day of the actual attacks, Carlyle was holding its annual investor meeting, with presentations to limited partners by the founders and other Carlyle partners and advisers. Former President George H. W. Bush had spoken the previous evening at dinner. Among the investors on hand: Shafiq bin Laden, one of Osama bin Laden's numerous half-brothers and a representative of a family that had invested $2 million in Carlyle's second flagship buyout fund (a $1.3 billion pool).[5]

Michael Moore's documentary *Fahrenheit 9/11* seized on the situation, drawing the connection between Bush's Carlyle ties and bin Laden, suggesting Carlyle was far more nefarious than a simple Washington influence peddler, especially given its close ties to the defense industry. The firm and the bin Laden family ended their relationship later in 2001, but the association was persistent, and while dissipated, still lingered a decade later. After Osama bin Laden was killed by a team of U.S. Navy SEALS in 2011, Fortune's Dan Primack mused in an online article whether enough time had passed whereby Carlyle could take investments from the bin Laden family again.[6]

Broadening its adviser base beyond the government made sense. The number of defense-related deals is finite, and Carlyle was confident its reputation had evolved to the point where it would continue to see almost any deal worth doing in that area, often before anyone else. The founders also surmised that the model of having experienced, well-connected advisers to help open doors could easily translate to the broader corporate world.

The firm chose former IBM's Gerstner as Carlucci's successor in 2003. Gerstner, who retired as Carlyle chairman in 2008, helped usher in an era of partners and advisers with roots outside the Beltway and in the Fortune 500. Carlyle in 2005 hired former Bank of America Chief Financial Officer James Hance as a senior adviser to consult on financial deals. Other advisers included former 3Com CEO William Krause.

Even while bulking up on corporate expertise, Carlyle continued to hire from the ranks of government and government contractors. Arthur

Levitt, the former chairman of the Securities and Exchange Commission, and former Air Force Chief of Staff John Jumper were tapped as senior advisers.*

■ ■ ■

The firm used its well-connected advisers to begin a relentless expansion throughout the world and Rubenstein's wanderlust led Carlyle beyond the United States faster and more meaningfully than any other major private-equity firm. Fund-raising trips doubled as location-scouting missions as Carlyle pieced together a growing web of funds designed to exploit a combination of its capital and local expertise.

Carlyle from the early days was active in tapping the vast and secretive wealth of the Middle East, where Rubenstein's willingness to visit in person, and often, played well into a culture that not only prizes, but demands, long-term relationships in business.

That work reached a milestone in 2007, when Carlyle announced that Mubadala bought a stake in Carlyle. The deal was a variation on Carlyle's theme of going local in overseas markets. This was a way to get even deeper into a somewhat mystifying part of the world. At the same time, Mubadala got access to Carlyle beyond what was available to an ordinary limited partner. The fund owned a piece of the firm itself.

Mubadala, while backed by the government, isn't a typical sovereign wealth fund. In Abu Dhabi, that's handled by ADIA. Mubadala's mission is to make investments that more directly benefit the emirate and it spent its first few years assembling an eclectic portfolio. Beyond the Carlyle stake, Mubadala sponsors a Formula One team, an association it used to bring a car race to Abu Dhabi. The fund also made an audacious, and so far losing, bet on perennial runner-up chipmaker Advanced Micro Devices, creating a joint venture that announced plans to open a semiconductor factory in Abu Dhabi.

Mubadala also played a key role in helping the founders begin to reap riches from what they created. In 2010, Carlyle took a $500 million loan from Mubadala in large part to pay a dividend to the owners, including the founders and the California Public Employees' Retirement System.

---

*Levitt also serves on the board of directors of Bloomberg LP.

Carlyle repaid the loan in late 2011 and early 2012, a move that helped avoid Mubadala converting the debt to equity at a discount to the IPO price.

Mubadala was a key tenet of establishing the firm as global in its approach. Carlyle's founders argued their version of diversification—geographic—put them on that path before any of their competitors, including Blackstone. That view was crucial to Carlyle's pitch for one of its most important deals, the long-mulled initial public offering.

The founders, all headed toward their sixties at the time, seriously contemplated going public back when Schwarzman got his deal done and Kravis got as far as filing an S-1, in 2007. Just as the credit crisis derailed KKR's plans and diverted that firm into a European two-step to an NYSE listing, the state of the financial world scuttled any plans for Carlyle to gain a public listing.

By 2011, the founders were more than ready and saw the year shaping up to be a perfect environment to prime the market's interest. A lack of exits in the post-credit crisis era meant there was a backlog of companies to sell or take public, which helped distributions and therefore profits. More friendly credit markets allowed new deals to get done. And importantly, limited partners were ready to commit money again, helping accelerate Rubenstein's money-raising machine.

The firm took additional steps to bolster assets under management and business expansion. The founders hired Morgan Stanley's Michael "Mitch" Petrick to build out a credit business and pulled off the acquisition of AlpInvest, a European private-equity fund-of-funds whose broad portfolio immediately goosed Carlyle's total AUM and gave it a new line of business. Carlyle also bought a stake in a hedge fund, Claren Road.

The moves bulked Carlyle up to an extent that it and Blackstone were getting ever closer in terms of assets under management, a fact not lost on those at either firm, from the top executives on down. Privately, they sniffed at the composition of each other's assets. Blackstone was heavily weighted toward hedge funds, Carlyle's AlpInvest number included holdings in other private-equity funds.

The new businesses were meant to learn from Blackstone's experience as a public company, which underscored investors' desire for predictable streams of income and smoother trajectories for the overall profits. Petrick's business accounted for 24 percent of Carlyle's profit in the first nine months of 2011.

At Carlyle, moves to diversify from a product perspective failed before, sometimes spectacularly. A hedge fund, Carlyle Blue Wave, was shuttered in July 2008 after its assets dropped by more than 30 percent, to about $600 million from the $900 million the fund started with in March 2007. The fund dropped 10 percent in 2007, and had gained 2 percent for 2008 when it was liquidated. Comparable funds had returned an average of 4.8 percent from March 2007 to the closure.[7]

The Blue Wave closure felt less traumatic than another failure a few months previous. The more public misstep came with Carlyle Capital Corp., a publicly traded debt fund that collapsed earlier in 2008. Designed to invest in mortgage-backed securities, the fund initially won support from private investors, including many of Carlyle's long-time limited partners in its more traditional private-equity funds. The three Carlyle founders put their own money in; other Carlyle executives followed their lead. Altogether, Carlyle employees had $230 million on the line.

Carlyle Capital went to raise money in the public markets in 2007, even as the market was starting to get shaky. That was apparent in the fund's own offering, which was cut by 25 percent. Public investors put up more than $300 million. Combined with Carlyle money and private investors, the fund's total equity was about $900 million.

A lawsuit filed after the collapse said Carlyle marketed the fund as aiming for leverage of around 19 times, meaning Carlyle would borrow up to $19 for each dollar of equity. The lawsuit said the actual leverage was more than 30 times.[8]

In such situations, such a bet goes wrong if the price of the underlying assets fall so much that lenders can make margin calls, and that's just what happened. Carlyle pressed the lenders, which included huge banks like Citigroup and Deutsche Bank, to refinance the debt. Those negotiations, which Carlyle described at the time as "exhaustive," failed. And so did Carlyle Capital, which had to be liquidated to meet those margin calls.

The Carlyle Capital collapse in March foretold a coming storm far beyond the firm, predicted ominously in coverage at the time. "Carlyle won't be the end of it," Greg Bundy, executive chairman of

Sydney-based merger advisory firm InterFinancial Ltd. told Bloomberg News at the time. "There's more to come. The problem is no one can give you an educated guess about how much."[9]

Even an educated guess probably would not have come close to what happened later that year. While Carlyle Capital certainly resonated within the firm as its single biggest failure to date, it was ultimately a kitchen fire compared with the apocalyptic blazes that scorched Wall Street later that year, bringing the global financial system to the brink of collapse.

The failures of CCC and Blue Wave didn't diminish the founders' ambitions and their conviction that building the firm beyond private equity was not only desirable but necessary to keep satisfying investors, both the limited partners and their anticipated public shareholders. What Carlyle knew was that they needed a dedicated effort that would give them tighter control over any new businesses and for that they needed someone to run the show who ultimately was in the mix of the firm's most senior levels. "We decided there had to be someone on the operating committee who owns it," Youngkin said.

Rubenstein went into recruiting mode to find someone to fit the bill.

One morning in early 2010, Mitch Petrick was in Vail, Colorado for a family ski trip. He'd recently left Morgan Stanley after two decades, a month after a management overhaul led to his demotion from the head of sales and trading at the Wall Street firm. He was weighing his options and had already laid the groundwork for his own, independent firm. David Rubenstein had arranged this meeting at Lodge at Vail to convince him otherwise. Petrick sent the rest of his family to the slopes and listened.

The two men repaired to the empty bar, where the odor of beer and the previous night's après-ski revelry was still hanging in the air. An atypically casual Rubenstein, clad in khaki slacks and a sweater, went to work on Petrick. "He is the consummate salesman," Petrick said. "He was very persuasive that this made a lot more sense than doing it on my own."

Rubenstein laid out a vision for Petrick akin to the yellow legal pad he'd shown Pete Clare almost two decades earlier. Petrick's business, now known as Carlyle Global Market Strategies, or Carlyle GMS, would be a brand in its own right. Its aim would be to go into every corner of the world just as Carlyle did in private equity. The difference from previous efforts would essentially be Petrick and a strong mandate from the founders.

"This is the difference between running a fund and running a business," Petrick said. "There's an institutionalization above it and much better transparency on what we're doing and how we're doing it. That's not to say we won't run into problems, but we'll know how we got there. You can't draw a Plan B in the middle of the battle."

The devotion of human and financial resources to Petrick's business marked the biggest shift in Carlyle's evolution since its decision to move beyond one fund two decades previous. Its success will be crucial to ensuring the firm does in fact keep growing. "This place is not just a private-equity firm anymore," Petrick said.

■ ■ ■

Carlyle's decision to restart discussions around its IPO was an indication that the industry's boom and bust was far enough in the past and even before the registration was filed, the Carlyle IPO became a hot topic on Wall Street. Here was a brand-name financial firm contemplating an offering of itself, a sign that the smartest dealmakers thought it might be time to do another big deal. Blackstone's IPO still resonated in private-equity and Wall Street circles as a perfectly timed IPO, at least from the perspective that Schwarzman and Peterson were able to get paid handsomely for their stakes.

A leaner and somewhat chastened group of big underwriters scrambled to pitch Carlyle in the summer of 2011. The three founders, Youngkin, and CFO Friedman entertained presentations from the banks, most of whom sent not just their investment banking heads but the CEO of the whole bank, to make the case.

Stories about the horserace popped up in newspapers, wire services, and on business news channels. In the end, JPMorgan Chase, Citigroup, and Credit Suisse won the coveted lead spots on the offering. Despite an ugly turn downward in the equity markets during the second half of 2011, Carlyle pushed ahead with the initial filing, with the notion that it would be ready if and when markets recovered.

Just as with Blackstone almost five years earlier, dealmakers, bankers, and journalists were eager to get a look beneath the covers, specifically at the pay details. After an austere few years, folks wondered whether there was still huge money to be made in private equity.

Carlyle gave its answer late one January Tuesday in an amended registration filing that detailed compensation. The three founders had collected a combined $413 million in 2011, the vast bulk of it coming from distributions from its funds. Each founder got $134 million, plus a $275,000 salary and a $3.55 million bonus. By comparison, Schwarzman had earned $398.3 million in 2006, the year before Blackstone's IPO.

The compensation of the founders was one of several areas where Carlyle bucked convention in its filing to go public. The firm made it clear that unlike most publicly traded companies, it wouldn't form a compensation committee to set founders' pay. That would remain in the hands of the founders themselves, as it had from the beginning. In another case, Carlyle proposed that it would settle disputes with shareholders through confidential arbitration and prohibit class-action lawsuits from being brought against it. After consulting with the Securities and Exchange Commission, and facing concern from Carlyle investors (many of whom are active shareholders in public companies in addition to backers of buyout funds), Carlyle dropped the provision. The decision came just as a handful of U.S. senators pressed the S.E.C. to block the offering because of the arbitration clause.

■ ■ ■

In early February 2012, I sat with Rubenstein in front of hundreds of students and executives at Columbia Business School's annual private-equity conference. The title for the conference was "Out of the Storm but Not Out of the Woods," and the morning keynote was a discussion between Rubenstein and Clayton Dubilier & Rice founder Joseph Rice, one of the early practitioners of private equity whose firm bridged the eras of financially driven deals to ones that required dedicated operating teams.

It was at least Rubenstein's second public speech in 72 hours; two days earlier he spoke at a Bloomberg-sponsored conference on China. The elephants in the room that morning on Columbia's campus were the IPO, which Rubenstein studiously avoided discussing, and Romney, which he and Rice did take on.

The appearance was classic rapid-fire Rubenstein, from wry jokes to a précis on the U.S. debt crisis, complete with a series of figures and back-of-the-envelope calculations about what impact changing the tax rate of private-equity firms would have on the country's budget deficit. And a full-throated defense of the industry, along with a concession that the demands change as the scope of influence widens: "If you own a lot of companies on behalf of your investors, you have a social responsibility," he said.

And when the hour was up, he posed for a quick picture with conference organizers, slipped out a stage door, and jogged to his waiting car. He immediately joined a conference call, finished it, and was back on his plane by the afternoon.

Chapter 3

The L Word

Steve Schwarzman and James B. "Jimmy" Lee, Jr. were elated. It was the summer of 1989, and the two men had just finished a marathon negotiating session to buy CNW, a railroad company, for $950 million. The auction had been fierce. Schwarzman and Lee, a banker from Chemical Bank who was providing much of the debt financing for the deal, had worked on one floor of a Chicago law offices, bidding late into the night against a rival bidder tucked in a separate conference room one floor below.

When the deal was finally won, with Chemical providing $585 million in loans for the purchase, Lee wanted to mark the event with some sort of celebration. Blackstone had arranged a tiny chartered jet to ferry the pair back to New York, and Lee finagled two Heinekens before they got on the plane. As they took off, the two men, wedged uncomfortably in the back of the plane, clinked glass bottles.

At the time, the pairing was a marriage of convenience. Blackstone had yet to mark its fifth birthday, and Schwarzman was still figuring out exactly what the firm should be. He knew there were deals to be done, and that he needed financing to do them.

Jimmy Lee was eager to win clients and build a book of business at Chemical, and later Chase's investment bank. He knew he wasn't Schwarzman's first call (because he'd told him so). So he decided to make himself indispensable as Blackstone's financier and later adviser on M&A.

Lee was playing in an area once dominated by Drexel Burnham Lambert Inc., specifically by Michael Milken. It was Milken, a Drexel trader, who pioneered the use of high-yield, noninvestment-grade bonds (aka junk bonds), often in hostile takeovers. Drexel and Milken helped fuel the surge of mergers and acquisitions, including leveraged buyouts, during the 1980s. Milken was indicted for securities violations tied to insider trading, triggering Drexel to file for bankruptcy in 1990.[1]

While that eliminated a major provider of debt for LBOs, Drexel was a de facto training ground for a number of men who went on to create or work at major private-equity and investment firms. Most notably, Leon Black, Joshua Harris, and Marc Rowan—all former Drexel executives—went on to create Apollo Global Management.

New York-based Apollo has risen to become one of the biggest private-equity managers, best known for pursuing deals where it can use its expertise around complicated debt situations. Its investors give the firm broad latitude to invest not only through pairing equity with loans and bonds, but by buying debt at discounted prices as a way to eventually own the company, or in a bet that the company's debt doesn't reflect its underlying value.

Drexel's demise gave Lee a huge opening to become a major provider of debt for leveraged buyouts. Schwarzman and Lee pulled off dozens of deals in the mid-1980s through the 1990s. Two decades later, evidence of a relationship that evolved into a friendship peppered the deal memorabilia lining Lee's office in the executive suite of JPMorgan Chase, where he is vice chairman. On the end table in Lee's sitting area are two pictures, both featuring Schwarzman.

One has the two men standing with JPMorgan CEO Jamie Dimon at a New York Public Library event in 2008 honoring Lee. The other, much older, picture shows Schwarzman presenting Lee with an award, one of a number that each has given the other over the years. Lee's relationship with private equity isn't limited to Schwarzman and Blackstone. He and his bank have financed deals from TPG's seminal takeover of Continental in the 1990s to the record-setting LBO of TXU, by KKR and TPG, in 2007.

Schwarzman was his willing guinea pig in those early days, as Lee searched for his competitive edge and Schwarzman started doing deals at a more rapid pace. Lee's innovation was creating the syndicated loan market, which provided the foundation for a financing system of one-stop shopping, combining the loan business with the bond business. The first such deal, engineered by Schwarzman and Lee, was Blackstone's 1994 purchase of UCAR International, where Chase underwrote more than $1 billion of debt and equity. "We experimented together," Lee said. "It was like the late 1960s and 1970s in rock 'n roll."

■ ■ ■

Private-equity money is somewhat ordinary until it's paired with debt. This borrowed money—the leverage in a leveraged buyout—is what gives private equity the chance to be a wildly lucrative business. Were debt removed from the equation entirely, the entire model would break down, simply because managers couldn't deliver the returns to their investors, and reap the rich fees for doing so. Debt is the jet fuel that makes it all possible. Private-equity managers argue that prudent use of leverage (emphasis on the prudent) is not only reasonable but necessary, and part of running a healthy business that manages its cash appropriately and uses tools including debt to most appropriately grow.

Still, leverage also has been one of the biggest drags on private equity's reputation. As anyone who's ever had a mortgage or a credit card knows, borrowing money comes with inherent risk. Whoever is lending it demands that it be paid back on certain terms. Throughout private equity's history they've found eager lenders, the equivalent of the credit card companies who carpet-bomb college campuses with offers.

When a private-equity firm wants to buy a company, it uses a mix of money from its own fund (equity) and some amount of borrowed money, usually in the form of bonds and loans. The money is borrowed using the target firm basically as collateral and the amount and terms are based on the company's perceived ability to pay the interest, and ultimately repay all the debt.

It's a variation on the economics of purchasing a house using a mortgage. The buyer uses a blend of his own cash and a substantial bank loan to fund the purchase. Assuming the value goes up, the return is based on earning a multiple of that small amount of principle, after the loans are paid off. Let's say you buy a house for $100,000, using $20,000 as a down payment and an $80,000 mortgage. If you were paying the entire purchase price in cash, you'd need to sell it for $200,000 to double your money.

But you have leverage: borrowed money. That means you only need to sell it for $120,000 to double your money ($120,000 sale price minus the $80,000 loan = $40,000 profit). If you do sell it for $200,000, you'll make five times your money.

There are more similarities that make an LBO enticing from a profitability standpoint. Just as with a mortgage for a house, interest on corporate debt is tax deductible. Author and Bloomberg columnist William Cohan put it succinctly: "Since corporate debt is the mother's milk of a leveraged buyout, there would be no private-equity/LBO industry without this huge tax benefit."[2] He went on to argue that this tax benefit is effectively a public subsidy of the business, since the rest of us end up making up the difference for revenue that would otherwise come from the LBO-backed companies. The private equity industry has staunchly defended the tax deductibility of debt, noting that its use is far from limited to leveraged buyouts. Beyond homeowners, corporations not owned by private-equity firms enjoy the same benefit.

There is a philosophical element to the discussion around debt that I repeatedly encounter in my exploration of how the money flows into, around, and out of private equity. Practitioners describe it as a vital tool in delivering superior returns to their investors and themselves. They argue that debt provides a level of discipline in running companies crucial to its long-term success and that successful companies that aren't controlled by private equity routinely use reasonable amounts of debt to fund growth, bet on new products and make acquisitions.

Critics see placing large amounts of debt on a company's balance sheet as nothing less than a destructive force that threatens all of our economic well-being. Their argument goes that forcing a company to divert cash to service debt crimps its ability to invest and grow. That just as a person or family shouldn't overextend themselves in a house they can't afford, private-equity firms shouldn't place debt on a company that it won't ultimately be able to pay off. Too much debt can overcome a company, sending it into bankruptcy and putting people on the streets.

Leaving aside the philosophical argument around the use of debt, here's how it's used in an LBO. The money involved is stacked in several layers for purposes of importance. At the top is senior debt, secured against the company. Below that are other slugs of debt, which are subordinate (that is, in the case of a default, paid back after the senior debt). As a debt investor, the higher you are in the debt stack, the less risk you're taking and, therefore, the lower your anticipated return.

While banks had been in the business of providing the senior debt in the form of bank loans, Lee pushed deeper into the stack. A relentless salesman, he found that he could provide the next, riskier, level of financing by immediately selling portions of it to other investors, his clients. The syndicated loan market was born.

While private-equity executives often contend that they are not part of Wall Street, a point made repeatedly during the depths of the financial crisis, during the height of the Occupy movement, and to every regulator or legislator who would listen during all of that time, the debt part of the equation inextricably ties buyout firms to investment banks and other lenders, as well as hedge funds.

Big banks like JPMorgan and Goldman Sachs have evolved into the primary providers of debt for leveraged buyouts and as the private equity industry has grown, groups of bankers devoted to what bankers call financial sponsors (just another name for private-equity firms) have flourished, especially when deals were coming fast and furious. So just as investment bankers build careers specializing in calling on techno- logy companies, retail concerns, and oil and gas partnerships, some spend their days and nights thinking about the likes of Henry, Steve, and David.

Banks have a complicated, but extraordinarily lucrative, relationship with private equity. The biggest buyout firms have become some of the

firms' best clients, each paying hundreds of millions or more each year
to Wall Street. Freeman & Co., a New York consultancy, estimated
that in 2007, the likes of KKR and Blackstone paid Wall Street firms
a staggering $16.3 billion in fees. That figure had fallen to a still-
substantial $7.65 billion in 2010. Almost half of that came from the top
20 firms, Freeman found, underscoring how much of the private-equity
business is dominated by a small cadre of institutions.[3]

Private equity also sits in a fast-paced, cutthroat corner of Wall
Street devoted to mergers and acquisitions, an area that has spawned an
ecosystem of bankers, accountants, lawyers, and consultants all devoted
to "the deal." Merger activity mirrors the broader economy, which
affects companies' appetites to acquire, and certain industries go through
periods of consolidation and divestiture. At no time since 2000, though,
has total M&A activity worldwide dipped below $1.1 trillion. It peaked
in 2007, largely driven by leveraged buyouts, at just over $4 trillion in
deal volume, according to Bloomberg data.

Private equity's prominence in the broader M&A discussion, as
measured by a percentage of deals that are buyouts, varies, depending on
a number of factors, including debt and the willingness of corporations
to sell divisions and compete with LBO firms for deals. In 2007, private-
equity deals accounted for 20 percent of announced M&A transactions
by dollar volume, Bloomberg data show. In 2009, at the depths of the
credit crisis, private equity deals were less than 7 percent. By 2011,
they'd regained their place, accounting for just less than 17 percent.

Any explanation of the leveraged buyout boom of 2005 to 2007
inevitably includes the phrases "cheap debt" or "easy credit." The
parallels to what led to the housing crisis are hard to ignore. Just as
financing was available for homebuyers to buy houses beyond what
they thought they could afford, so too was debt available for private-
equity firms to eye targets, bid up prices and buy companies that had
previously been far beyond their reach.

Part of it was the size of the equity funds they'd collected from
pensions and endowments eager, and in some cases desperate, for the
returns buyout firms had historically delivered. The other crucial
piece was the debt available, mostly through the high-yield market. The
high-yield (meaning high interest paying) market is something of a
catchall term for debt that is non-investment grade. Because of that

grade (given by credit rating agencies), investors demand to be compensated for the additional risk through more yield (interest) than they'd get from safer bonds issued by investment grade companies or the government. High-yield bonds are more colloquially called junk bonds.

During 2005 through 2007, the high-yield debt market was perfectly situated for the purposes of leveraged buyouts. Investors were eager to invest in debt vehicles like collateralized loan obligations (CLOs), which were assembled by banks by piecing together lots of loans and then dividing them into slices according to risk. Junk bond funds also thrived, so there were willing buyers for both loans and bonds.

Banks also used a number of products that helped fuel the boom. One was "staple financing," whereby the bank selling a company delivered the pitchbook for the deal with a separate document that offered to underwrite the debt financing for the proposed transaction at the same time it was pitching the sale. The terms for the debt were typically stapled to the book. That made it easy for a private-equity firm to pursue a deal since a key part of the transaction was already locked up. Many decried the practice as unsavory. In 2010, as banks revived lending for new deals, some with staple financing, the *Wall Street Journal* noted the trend: "[S]taple financing has its risks: Namely, potential for conflicts of interest, as investment banks advising a seller may have incentive to favor a buyer who takes advantage of the bank's offered financing."[4]

The investment banks had other tools in their arsenal, including what were known as "covenant lite" loans, which were made without some of the tests that would trigger default. Those sorts of arrangements gave private-equity firms confidence that even if what they bought struggled financially, it wouldn't trip the covenants that could lead to default. Then there were equity bridges, whereby a bank would "bridge" the equity part of the deal. That is, the bank would take part of the equity if the private-equity firm wasn't able or willing to speak for it, allowing the deal to move forward. All of those elements meant there was lots of available equity and lots of available debt. Combined with a go-go economy, it was a potent cocktail for the buyout industry. And buyout firms went on a bender. To continue the comparison to the consumer housing market, just like would-be homeowners coaxed into more house than they could ultimately afford, private-equity firms pushed the envelope with the help of eager financiers.

For context, KKR's seminal takeover of RJR Nabisco in 1989 stood as the largest-ever LBO for about 17 years. When KKR itself, in partnership with Bain, finally topped that with the HCA deal in late 2006, HCA held the top spot for only three months. Nine of the 10 biggest deals in the history of private equity happened from 2005 to 2007, the lone outlier being RJR.

The amount of debt layered onto companies during the leveraged buyout boom terrified some industry observers, and even some private-equity practitioners, as the credit crisis set in during 2008 and into 2009. Observers fretted over a "wall of debt"—money committed to LBOs from 2005 to 2007 that companies couldn't pay off and for which there was no market to refinance.

Surprisingly, even shockingly to some, there was no collective collision with that wall, though some companies struggled. The private-equity owners seized on a friendly credit market in 2010 to refinance billions of dollars of debt, pushing back maturities or forcing existing debtholders to trade in near-worthless debt for new paper that could be worth something down the line. They also benefited greatly from elements like covenant lite loans that allowed them to operate with debt ratios that under different circumstances might have triggered default.

Yet the amount of debt committed to leveraged buyouts during that period left lingering questions about how much debt was too much, and the dangers of leveraging a company just because you could. One complicated lesson of the boom and bust is Freescale Semiconductor, the chipmaker taken private by a group of private-equity firms in 2006 in the biggest LBO of that type of company ever. While the final chapter on the company has yet to be written, its troubled recent history makes a strong case that not every company can bear the burden of heavy borrowings.

■ ■ ■

Freescale began as part of Motorola, the legendary Chicago company that effectively invented the modern mobile phone. For decades, the semiconductor division had a captive customer that was helping define the modern electronics industry. Under pressure from its public share-holders who argued the unprofitable chip business was a drag on the broader company, Motorola announced in 2003 it would spin out what became Freescale. The spin was completed in late 2004 and Freescale's stock performed well. It was trading around $30 a share when word leaked that Freescale was entertaining buyout offers.

As the LBO boom began to crest in 2006, there was virtually no company that wasn't a potential target, given the aforementioned glut of both equity and available debt. Semiconductors are a notoriously cyclical industry historically, owing to the huge capital expenditures necessary to build chip factories, known as fabs. Profits ebb and flow dramatically, based on when a company has to shell out for a new fab, as well as the shrinking margins for semiconductors as they give way to the next generation of products.

To be sure, some of the most successful companies in U.S. history are chip companies, including Intel, Qualcomm, and Texas Instruments. Those companies and others helped define the modern technology industry; Intel was and is a central force in Silicon Valley, widely considered the cradle of American innovation. Semiconductors are the vital brains in electronics. In Freescale's case, the company's products were found in the dashboards of cars and video game systems among hundreds of other products.

Flush with cash and with easy financing offered, a handful of the world's biggest buyout firms weren't scared off from Freescale. They saw an underperforming, undermanaged, and overall neglected company that could benefit from a few years outside of the unforgiving public markets. A bidding war erupted and in the end, four firms—Blackstone, Carlyle, TPG, and Permira—agreed to buy Freescale for $17.6 billion, a 30 percent premium from where it was trading when word of a potential deal leaked. As soon as the deal closed, Freescale became the most indebted semiconductor company by a wide margin. Within months, the global economy began to unravel. Freescale watched as Motorola, still among its largest clients, and automakers, another key customer, faced unprecedented declines in their own businesses. That pain hit Freescale hard.

The private-equity owners scrambled, divvying up work among the parties to focus on the balance sheet, the company's operations, and its management. Michael Mayer, the CEO who'd overseen the divestiture from Motorola, stepped down in February 2008. The owners recruited Rich Beyer, the CEO of chipmaker Intersil, to run the company. When he told a fellow CEO he was going to run Freescale, the colleague asked, "Why would you join such a crappy company?"[5]

Beyer undertook a massive restructuring effort, closing three factories and reducing the number of design centers to 23 from 66. The owners engineered a debt swap to push out the chipmaker's borrowings, reducing debt by $2 billion. The efforts culminated in a 2011 IPO that was far from a glorious exit for the buy-out firms. All the proceeds went to pay down debt. The valuation for the IPO of $18 a share was 50 percent less than the average price paid by the owners.

By early 2012, Freescale was stabilized, if barely. Freescale's market capitalization was $3.7 billion, The company's debt load, once in excess of $10 billion, had been pared to a still-large $7 billion. The deal stands in part as a cautionary tale for LBOs, especially those negotiated amid frothy equity and debt markets. While Freescale has struggled, its owners are quick to point out that it did not, in fact, default on its obligations and did not file for bankruptcy. They make the case that the exogenous economic forces that crushed the company during the financial crisis might well have overtaken the chipmaker and forced a fire sale, and that its ability to have focused management and ownership ultimately helped it live to fight another day. The lack of clear lesson only serves to underscore the *ultimately complexity* of these deals, where numerous variables collide to determine the fate of a company.

■ ■ ■

As the global economy, and private equity along with it, recovered in 2010 and 2011, a number of buyout executives were quick to point out the lack of defaults by private-equity-owned companies. An analysis of the biggest deals of the boom shows that largely to be true and while "not going bankrupt" is far from the definition of a successful deal, the doomsday scenarios didn't play out in spectacular fashion. There were some failures. KKR's Capmark, a commercial real estate lender, sought bankruptcy protection in 2009. That followed retailer Linens 'n' Things, backed by Apollo, which filed in 2008.

In early 2010, there was a rigorous debate over how defaults by private-equity-backed companies compared with non-LBO backed concerns. Boston Consulting Group helped stir up the discussion, predicting that almost half of the companies bought by private-equity firms would default on their debt within three years.[6] Defaults have yet to accelerate. Historically, defaults have actually been lower for companies that have been through a private-equity transaction, according to at least one research paper. The study, by Per Stromberg at the Stockholm School of Economics, found an annual default rate from 1980 to 2002 of 1.2 percent for LBO-involved companies, versus a default rate for U.S. corporate bond issuers of 1.6 percent for the same period.[7]

The ambitions of the private equity industry rise and fall largely on the availability of debt, a lesson underscored by the lack of deals in the wake of the credit crisis, when banks weren't able to lend and the funds that bought the loans backing LBOs largely evaporated.

In 2007, the notion of a $100 billion leveraged buyout, was kicked about with abandon, and modeled by eager analysts inside every bank and major buyout firm. In 2012, the notion of a deal that size was simply laughable. Since the Hilton deal, announced in mid-2007, the largest buyout announced was a KKR-led consortium's $7.2 billion takeover of Samson Investment Co., an oil exploration concern, according to Bloomberg data.

The debt wasn't there to the extent that it once was. One of the easiest ways to measure it was through the percentage of the price that comprised debt versus equity. This was one of the most fundamental changes from the earliest days of the industry, when a private-equity fund could provide 5 to 10 percent of the purchase price and borrow the rest. Data showed that especially for smaller deals (under $1 billion), debt comprised only 46 percent of the purchase price in 2011 on average, down from 57 percent in 2006, near the peak of the boom, according to researcher Pitchbook. Transactions above $1 billion were able to get 61 percent of the purchase price in debt, down from 67 percent in 2006.[8]

Equity, however, was more than available from eager buyout firms. Much was written and discussed about the industry's "dry powder," the colloquial term for committed, uninvested money. Firms collectively had around half a trillion dollars of dry powder, according to numerous estimates, having sat on the sidelines for much of 2008 and 2009. The relative scarcity and cost of debt meant the dealmakers couldn't buy with abandon. One lesson of the boom and bust was clear: Be careful what you buy.

Chapter 4

"When Was the Last Time You Bought a Toilet Seat?"

Dollar General

R ichard Dreiling stepped onto the balcony outside the bar of the Dream Hotel in New York on the evening of November 13, 2009, and took a deep breath. As a light rain began to fall, exhaustion overcame him. He went back inside with his wife Ellen, told his colleagues good night, and went back to his hotel to sleep.

It was the end of a long day. That morning Dreiling had stood on the balcony of the New York Stock Exchange and rung the opening bell in honor of Dollar General's return to the Big Board via a public offering. It capped two weeks of pitching institutional investors on the story, repeating an hour-long presentation 9 or 10 times a day over breakfast, lunch, and dinner and everything in between in almost a dozen cities, from New York to Denver to Los Angeles, sometimes circling back to the same place for more meetings. It also capped a two-and-a-half-year reinvention of a discount retailer that had lost its way, floundered for a plan, and eventually succumbed to a rich takeover by KKR at the height of the LBO boom.

Dreiling, who started his career in retail as a stock boy in Kansas City, was the primary architect of the reinvention, charged by KKR with burnishing a chain that dated back to the 1930s in Kentucky and had once operated under the motto "The Town's Most Unusual Store." For a massive chain (10,000 stores in 39 states), the company retains more than a whiff of eccentricity. I had been told that to really understand Dollar General, I had to go there, to the company's head-quarters in the northern suburbs of Nashville, in an enclave called Goodlettesville. There, perched on a hill is a two-building, four-story complex. Their addresses are One Integrity Place and Turner One, a nod to the company's founding family.

The first thing you notice is the bears, massive metal statues of bears climbing over the fountain in front of the headquarters, one lying lazily on a nearby stone bench. Just inside the door is another bear (he was wearing a Santa hat on this particular December day). The bears were put there by one of Dreiling's predecessors, Cal Turner Jr., the son and grandson of Dollar General's two founders and its CEO for more than 20 years.

Off to one side of the atrium inside the front door is the "Hall of Values," a mini-museum of Dollar General's history, complete with a Southern baritone voice-over with a banjo and fiddle as background music. Walking counterclockwise through the room, the story of the company unfolds. Cal Turner Sr. and his dad, J. L. Turner, opened in 1939, a single location in Scottsville, Kentucky, under the name J. L. Turner & Son Wholesale. The elder Turner had dropped out of school when he was 11 years old; much of the company's philanthropic efforts centers on education and literacy.

By 1955, the Turners had decided to sell directly to consumers, intrigued by the allure of "dollar days" at department stores. What if, they wondered, there was a store where that was true every day? A big part of the initial strategy was to buy huge amounts of unwanted goods at a low price and then resell them. Cal Turner at one point negotiated with a vendor to buy reams of pink corduroy he made into pants and then successfully sold for $1 a pair.[1] The company expanded and was generating more than $1 million in annual net income by 1967, and a year later Dollar General went public. Cal Turner Jr. took over from his father as CEO in 1977 and the company kept growing by opening new stores and eventually making acquisitions. In 1983 and 1985, the company bought almost 500 additional stores and then struggled to integrate them into the existing company. With sales growth at a near-standstill, the company stopped advertising altogether in 1985 to regroup and focus on the brand, a fact noted in the Hall of Values.

One part of more recent history that goes unmentioned in the museum is the company's settlement in 2004 with the U.S. Securities and Exchange Commission after an investigation over accounting irregularities. The company never admitted wrongdoing, eventually agreeing to pay $10 million to settle the probe. Turner resigned as CEO in 2002 and chairman in 2003 after repaying $6.8 million he received in bonuses and through exercising stock options in 1999 and 2000.[2]

■ ■ ■

Armed with funds from limited partners and with access to debt from Wall Street, private-equity firms are rarely interested in companies firing on all cylinders. Healthy firms can't usually provide the potential for returns that buyout managers have guaranteed their investors, and which will deliver the rich profits they're after. In an era where huge amounts of leverage are no longer available, the combination of cash and debt has to be aimed at companies where something dramatic can happen to the company, usually by making radical changes to the way the target operates. That often starts with who runs it.

Dreiling has a shock of white hair that gives him a passing resemblance to the late comedian Leslie Nielsen. Belying his long career in retail, he's engaging but efficient. In a store, he's taking everything in. Around a table, he's sizing people up. He's quick with a compliment. Analyst queries on calls are often met with "That's a great question" before he launches into an answer.

It was just outside the Hall of Values where Dreiling first met the company's corporate staff, in January 2008. He walked into the atrium and stood on a small stage—set up in front of a bear—facing a banner that said, "Welcome Rick Dreiling." He took one look at that and thought to himself, "I hope like hell they're still saying that in 90 days."

There was reason for apprehension. Several months before Dreiling's appearance, they'd met their new owner, represented by a fellow named Michael Calbert, a former grocery store executive who'd spent the past seven years at KKR buying companies like Toys "R" Us. Calbert and Raj Agrawal, another KKR partner, along with Dollar General chief financial officer David Tehle and interim CEO David Bere, had spent the past nine months mapping out Dollar General's strategy. Part of the process had been picking someone to run the company. Now here was the guy they'd chosen.

While KKR was convinced it had made a winning deal, it was nonetheless a massive bet, especially in the face of an economy that was wilting and on the verge of cratering. KKR and its banks had barely been able to secure the financing needed to close the deal the previous July as the credit markets that had fueled enthusiastic deals earlier in the year locked up.

That day in January, Dreiling knew he had to be reassuring. He broke the ice by referencing a story in the local paper that had referred to KKR bringing in its "turnaround expert."

"I don't know who this turnaround expert is, but it's not me," he told the employees gathered around him and peering down from the three balconies overlooking the atrium. "This is your company and I have to earn your respect."

Despite working for decades in California and then New York, Dreiling maintains his Midwestern charm, which played well in the South. He got a taste of Southern manners a early on in an elevator, when an employee recognized him and said, "It's nice to meet you, Mr. Dreiling." Dreiling said, "I'm not Mr. Dreiling. My name's Rick." The response: "Well, it's nice to meet you, Mr. Rick."

On another elevator ride, when two employees didn't recognize him, he overheard a conversation that worried him, and underscored the lack of direction at the company. One turned to the other and said, "What do you think the program of the week is this time?"

That sort of confusion is where private-equity firms say they thrive.

Owning a company is where the rubber meets the road for private equity, and in the journey that the money takes from those pensions and endowments, this is the stop that has the broadest implications for the most people. Investors, workers, executives, customers, and the private-equity guys all have something on the line here. The conversation in the elevator, and looking up at the expectant faces looking down into the atrium, reminded Dreiling this wasn't an academic exercise. This was the sort of deal that KKR should excel at, the sort of deal it had sold itself to its investors on for going on three decades.

■ ■ ■

The years 2006 and 2007 were the headiest of times for private equity, and KKR was the busiest of any firm by most measures. The firm had made its name by making deals, and the opportunities to buy things had never been better.

KKR went on a buying binge. In late 2006, they topped the long-standing record for the industry's largest deal (set with its own RJR takeover almost two decades earlier) with the purchase of hospital chain HCA. After Blackstone topped that record months later with Equity Office Properties, KKR came back with TXU, the $43.2 billion deal that stands as the biggest ever.

Among the busiest deal guys was Calbert. He'd arrived at KKR in 2000 after another KKR company, Safeway, had bought a Houston grocery chain called Randalls where he was the chief financial officer. KKR has an affinity for retail, and specifically supermarkets. The firm has owned at least five supermarket chains since its creation, most notably Safeway, which it bought in 1986. Over the following 13 years, KKR turned its $129 million stake into $7.2 billion (making about 56 times its money); it's one of the most successful deals in the firm's history.

The Safeway deal was preceded by KKR's ownership of Fred Meyer, where it earned more than nine times its money. While it owned Safeway, KKR for a period also owned Stop and Shop, where it ultimately made more than about 10 times its original investment. At Randalls, Calbert's company, KKR more than tripled its money when it sold the chain to Safeway. The record in grocery was not perfect. KKR lost about $250 million on its investment in Bruno's, which it owned from 1995 to 1999.[3]

Calbert had been something of an experimental hire, though in a typically deliberate way for KKR. While he was in talks to join the firm, KKR had decided to start a new division, an internal consulting firm known as Capstone, which would allow KKR to offer operational advice it normally would have to pay McKinsey, Bain & Co., or Boston Consulting Group for. To run that business KKR hired Dean Nelson, who had worked at BCG as well as Shell Oil.

But they wanted some deal partners with real-world experience instead of just fancy MBAs, and Calbert fit the bill. Once on board, he started ginning up retail ideas, the highest-profile being the 2005 takeover of Toys R Us, with Bain Capital and Vornado. The Dollar General deal was percolating inside KKR for at least a year before the company sprang its offer in the fall of 2006. From his perch at KKR's Menlo Park office, Calbert marshaled a group of analysts to come up with a thesis around dollar stores.

Running numbers only gets you so far, so Calbert went on the road himself. He enlisted industry contacts, including former Dollar General executives, to visit stores with him, usually down South, where Dollar General stores were concentrated. He'd chat up store managers and customers, gathering anecdotal evidence to match the quantitative analysis performed back in New York and California. By 2005, he wanted to buy Dollar General, but it was too expensive. So he waited.

It didn't take long. The following year turned out to be a disastrous one for the chain. Amid a booming economy, dollar stores were far from in vogue. Dollar General had more specific problems. Many stores were disorganized, and a long-standing practice of keeping leftover inventory on hand backfired, Calbert said. Already rumors about a takeover were swirling. In late November, CNBC reported that buyout firms Bain Capital and Cerberus were weighing offers, sending the stock higher.

The market got the clearest sense of the company's woes on November 29 of that year, when it told investors the day after CNBC's report it would close 400 stores the following year. The company estimated the closures, plus the cost of selling off excess inventory at deep discounts, would cost $138 million. The stock dropped 6 percent that day.

There was no mention at the time of KKR, but Calbert already had been working the halls of KKR and making his case. Not everyone mirrored his enthusiasm. Most investments can clear KKR's investment committee with five or six meetings; Dollar General took eight. Calbert's partners asked for more information, including a presentation from outside consultants on the business, as well as further consultation with a former chief executive of a KKR-backed retailer. Finally, they were convinced.

On October 5, 2006, Calbert made his approach, meeting with then-CEO David Perdue, former CEO Cal Turner Jr., and David Wilds, a director on Dollar General's board. Calbert told the trio that KKR was interested in conducting official due diligence ahead of a potential formal offer. As a public company, Dollar General's board had a responsibility to consider the proposal and the following day the board's governance committee was notified of KKR's approach; it was decided that the full board should be informed and consider its options.[4]

The board formed a committee, which then hired Lazard to give advice, adding the investment bank to a roster of counselors that already included Lehman Brothers.

KKR originally was teamed with TPG in its pursuit. Blackstone and Bain emerged as another potential bidding pair. As various investors and bankers trooped into Goodlettesville, anxiety swept through headquarters. "Confusion was the No. 1 thing," CFO Tehle said. "People are saying, 'What does this mean for me personally?' Everyone was very nervous, thinking 'I'm sure my job will be eliminated.'"

In late February, Lazard gave the bidders a deadline for "best and final offers." KKR, now without TPG, offered $22 a share, a 31 percent premium over the company's share price on Friday, March 9, when it submitted its offer. An analysis by Lazard had come up with two scenarios to value the stock, the high end of the range in the more aggressive scenario was $21.25 a share.

Dollar General, its lawyers, and bankers huddled in person and over the phone that day and Saturday. Blackstone and Bain asked for more time. Dollar General and its bankers consulted, then demurred and voted unanimously to accept KKR's offer on Sunday, March 11.

KKR announced that it would buy the company the next morning. Tehle stood in the area outside the Dollar General conference room where much of the deal had been negotiated and watched CNBC as the deal was announced via press release at 8 A.M., 7 A.M. Nashville time. Within what felt like seconds to Tehle, the commentators were discussing the deal, instantly analyzing the price. They deemed it a fair price. Tehle exhaled.

Calbert and Agrawal arrived and spent the next three days in Goodlettesville, first conducting a town hall for employees, then sitting with the management team in the board room and going through it "in a very calm and measured fashion," Tehle says. "We agree with your numbers," Calbert told the executives. "These ideas are coming from what you guys are giving us."

Everyone was excited, but they still had to close the deal. The first step was the cash portion, about $2.8 billion. With TPG out of the picture, the entire nut fell to KKR to circle up. Simply writing a check wasn't an option, since a commitment of that size could trigger issues related to how much of one fund could be in a single deal. KKR needed other people with money.

Craig Farr is an affable Canadian who ventured south of the border to work on Wall Street and never left. As head of U.S. equity capital markets at Citigroup, KKR was a key client and his relationship at 9 West was cemented through his work on the public offering of KPE, the firm's European fund. When Kravis and Roberts were mulling the notion of starting their own capital markets unit, they hired Farr, with a vague mandate to figure out how money should better flow into and around the firm and its deals. No one, Farr included, knew exactly what that meant. Inside KKR, he was like the new kid in school. Everyone was intrigued, but not quite sure what to make of him and his new assignment. Deal guys, used to handling all their own financings through existing Wall Street relationships, were uneasy.

As the Dollar General deal moved toward completion, Farr got his chance to prove his worth. "George (Roberts) called and said, 'Can we get this done?'" Farr said. "I'd been here for less than a year. Of course I said yes." Farr tapped Canada Pension Plan, with its hearty appetite for so-called co-investments that give investors the ability to put more money into a deal, for lower fees. Farr additionally convinced Wellington Capital Management, an existing public shareholder of Dollar General, to buy into the new deal. Goldman Sachs and Citigroup, which were helping arrange debt financing, ponied up cash from their private-equity arms. KKR had the money it needed. "Everyone saw tangibly how this could work," Farr said. "Before that, there were a lot of skeptics."

The combined equity was about 37 percent, a substantial portion by historical standards (in KKR's seminal RJR deal, the company put up less than 10 percent), but it still left more than 60 percent of the deal to be funded through borrowed money. The souring economy that was part of KKR's Dollar General investment thesis hit home fast, and uncertainty in the credit markets almost derailed the deal altogether.

"We assumed it was going to get done," Tehle said, "until we went on the road."

The debt for most LBOs is a mixture of loans and bonds, and the bonds are marketed to institutional investors by a team that includes salespeople from the underwriting banks (in this case Goldman and Citi) and executives from the company. Tehle and David Bere, the president and interim CEO, were tapped to represent Dollar General.

In the course of two weeks in late June, Tehle and Bere gave presentation after presentation for the road show. While they were confident they could pull off the plan, Tehle admits they were pitching a leap of faith through their PowerPoint slides, or "deck" in Wall Street-ese. "It was a great deck, a great story, but it wasn't a proven story," Tehle said. "People would say, 'You haven't done any of this yet.'"

Still, response was generally good for the first week. At the end of the day, the Dollar General executives would dial in to a call to get an update and everything seemed fine, until Sunday night. At 10 P.M., Tehle and Bere dialed in from their respective hotel rooms in Boston, where they were set to meet investors the next morning. "The tone is decidedly more negative," Tehle said. "Clearly, over the weekend things got worse."

During the call, one banker suggested they might have to pull them off the road and wait six months.

Tehle rang Bere in his room after the conference call and voiced his concern. Then he called Calbert and expressed anxiety about postponing the road show and the bond sale. "That's not going to happen," Calbert told Tehle.

In the end, the deal got done, with Goldman and Citi reducing some fees for buyers, holding some of the debt on their respective balance sheets. "They took some pain," Calbert said. Like KKR, though, they were all in, given their choice to not only underwrite the debt, but participate on the equity side as well. The deal closed on July 6. Now Calbert had to find someone to run the company.

Calbert and David Perdue, the Dollar General chairman and CEO at the time of the deal, had agreed from the beginning that Perdue would leave once the deal closed. With Bere as the interim CEO, Calbert began a methodical search for a new leader.

Dreiling wasn't an immediate candidate despite some shared history. The two men had known each other from their supermarket days, and Dreiling had worked for KKR as a senior executive at Safeway. He was at Safeway when the grocery chain bought Randalls, where Calbert was the CFO. They kept in touch for a few years after that deal, in 2000, when Calbert went to KKR and Dreiling went on to serve as chief operating officer of Longs Drug Stores. He went on to run Duane Reade, the New York-based drugstore chain owned by fellow private-equity firm Oak Hill Partners.

Dreiling hadn't paid a huge amount of attention to the Dollar General deal, or not much more beyond reading the headlines with everyone else. At around $7 billion it was only a biggish deal for early 2007. After all, KKR had bought TXU for six times that and bankers were fantasizing about a $100 billion leveraged buyout. A discount chain down in Tennessee was a one-day story.

A headhunter who wasn't working on the Dollar General search suggested that the two men connect. Calbert liked the idea and rang up Dreiling. Dreiling's reaction to Calbert: "You want me to run *what*?" He was flattered but relatively firm. He had a job and wasn't looking for a new one. "Do me a favor," Calbert said. "Go out to New Jersey and visit four or five stores and tell me what we need to do."

Dreiling complied, and reported back to Calbert. The KKR partner kept wooing. Calbert asked Dreiling to meet him in Phoenix in the fall of 2007 and spend a day touring stores, part of his standard procedure in assessing a CEO candidate. He was still proceeding with the quickly fading façade of asking Dreiling's advice. Dreiling was the fourth or fifth would-be chief he'd squired around. "You can tell a lot about how they act in the store," Calbert said. "Are they condescending to the staff? What do they look at?"

In the first store they walked into, he lost Dreiling in the relatively small store (most Dollar Generals are 7,200 square feet), and found him a few minutes later, chatting with the store manager. At another outlet, Dreiling called Agrawal over and pointed to the Gatorade display. "You have green and red, where's orange? Orange is the number-two seller and there's not even a tag here, so they clearly don't carry it. Why would you stock No. 1 and No. 3?" Agrawal didn't have an answer. In another store, Dreiling and Calbert were walking through the hardware aisle and saw a display of toilet seats. Dreiling asked Calbert: "When was the last time you bought a toilet seat?"

Halfway through the day, the two KKR executives walked out of a store ahead of Dreiling. Calbert said to Agrawal in the parking lot: "You've just met the new CEO of Dollar General."

Despite Calbert's certainty, Dreiling wasn't sold and KKR protocol dictated that a hire of this magnitude needed to be vetted by Kravis and Roberts.

The courtship was delicate. Calbert was positioning the meetings to Dreiling as a series of favors, casual conversations among friends about how to deal with this new company KKR had bought. After all, Dreiling had once been a part of the KKR family via Safeway, and had clear admiration for Kravis and Roberts personally. Over Thanksgiving, which Dreiling was spending in California, Calbert asked him to have lunch with Roberts, with the same instructions: "Just tell him what you think." The two men talked about their kids and life, and a little about Dollar General. Dreiling wasn't stupid; he knew this was at least a quasi-job interview and the more he talked about Dollar General, the more he wanted the job. Roberts asked him, on a scale of 1 to 10, how Dreiling would fit as Dollar General's chief. Dreiling said, "I'm a 12." Roberts was stonefaced. Later, he told Dreiling it was the first time in decades of asking people to rank themselves that anyone had rated themselves off the chart.

Now a full-on candidate, Dreiling was required to go through a battery of psychological tests administered by an outside firm, an hours-long exercise in a hotel suite with not much more than carrots to munch on, anathema to Dreiling, who prefers potato chips. A couple of weeks later, Calbert called and said Kravis wanted to meet. Arriving at 9 West late one afternoon, he was ushered into the small conference room adjacent to Kravis's office. While he waited, Dreiling noticed that a blue folder with the pysch consulting firm's name was sitting on the table, with his name on it. Kravis came in and the two men talked for an hour, a wide-ranging conversation similar to the Roberts lunch. As they walked out of the meeting room, Dreiling couldn't help but glance down at the blue folder Kravis now had in his hand. Kravis looked at the folder, looked at Dreiling and said, "By the way, you passed."

Now it was up to Calbert. As Christmas approached, he suggested he and Calbert get together, with their respective wives, who already knew each other. The men would play golf while the wives visited "and then we'd meet the girls for dinner," Dreiling said. On the course, Calbert gave him the offer.

Private-equity deals can be wildly lucrative for those involved, and the managers of the companies are no exception. It's an element any buyout manager will stress amid the talk of "aligning interests." In Dreiling's case, his salary is $1 million a year, relatively modest for the CEO of a large publicly traded company. The big money is in the stock. A government filing in April 2012 showed that Dreiling, who has sold a small portion of his stock, still owned about 1.54 million shares of Dollar General. Trading at $46 a share, that stake was worth roughly $70 million.

Back in 2007, all that was theoretical. Dreiling asked for some time to think it over. After all, he had a job that he liked, working for another private-equity firm, to boot. While he wasn't planning on returning to New York for another week, he called the partner at Oak Hill who chaired Duane Reade and said he was coming back early from vacation and wanted to meet. "Anyone knows that if your CEO calls saying that, you've got some sort of problem," Dreiling told me, laughing. Oak Hill asked for the weekend to put together a counteroffer to keep him at Duane Reade and Dreiling agreed.

He left his office near Penn Station in midtown Manhattan and stopped by Uncle Jack's, a local steakhouse, for his usual wind-down glass of wine. While he was chatting with the bartender, his cell phone rang. It was George Roberts, pressing his case with a personal appeal.

Dreiling, still slightly starstruck by the KKR mystique, assured Roberts he was thinking about it carefully. The next Monday, he accepted the job.

■ ■ ■

I wanted to see a Dollar General store through Dreiling's eyes, so we hopped in my rental car and drove to an outlet you can practically see from the conference room where we'd been sitting earlier, just up the hill at headquarters.

Clearly this was a showcase store and I felt a twinge of sympathy for the poor store manager who has to deal with folks from corporate popping in with visitors in tow. Dreiling walked me through the store, talking about changes small and large. Small: The strips that hang merchandise off the shelves vertically are now fixed to the shelf, preventing stockers from knocking them off when they replenish the shelves at night. Large: Store managers across the chain used to have autonomy over about 20 percent of what the store carried, meaning if you had a store run by an avid Elvis fan, it was stuffed with Elvis merchandise. Now store managers have autonomy over exactly zero.

They also have very little say about what goes where. Dreiling found that there often was little thought, or maybe different theories, about what should go where. Spices would be sitting on the same aisle as underwear and bras.

Every foot is accounted for. As we walk through, Dreiling notes that candles aren't big sellers, so next year they'll have four feet of shelf space instead of eight feet. Everything is about real estate here. Dreiling repeats "7,200 square feet" like it's a mantra.

There were no toilet seats in sight.

When he took over, Dreiling asked Tehle to rent about 50,000 square feet of empty retail space to create three prototype layouts that they could fiddle with. The byproduct of those experiments is what we see in stores today. "Now it's all tweaks," Dreiling said. Apparel has been elusive and they've conducted research to figure out how to get their core customer to buy. One result is less for women, despite women being the overwhelming majority of the Dollar General shopping public. They shop for their kids first, their husbands second, themselves third.

Another insight was understanding how categories of products dictated what brought shoppers in as well as what they ultimately bought. "Consumables drive the visit, non-consumables drive the basket," Dreiling said, in retailer-speak. Translation: You get them in to buy some eggs, you make money when they realize they need a birthday present, a new shirt for their son, and some school supplies.

With that in mind, every store now carries milk. As we walk through, he notes that they also have orange-flavored Gatorade.

Elements like the breakdown between consumables and non-consumables—along with same-store sales growth, expansion plans, and potential acquisitions—are the things that Wall Street obsesses over, better to build their models with and therefore make predictions about the company's earnings and ultimately their stock price. When I visited, Dollar General was in the midst of meeting analysts from brokerage houses (known as the sell side) and institutional investors (the buy side). Dollar General caught the attention of some of the world's foremost investors, including Warren Buffett, who was among the 10 biggest shareholders of Dollar General as of late 2011. He more than doubled his stake during the third quarter of that year. His interest is especially interesting given that he's been a vocal critic of private equity, with which he's sometimes gone head to head in buying companies. In a 2010 speech that was pre-recorded and played at corporate governance conference, he said Berkshire Hathaway had avoided buying companies outright from buyout firms in part because they "don't love the business" in the same way long-time owners do. His preference is to keep owners after the acquisition to take advantage of their "passion" for the company.[5]

Part of the attraction for Wall Street about the Dollar General story is the relative outperformance of the company versus Family Dollar, which fended off its own takeover in 2011. That approach, from activist shareholder Nelson Peltz, spurred more interest from other hedge funds. Bill Ackman bought shares of Family Dollar in 2011 and told an investment conference in New York that year he believed he could make money if Family Dollar could replicate Dollar General's success.[6]

I asked Dreiling whether he worried he'd given his competitors a blueprint they could use to beat him. "There are no secrets in retail," he said. "It's not about the plan. Everybody's got an idea. This is about executing the plan."

■ ■ ■

For some of the execution, Calbert and later Dreiling turned to KKR's in-house operations squad known as Capstone. The group had advised

Calbert during due diligence and was responsible for helping the deal team write a 100-day plan for Dollar General. Within weeks of the deal being announced, a small group landed in Goodlettesville. Three Capstone executives were there for 100 weeks. Dean Nelson, the head of Capstone, also sat on Dollar General's board for a period. Like their counterparts at other private-equity firms, the KKR operations experts had to walk a fine line. Like Dreiling's analysis of the blueprint, Nelson said his team has to essentially cajole and enable: "These are things the companies have thought of. You have to figure out how to help them do it."

In Dollar General's case, Capstone went about ruthlessly figuring out a plan to "remerchandise" the stores. No SKU was sacred and each one had to be analyzed in terms of profit per square foot. The stores were carrying four brands of batteries. That was deemed too many. Solution: Cut it to two and let the manufacturers duke it out.

Fixing the private-label offerings was a crucial part of merchandising and the quality challenges there quickly came into sharp focus when a rat had been found in a Dollar General private-label package of green beans.

Nelson put the entire private-label project in the hands of Rebecca McKillickan, who spent two years reassembling the business. Dreiling, an avid diet soda drinker, took a special interest in private-label colas after he sampled the product and practically spit it out. It turned out the supplier had altered the formula—the "brix" in cola-speak—in order to save money. "He reformulated that product himself," Nelson said of Dreiling.

Hundreds of miles from headquarters, there is evidence that Dollar General is a sprawling work in progress. A few days after Christmas, I wandered into the Dollar General in my wife's hometown, a town called Walton tucked in the Catskills in upstate New York (population 6,596). It's a classic rural location for a discount retailer, so much so that there's a Family Dollar a quarter-mile away, just a couple blocks up Delaware Street.

On this quiet December morning, the store was in the process of shifting out of Christmas mode, with deep discounts on holiday items, from labels to ornaments. Many of them were already gone, and one set of shelves had a sheet faxed from a central location laying out how to properly display Valentine's Day candy and gifts. On my way out, I spotted a local touch: bright orange t-shirts to support the local high school sports team, the Walton Warriors.

This particular Dollar General is far from the gleaming palace a few blocks from Dreiling's office, but there were signs it could get there. While it's not the town's most unusual store, it's got the potential to be a new generation of general store in towns like this.

By the spring of 2009, a handful of executives inside Dollar General and at KKR realized they were far ahead of where they'd planned to be and that a public offering was possible, maybe even that year. In May, Dreiling held an offsite strategy meeting with his direct reports and invited Calbert in for part of the day. Calbert broached the idea of an IPO with the managers, who greeted the idea enthusiastically.

A key element behind Calbert and KKR's thesis about Dollar General in 2006 and 2007 was that the economy had crested and would soon turn their way—that is, people were going to be looking for places to save money. They were right, and startlingly so, Calbert and Dreiling said. "What the economy did was the trial that made everything happen faster," Dreiling said. A spooked U.S. consumer started looking for ways to save money through the recession, and then held on to some of those habits in the fragile recovery.

The typical Dollar General customer lives in a household that makes about $40,000 a year. Dreiling's job is to make sure she's happy, while also wooing a couple of other sets of customers. Dollar General categorizes these shoppers as "trade-downs" and "trade-ins." Trade-downs are folks who are coming to Dollar General out of personal economic necessity, who've decided they can't afford to buy what they need at Target anymore. They typically make higher than the average customer, up to about $70,000 a year, but are looking for every place they can to save money. Trade-ins are the relatively wealthy customers who shop for food at a traditional or even high-end grocery store, but save on, say, household cleaners at Dollar General.

The IPO provided another interesting test case. It would be the first time that KKR Capital Markets would underwrite a stock offering. For Dollar General CFO Tehle, that made a big difference. "Any other firm, they are looking to sell you something, that's their job," he said. "With KCM, you feel like they're a partner to the business." The IPO filings outlined how much KKR and the other investors stood to gain, after only a couple of years work. The equity investors paid an average of $8.76 for each share of Dollar General they owned. At the IPO price of $21 apiece, the paper gain was more than double. In May 2012, Dollar General was trading above $46 a share.

KKR sold only a small amount in the IPO, and the firm has sold down its position in secondary offerings, five of them as of April 2012, each at a higher stock price, including $45.25 in 2012. In December 2011, Dollar General opted to use some of its excess cash to buy some of KKR's shares back, reducing the number of shares outstanding, a key for the debt ratings agencies.

For KKR, Dollar General was a much-needed win from its LBO boom buying spree. TXU and First Data continue to struggle and are unlikely to be sold for much more than what KKR and its investors paid for them.

For Tehle, a friendly but serious man, standing above the NYSE that November morning resonated on a personal level. He'd been at the company at its depths, staring down the barrel of a corporate existential crisis. He hadn't known whether he'd be part of the new, KKR-led regime. He'd sat on the phone and wondered whether the deal that he'd believed in and helped navigate would even get done, in the teeth of those ugly credit markets in 2007.

"It was elation," Tehle told me during the headquarters visit. He was wearing a pink shirt with French cuffs. The cufflinks are a square that says "DG" with "NYSE" underneath it, a token from the IPO celebration; Dreiling has a pair of his own. "No one thought it would happen that quick. This is what we were all working for."

Chapter 5

Modern Art

Inside KKR

T en thousand bucks.

Henry Kravis and his cousin George Roberts each scribbled out a check in that amount, smaller companions to the $100,000 draft their more established colleague, former boss and partner Jerome Kohlberg, had written.

That formed the entirety of the start-up capital for what became Kohlberg Kravis Roberts & Co., known then unofficially, and now officially, as KKR. None of the three men would ever need to put any more money in. The two cousins would become billionaires several times over. Kohlberg would go on to create his own firm the following decade after disagreeing with the cousins on the strategy of the firm. Kohlberg & Co., based in suburban Mt. Kisco, New York, has invested in the likes of sporting goods maker Bauer, Christian publisher Thomas

Nelson, and Central Parking. He also personally owns the Vineyard Gazette, a newspaper on Martha's Vineyard.

Today, the original bank documents hang framed near Kravis's corner office on the 42nd floor of KKR's headquarters at 9 West. A gift from JPMorgan's Jimmy Lee, the matting features logos of companies KKR has bought in the intervening years, from Safeway to Motel 6. Since Lee tracked down the documents, KKR has gone on to buy everything from Del Monte to Oriental Brewery. At three different points, it's held the title of pulling off the biggest leveraged buyout in history.

By dint of one of those deals, the $30 billion purchase of RJR Nabisco in 1989, KKR is the most famous of all the leveraged buyout firms, at least by the measure of asking a random passerby or a relative over Thanksgiving dinner. The extraordinary details of that hotly contested deal gave rise to *Barbarians at the Gate*, one of the most compelling business stories of all time. The book, by Bryan Burrough and John Helyar, captured vividly the backroom dealings, outsized egos, and gamesmanship that people on Wall Street recognized as being all too accurate and everyone else reacted to with some combination of admiration and horror.

Just as *Barbarians* stood the test of time, so did the RJR deal in terms of its stature in the industry's history. Despite talk at the time that it was representative of a wave of megadeals, none came close. For almost two decades, no firm was able to top it in sheer dollar volume, and that may be part of the reason the deal, and the epic account of it, remain so closely associated with KKR and inform its public image to this day.

■ ■ ■

KKR's New York headquarters are majestic. Security is tight, with a guard posted behind glass before a visitor can pull open the wooden doors that open onto a view of Central Park. The carpeted halls are lined with art from Kravis's own collection, which tends toward the modern. His wife, Marie-Josée Kravis, curated what's on display around KKR headquarters, picking from the Kravises' wide-ranging art collection. While the corridors have mostly understated modern art, some of the meeting rooms feature more provocative pieces. There's a small meeting room down the hall from Kravis's office with two massive Cindy Sherman photographs hanging on opposite walls, from a series the artist did featuring what can only be described as creepy clowns.

Vestiges of the earliest days are sprinkled throughout the offices of KKR, beyond the bank paperwork framed in the anteroom to Kravis's office. In the small library adjacent to his office, where he holds most meetings, there's a picture of Joe and Rose's, the restaurant in midtown Manhattan where Kravis and Roberts had dinner right after they left Bear Stearns. The site of the restaurant is now a Dress Barn.

Any conversation with someone who works or has worked at the firm, including the cousins, makes it clear that Henry and George together are running the show. There are no other major investment firms today beyond theirs whose figurative DNA is linked to actual shared DNA.

Henry and George have known each other for 66 years, dating back to a family vacation the Tulsa Kravises and the Houston Robertses took to Marblehead, Massachusetts. Not surprisingly, neither remembers the trip, though as the two grew older, and closer, both their parents reminded them of that first meeting. As children, they saw each other frequently, and Kravis is fond of saying their last major disagreement was over a bicycle when they were seven years old.

George was visiting Henry, who'd just gotten a new bike. George wanted to ride it. Henry didn't want him too. Scolded for not being a better host, Henry got chased into the house, where he promptly ran smack into a wall, injuring his face to the point where he had to go to the hospital. Argument over.

Beyond middle school and summer camp, use of the term "best friend" is limited, and yet Kravis uses it frequently to describe Roberts. For decades, they spoke one-on-one every day by phone or in person. In the modern era, they typically are involved in some sort of meeting or group communication on a daily basis, though they've fallen out of the daily check-in habit.

Still, the ethos was set. The two men, known as "HRK" and "GRR" in firm correspondence, are by all accounts inseparable philosophically. "It's very clear they have a pact, and it's very strong," said Craig Farr, who runs the firm's capital markets business. This partnership pervades every aspect of the firm. While each man speaks for himself, it is clear they're also comfortable speaking for the other. Any statement to the press or investors of any magnitude comes from both of them. During our conversations, Kravis constantly referenced "George and I" when describing decisions large and small.

"We're two people, with one voice," Kravis said. "If we disagree, we talk it out. If one of is totally against it, it's not happening." In another conversation, he referred to KKR as a football team "with a two-headed quarterback." When I asked Roberts how it trickles down through the firm, he compared it to a healthy relationship between parents that models behavior for their children. "There's no agenda between Henry and me," he said. "That reinforces everything we're trying to do at the firm."

With two long-standing founders so in synch, and still firmly in control of their creation, the culture is thus undoubtedly a reflection of them. And that culture is a serious, driven one, with 9 West, Menlo Park, and every KKR office living shrines to overachievement. They preach discipline, and "relentless" is a word I heard over and over again.

While the RJR deal turned out to be an outlier in terms of size for that period, the notion of Doing The Big Deal is quintessential KKR. The firm has underscored that in the decades hence by buying big-ticket, high-profile companies. Its partners are at times painfully methodical, but ultimately hyper-confident in their strategy. The line between rigor and mania is a thin one, and there's a drive to be *the best* that seems to exist in slightly sharper relief in the halls of KKR. Maybe it's the art on the walls, maybe it's that everyone is impeccably dressed. Maybe it's the lack of irony and sense of absolute focus that pervades every single conversation. It manifests itself mostly in the way KKR chooses who ends up working at the firm. I heard stories of rounds of interviews stretching over months, with meetings that numbered in the thirties or forties. Up until a decade ago, when it became logistically impossible, any candidate of significance met every single partner. Recalling his hiring in 1993, chief administrative officer Todd Fisher said, "The process was shocking in terms of its intensity."

■ ■ ■

As is the case at other firms who haven't gone through any sort of CEO succession (Carlyle being the other prime example), the chemistry between the founders is seen as a crucial asset. The power of that partnership and the underlying personalities, too, make a multibillion-dollar question mark for all of KKR's investors, both public and private. Kravis told his public shareholders in 2011 that he and Roberts are keenly aware of succession planning. "You have to be assured that George and I think about this every day," he said at the March investor meeting at New York's Pierre Hotel. "We talk about what will be the future at KKR and you can't run any company, in our view, unless you build a very deep bench of people."

The best-known face of the firm beyond the founders is Scott Nuttall, whose title, Head of Global Capital and Asset Management gives him a broad portfolio overseeing all of the firm's money-raising activities and newer lines of business. In addition to sitting on the management committee, he's also the firm's primary senior executive voice to public shareholders through the quarterly conference calls with Wall Street analysts and investors.

Nuttall captures the firm's relentless discipline and Kravis's and Roberts's insistence that KKR wasn't about one or two men. During one conversation, he parried any attempt to talk about himself, constantly pushing the discussion to the firm. Yet he has quietly gained more and more responsibility since his arrival at KKR in the early 1990s after working for a short stint as an analyst at Blackstone. His current role makes him among a handful of people who could potentially run the firm, especially since he's been a deal guy as well as worked in management overseeing some of the newer initiatives as well as an expanded fund-raising effort.

Having spent most of his adult life so far at KKR, Nuttall is well indoctrinated, to the point where he, too, thinks constantly about KKR's legacy. "Firms that found industries tend to get passed by," he said. "We need to make sure that doesn't happen. We all walk around with that anxiety, and that's good."

Nuttall is a wunderkind in a house full of them. William Sonneborn, who runs KKR Asset Management, is 42 years old. Frederick Goltz, based in San Francisco like Sonneborn, is 41.

Sonneborn arrived at KKR through an approach in early 2008 by Nuttall, who initially wanted to explore a KKR-sponsored employee buyout of money manager TCW, where Sonneborn was president. A phone call prompted a visit to 9 West, where Nuttall quickly determined that he didn't want to buy TCW, but he did want to hire Sonneborn. He quickly introduced him to Kravis and, with his blessing, invited Sonneborn to the firm's annual firm meeting, which happened to be taking place a couple of weeks later not far from where Sonneborn lived.

That's where Sonneborn got the full picture of KKR. He arrived at La Costa—a resort in Carlsbad, California, which KKR owned through a real estate partnership, that was the regular site of the annual meeting—for more than two dozen interviews with various partners, and his initial meeting with Roberts. One of his most striking impressions was numerous KKR executives in various states of injury incurred through the sports portion of the meeting. "These were, after all, very competitive, type-A people," Sonneborn said.

The sports component was relatively new to the meeting, and a brainchild of Goltz, by then a 12-year veteran of the firm who was in KKR's first analyst class. Looking for a way for himself and his colleagues to blow off steam, he'd cast about for the right sport and chosen soccer. Roberts, perusing the agenda ahead of time and showing how deep he was willing to get into the details, questioned Goltz's decision, worried about too many people getting injured and insisted he offer volleyball as well. Goltz acceded to the boss, but noted later that all the injuries, including broken fingers, came from the ranks of volleyball players. "The problem is, you can't really gloat with George," he told me.

Goltz's deep affinity for Roberts dated back to a time when he joined a firm that had a total of 22 executives. A native of western Pennsylvania who went to Wall Street after the University of Pennsylvania (he also earned an MBA at INSEAD after joining KKR), he briefly tried to convince Roberts to let him stay in New York. Roberts insisted the job was in California. Goltz joined an office of less than 10 people, which at the time had a single laptop that whoever wanted it had to sign out for the weekend.

The firm meetings then were held in Vail, since the two dozen participants could stay at some houses there owned by Kravis and longtime KKR partner Paul Raether. A defining moment for Goltz at his first gathering was a high-stakes poker game where "the house" extended him and a few others credit for their bets. Goltz, then a brash young man, lost badly. As he left for home, he wondered if the debt was real. Then he got the bill. "It wasn't about the money," he said. "It was about the lesson. Ultimately, you're accountable."

Goltz went on to co-head the firm's energy business and then raised his hand for a new effort in 2008: KKR's attempt at a dedicated fund for mezzanine lending, the high-interest debt used in leveraged buyouts or by companies who can't get traditional bank loans. The decision to pursue the business was classic KKR. "The amount of time we agonized about getting into the business was measured in years," Goltz said. They finally chose mid-2008 as the entry point, only to watch the world collapse around them. "What looked like a straightforward process became a three-year process," he said. Goltz suffered through dozens of fruitless meetings with would-be investors paralyzed by the global credit crisis but interested to hear KKR's take. When the world right-sized, he was finally able to raise the money, and in late 2011 KKR announced a $1 billion mezzanine fund.

Sonneborn and Goltz both said the effort, along with a similarly tortuous path to an infrastructure fund launched around the same time, epitomized the firm's ethos, one that largely values an excruciatingly methodical approach that at times leaves it behind its more aggressive competitors. "We're deliberate in making a decision and then dogged," Goltz said. "As transformative as the last 10 years have been for the firm, it's not like we're going catch as catch can. That is just not in the DNA."

So it's left to Goltz and Sonneborn and their ilk to fiddle where they can. Sonneborn's relative newness, his responsibility for the most recent business expansions, and working in an outpost in San Francisco give him license to try new things. While the office has the signature KKR touches—the 50th-floor office provides views of the Pacific Ocean looking over the Golden Gate Bridge, making 9 West's vistas seem almost quaint—Sonneborn is pushing the envelope. In March 2012, he abandoned his office to sit on a newly expanded trading floor to accommodate the growing non-private-equity business. "We're trying new things," he said. "We have younger people and newer businesses."

That's balanced by peers who've spent decades with the firm. Michael Michelson, the co-head of North American private equity, joined the firm in 1981 after working with KKR as an outside lawyer at Latham & Watkins; his fellow co-head, Alexander Navab, joined in 1993. Raether, who heads the firm's portfolio management committee, arrived at KKR in 1980.

In 2009, Kravis and Roberts decided to elevate Todd Fisher, who joined them in 1993, to the newly created position of chief administrative officer. The process of getting Fisher into the job wasn't easy. He'd initially led an effort to hire an outsider to fill the job but the two cousins ultimately decided they wanted someone internally to take it. "It was a bit of a shock to the system," Fisher said. "I couldn't tell if it was a promotion or a demotion." Kravis separately conceded to me that he and Roberts had a hard time giving responsibility to Fisher and other senior managers, a tendency Fisher was well aware of. "It was not an easy set of conversations," Fisher said. "It involved a lot of people I was going to have to interact with and that I'd have a say over what got done. They swallowed hard and said, 'We want to do this.'"

Fisher now has responsibility over legal, public affairs, and finance. He gets a chance to shape the future of the firm, all the while shaping KKR in the mold of how it began. "We were operating as a boutique and we were changing ourselves into an institution. How do you add 600 employees to 300 and retain your unique culture so you don't get consumed by the culture of people coming in?"

The long tenures of the majority of executives, coupled with Kravis's and Roberts's role in hiring just about every one of them, mean the cousins have the ability, and use it, to call up just about anyone in the firm, at any time. "Regardless of how neat the org chart looks, they reach down deep and talk to people they've known for a long time," Goltz said. That serves to give managers an extra incentive to keep the two CEOs appraised of all the important things going on.

Going forward, one potential scenario has Kravis and Roberts ceding the CEO duties to another pair of executives, both of whom would likely be long-time KKR members. The cousins are likely to replicate the bicoastal scenario that has seemed to help balance their own leadership of the firm and, given the evolution into non-LBO businesses, at least one of the pair would come from outside the private-equity group.

Kravis insisted to me that no decision had been made as to what the post-HRK and GRR landscape would look like in terms of organizational structure, specifically whether it would be a single CEO or a couple of chiefs. Even with Kravis's "deep bench," there is simply no way any one person, or pair, will bring exactly what the cousins do. For a couple of guys under six feet tall, they cast long shadows.

■ ■ ■

Leaving Bear Stearns also made the founders focus on the type of firm they wanted to run. On what would be his last day at the firm, Kravis showed up from a business trip to find his office locked, with a guard posted outside. Kohlberg's resignation earlier, and the announcement that Kravis and Roberts were leaving as well, triggered Bear Stearns to clear out Kravis's desk and retain his files. Thirty-five years on, he still told the story with some indignation, and in detail, right down to the accent of the security guard.

Their uncomfortable departure, and the whole experience of working for someone else and then at a very young age deciding not to, have made Kravis and Roberts near-obsessives about the culture of the firm. During one interview, Kravis mentioned twice that I should see the cultures and values list that the firm hands out; it's prominently featured in the firm's annual report.

Over the course of more than a dozen interviews with KKR executives, the message was startlingly consistent from all of them, who swore they hadn't been coached. They chalked it up to Kravis and Roberts, who relentlessly drive their own personalities into the fabric of everyday KKR life. The work ethic is Midwestern humble can-do infused with a hearty dose of Wall Street ambition. KKR is a firm of strivers.

One of Kravis's favorite interview questions is about what an applicant has read. In a business school twist, he asks candidates to describe their personal balance sheet—that is, what they perceive to be their assets and liabilities. He said he presses anyone who comes to see him to show they are well-rounded; he assumes if they've gotten to this point they're smart. He was intrigued by Joseph Bae, who now runs KKR's Asian private-equity operation, because Bae had debated on whether to pursue a career as a concert pianist. Marc Lipschultz wrote an in-depth paper in college on Dante. Both men now serve on KKR's management committee, the group involved in all major firm decisions.

"It's a much longer process to hire people," Kravis said. He and Roberts insist on candidates meeting as many people as possible before they extend an offer, to avoid the perception that anyone is "Henry's guy" or "George's guy" and therefore starting at an advantage that quickly sours. "We want people to come in with the most wind at their back."

Roberts, knowing the interviewing rigor of his colleagues, uses his time as a sort of KKR personality litmus test. He presses interviewees to talk about a failure that affected them, even if it wasn't of their doing, sometimes as personal as a parents' divorce. Goltz said he walked out of his interview with Roberts having not talked at all about business. "The whole conversation was about my family and how I grew up," Goltz said. "He was much more concerned about, 'Is this a person I want to work with?' "

That approach has manifested itself for anyone with hiring responsibility as what's alternately referred to as the "dinner test" or the "taxicab and waiter test." Because these are men and women who measure everything, a standard interview element is taking the candidate out for a meal and actually counting how many times they say "please" and "thank you" to the staff. Sonneborn said would-be employees have gone through months of interviews only to flunk that test. "We want to know how they treat people they're never going to see again," Roberts said.

■ ■ ■

There are two baseball bats tucked in one corner of Kravis's library. One's a Louisville Slugger from Joseph Plumeri, who Kravis convinced to become CEO of insurance broker Willis, which KKR took private in the late 1990s. The other was a gift from David Knowlton, a long-time investment banker.

Knowlton first met Kravis in the mid-1980s as a young banker at Manufacturer's Hanover/Chase. KKR was at the time using other banks for most of its financing; Knowlton's boss gave him responsibility for establishing a relationship with the firm to pitch ideas for potential deals as well as business for the bank. Knowlton's first stop was a lunch with Richard Beattie, KKR's longtime outside counsel at Simpson Thacher.

His advice about KKR, Knowlton told me, was: "Call on the entire firm and don't forget George and Henry."

Beattie helped arrange a lunch at 9 West for Knowlton and within a year, they'd worked on two KKR deals. Knowlton developed a relationship with Kravis that has stretched nearly two decades.

Knowlton went on to start Watch Hill Partners, which was subsequently sold to FBR Capital Markets. In 2011, he created New York-based Three Ocean Partners. Kravis was quoted in the press release announcing the firm and agreed to spend time with Knowlton and the rest of Three Ocean to impart his wisdom. His advice, Knowlton said, to the young associates about how to succeed in an increasingly transactional Wall Street: "Be interesting, be relevant."

In a way, the modern KKR culture is a reflection of the maturing of not just the firm, but the industry, and of front-man Kravis himself. Early Kravis was a carouser, according to accounts including *Barbarians*, which tells tales of a thirty-something Kravis working hard and playing just as intensely, notably riding a motorcycle around his apartment at a birthday party.[1] That behavior appeared to crest around the time of the RJR deal, the swashbuckling tactics on display in the deal a reflection of Kravis's M.O. His wife at the time was Carolyn Roehm, a fashion designer, and the two cut a distinct figure through the Manhattan social scene.

In the twenty-first century Kravis is a different animal. Now in his late 60s, he has taken on a more statesman-like role. His wife Marie-Josée is said to have a deep impact on that approach. An economist by training, she has served on a number of corporate boards, including LVMH Moet Hennessy Louis Vuitton, the world's largest maker of luxury goods, and advertising company Publicis. With her husband, she's deeply involved in the Henry R. Kravis Prize in Leadership, an annual award given in conjunction with Claremont McKenna, Kravis's and Roberts's undergraduate alma mater.

Kravis, by virtue of living in New York and moving constantly within the close-knit, constantly overlapping world of high finance, has an ability to immediately disarm with a charming word. His philanthropy, especially to some of Manhattan's better-known cultural institutions like the Metropolitan Museum of Art, makes him a bold-faced name. He's probably the longest-standing major private-equity manager

on the New York charity circuit and has served on the board of Mount
Sinai Hospital. He's also been deeply involved in the arts, with a wing at
the Metropolitan Museum of Art named for him; Marie-Josée serves as
president of the board of trustees at New York's Museum of Modern
Art. Kravis himself also has been involved in economic development in
his adopted hometown. He created the New York City Investment
Fund and serves on the board of the Partnership for New York City.

His recent headline gift was a $100 million gift to Columbia Business
School, where he earned his MBA in 1969 and is now co-chairman of the
Board of Overseers. The gift was designated to fund the construction of a
new home for the business school, part of a $6.3 billion project to create
a new Columbia campus in West Harlem.[2]

Kravis told me he's opted to focus his philanthropy on groups tied
to education, culture, and medicine, three categories that obviously give
him a huge set of options. He's increasingly interested in applying
lessons learned in his day job to charity. "I love starting something new
or fixing something," he said.

■ ■ ■

KKR's Menlo Park office sits in a tidy low-rise building along
Sand Hill Road, the thoroughfare where the world's best-known
venture capital firms are tucked into similarly unassuming structures,
minutes from Stanford University, and less than an hour's drive from
San Francisco.

The echoes of 9 West are unmistakable throughout, the office itself
feels like the more relaxed California cousin to its New York counter-
part. Fruit smoothies are served every afternoon. Roberts, while more
reserved than Kravis, has a quiet folksiness to him. Unlike at 9 West,
where lunch is consumed in waves (senior partners tend to eat early,
younger associates later), the Menlo office is small enough that the group
eats together. For a time, to encourage conversation, Roberts handed out
a list of recommended books and asked his colleagues to deliver one-page
book reports (he borrowed the idea from Britt Harris, the chief investment officer of the Teacher Retirement System of Texas).

The art in Menlo also skews modern, the result of a wholesale
changeover when KKR moved the West Coast private-equity team

from San Francisco down into the Valley in 1999. In part to help shake up the firm, he ordered the previous art collection, populated by more traditional paintings from schools like the Hudson River Valley, auctioned off. The office now features far more modern art, from a small Warhol in a conference room near Roberts's office to several small video installations near the main reception area.

Roberts recalled how much his colleagues resisted the change. "Everybody hated it at first," he said. To win them over, Roberts had the woman who had helped curate the collection to come to the office for a mini-tutorial for the staff.

Roberts is far more understated, and his desire to move to California more than three decades ago wasn't just about liking the mild climes of northern California. He's much less comfortable in the spotlight, and slower to warm up than his more gregarious cousin. "He's intense and much more intimidating at first," Sonneborn said. "It took me awhile to be myself around him. Now he's a mentor." He's been known to sound the call for a return to basic principles and manners, once reminding the entire firm of the power of a simple hand-written note.

Roberts has mostly focused his philanthropy near his home base in northern California, serving on the boards of San Francisco's symphony and ballet. His own entrepreneurial streak led to the creation of the Roberts Enterprise Development Fund, a "venture philanthropy organization," according to its website.[3] In 1990, Roberts was among the first to try to apply private-sector metrics to the world of non-profits and philanthropy. "I was looking to do something that that if we didn't do it, it wouldn't get done."

He hired a consultant to study homelessness, a pressing issue in San Francisco, where the mild climate and relatively liberal values have led to a high homeless population. The first effort, to financially support homeless women who'd been the victims of domestic abuse, was, Roberts said, "a total failure" because the women often went back to their abusers once they had a little bit of money.

With REDF, Roberts has looked for ventures that will hire what he called the bottom 5 percent of society. One such group, a San Francisco-based organization called Juma Ventures, won several concessions including two Ben & Jerry's Ice Cream stands at Candlestick Park, home of the National Football League 49ers. Through that and other programs, REDF has helped get jobs for more than 6,500 people, Roberts said.

■ ■ ■

Cousin-to-cousin meetings are where the seminal decisions regarding the firm are made. It was in Kravis's small meeting room that he and Roberts sat in 1999 and mulled over the future of the firm that bore their names, one of a series of philosophical explorations. At a partners meeting around that time at the Doral near Palm Springs, the two men were visiting when George turned to Henry and said, in his typically blunt way: "Are you having any fun? Because I'm not." Kravis admitted he wasn't. Roberts pushed it further. "We're making a lot of mistakes," he told his cousin. They both knew instinctively that things were going wrong and they were trying to understand why. As they spent two days talking it over, Kravis zeroed in on something: the closing dinner.

The closing dinner is a tradition in the world of mergers and acquisitions, a fancy meal after everything is documented and signed, to celebrate the consummation. It brings together the deal guys from the private-equity firm, the investment bankers and lawyers and others involved in the transaction, to eat and toast the success of at least getting the deal done. What Kravis started thinking about was what's become an axiom for him over the past few years: Don't congratulate me when I buy something. Congratulate me when I sell it.

What he told Roberts back in 1999 boiled down to this: "The team would come out of the closing dinner and start working on the next deal." It represented a broader mindset that was pulling the firm down. Everyone was everywhere, and therefore nowhere with any focus. That was showing up in the numbers. After the 1986 fund returned a staggering 7 times investors' money, the 1993 pool had given back 1.7 times what limited partners put in. The 1996 fund's multiple was 1.8 times.[4]

The firm had made some bad deals in telecommunications as the technology boom heated up. A survey of investors showed that their prized limited partners liked them but had virtually no idea what KKR actually did, beyond give back more money than they'd started with.

Kravis and Roberts initiated a multi-faceted approach. They decided each investment would have a 100-day plan, like General

Electric had for its businesses, forcing the dealmakers to think beyond the closing dinner. The pair, who'd been content to have every partner be a generalist, organized executives into industry teams (initially 12 groups, later pared to nine). "We made it clear that we expected them to understand an industry from the bottom up," Kravis said. "Go to trade shows, meet with purchasing managers, marketing and sales managers, really get into the flow of whatever the business was."

KKR also decided to open its first international office. After debating whether to go to the United Kingdom or Germany, they decided to open in London in 1999. They sent Edward "Ned" Gilhuly and Todd Fisher over to bring the KKR way of doing things.

The global expansion foretold even bigger changes that would test the cousins' ability to sustain their prized culture. Succession plans took a potential hit in 2005, when Gilhuly and Scott Stuart, who'd headed the utilities and consumer products groups, left to start their own firm. The departure was rare and involved two men "widely believed to be the best and brightest of the next generation at KKR."[5]

Around the same time, Kravis and Roberts were exploring ways to expand KKR beyond private equity, an effort that made sense on paper given the firm's well-known brand, but was difficult in practice. The first major effort was in credit and the firm set up KKR Financial in 2004. The publicly traded fund was meant to buy debt in situations where KKR determined it couldn't play an investment idea through a traditional leveraged buyout. "We were frustrated when we'd go to a meeting with an idea to buy a company and the CEO would say, 'We have no interest in going private or selling a subsidiary'," Kravis said. "Those were very short meetings."

KFN, as it was known because of its stock symbol, endured a troubled few years, barely surviving the credit crisis because of investments in mortgage-backed securities. The CEO of the business, Saturnino Fanlo, left in 2008 and Kravis and Roberts gave responsibility for KFN to the KKR Asset Management subsidiary run by Sonneborn.

Kravis and Roberts saw another business opportunity in capital markets, specifically in raising equity and debt for companies they owned. Getting a piece of that business had the additional benefit of paring the amount of money KKR and its companies were paying Wall Street banks for those underwriting services.

Kravis had to assure bankers on Wall Street he wasn't looking to put them out of business. In reality, KKR doesn't act as lead manager on any deals, only as a co-manager. Farr, the KCM head who'd come over from Citigroup, preached the same message, telling banks that the strategy was in part about winnowing out smaller relationships. "It's been a huge work in progress," he said. "Where we pay our fees has become much more concentrated." And as Farr found ahead of the Dollar General deal, an arguably tougher audience was a group of KKR partners who were having a hard time embracing anything that wasn't straight-up dealmaking.

"At the beginning, it was so hard to get people to think outside of private equity," Kravis said, referring to both capital markets and KFN. "It was hard for PE guys to accept capital markets at first. They looked at them as a vendor." Kravis and Roberts set about preaching a one-firm message at every partners' meeting, a vision that it took to the public as well. At the firm's first meeting for its public shareholders in 2011 he and Roberts, along with Nuttall and most every executive who spoke, repeated the phrase "one-firm approach."

Part of making the case for teamwork was to remind each employee of the firm's pay structure. Kravis described the experience at Bear Stearns as formative in a number of ways, including how the founders decided they would pay their employees. Like many Wall Street firms, Bear Stearns had an "eat what you kill" culture whereby your compensation was largely based on what business you brought in. Kravis described a culture where you locked your office or your desk when you went home at night so no one took clients or business ideas.

The KKR founders decided that everyone would have a piece of the firm, however small. During end-of-year reviews in the early days, Kravis would walk each employee through the compensation, consisting of salary, bonus, and then carried interest. To the rank and file that seemed at best difficult to understand, and at worst, essentially made up. That's why Kravis and Roberts took to personally walking around the office handing out distribution checks. In one memorable case in the 1980s, the sale of a single portfolio company meant secretaries each got a one-time $80,000 check for their participation in that deal hand-delivered by the bosses.

The underlying theory exists today. KKR has one "carry pool," that is, a single pot where all the profits from its funds pour into each year. While compensation is tied in part to how well an executive did in his or her individual business line, the single pool gives management wide latitude to reward behavior that inures to the benefit of all KKR. "It helps make it feel like it's bigger than any one person," Sonneborn said. "It's the difference between being a firm and a franchise."

While becoming enormously wealthy along the way through the funds (the cousins are mainstays on the Forbes richest Americans list) Kravis and Roberts chipped away at their ownership of KKR during the 1990s and into the new millennium, in part to ensure they could keep spreading some portion of the firm's ownership through the growing ranks. When KKR finally got its public listing on the New York Stock Exchange, everyone learned the numbers. The two cousins each owned a little less than 14 percent of the firm, a figure Kravis said he thinks surprised some people.

The decade following Kravis's and Roberts's seminal meeting to reset the direction of the firm also saw the cousins begin to come to grips with its profile and its place in the broader and economic landscape. While the RJR deal, and the publication of *Barbarians* several years later, had thrust the firm into the public eye far more than their peers, KKR still largely maintained the mindset of a private partnership.

The buyout boom that began in 2005, accelerated in 2006, and crested in 2007 changed all of that. Even excluding RJR, KKR had historically owned a number of companies with recognizable brand names, from the Safeway supermarket chain to Regal Cinemas. But the deals it undertook in the middle of the century's first decade dwarfed all of the previous efforts on most every measure.

From 2005 to 2007, KKR announced $244.5 billion worth of deals, according to data compiled by Bloomberg. That's more than triple the value of all the deals KKR announced from 1988 through 2004, the data show ($70.5 billion). The company also was buying companies that served everyday consumers, from Toys "R" Us to Dollar General, as well as companies that served businesses, companies like First Data and SunGard Data Systems. Every one of those deals was worth $7 billion or more.

Kravis and Roberts decided in 2006 to sell shares in Europe for a fund called KKR Private Equity Investors, which traded in Amsterdam. The fund was designed to raise money to co-invest in KKR deals, and did so. A few other things happened along the way: The fund didn't do especially well, it gave the firm a window into being public, and the public a glimpse into the firm, and it ultimately provided a roundabout way to get KKR itself publicly listed after a stalled attempt in 2007.

KPE went public in 2006 at $25 a share, and it never saw that price again. Public investors, as Steve Schwarzman would learn when he took his own firm public, were puzzled as to how to value illiquid investments in private-equity funds. Illiquidity took another form in the case of KPE; since few people bought the stock, it was thinly traded.

Through quarterly earnings reports, KPE did provide a sense of how some of KKR's investments were performing; since KPE was an investor in many of the deals, it disclosed publicly where KKR was marking those holdings. Kravis and Roberts alternated giving commentary on the quarterly conference calls, providing the broader world an opportunity rarely afforded beyond KKR's limited partners—the worldview of an increasingly important investor putting money to work around the world.

With KPE not living up to its promise and KKR's efforts to get itself onto the New York Stock Exchange stalled, KKR and its lawyers came up with a clever solution, one that, even for guys used to complicated deals, was blazingly complex. The firm merged itself with the fund, which it already owned a part of, and the combined entity continued trading in Amsterdam. At the time of the merger, KKR told investors that it had the option to move the listing to New York within a year, which it did. KPE plus KKR became KKR (Guernsey) and then became KKR on the NYSE.

■ ■ ■

For KKR, nothing illustrated the new world of big takeovers more than its pursuit and ultimate purchase of what was then known as TXU, the biggest power producer in Texas. To win the deal, KKR and TPG employed a small army of outside advisers and relied on their own founders to win over environmentalists, regulators, and legislators. The experience of that deal, and what followed for both the company and private-equity industry, marked the beginning of a new era defined by more publicity and more scrutiny.

Announced with fanfare in 2007, Energy Future was headed toward being a bad deal from an investment perspective within two years, and the biggest deal in history may in fact end up being among the most disappointing for investors. By early 2012, a debt default was seen as virtually certain. Credit-default swaps, a financial instrument investors use to bet on whether a company will meet its debt obligations, put the chances of default at 91 percent within three years.[6]

At issue were natural gas prices, which were central to the business case to buy TXU in the first place. The buyers believed prices for natural gas would continue to rise, driving the price for wholesale power, which the company provides, higher. That would in turn increase the value of TXU. Along the way, they made other changes to the company, including shuttering some coal-fired plants and modernizing other facilities, but this was really a bet on gas prices. Instead, a recession in the United States crimped demand and, to make matters worse for Energy Future, huge stores of natural gas became drillable in shale deposits, mainly in Pennsylvania.

It's worth noting that KKR, ever opportunistic, seized on the shale boom and broader interest in natural resources to great success. Marc Lipschultz built a portfolio of shale-related companies, two of which KKR sold within roughly a year of buying them. Lipschultz tripled the value of one investment in 2011 through a sale of oil and gas leases in Texas. That followed a deal in 2010 where KKR quadrupled its money on a shale investment.[7] What ultimately undid TXU's investment thesis—natural gas supplies and prices—made KKR and its investors huge amounts of money through the shale plays. "Those are investments made on two different sides of a revolutionary change in the energy world," Lipschultz said.

Those deals were part of a typical grind-it-out strategy that dated back to 2000, when KKR created industry groups and they began swarming around strategies to make money in areas like energy. Oil and gas tied back to Kravis's and Roberts's own roots in Texas and Oklahoma; "this is anchored to the heritage of the firm," Lipschultz said.

With default effectively certain and their equity most likely wiped out, the owners sought to accentuate the positive. Even with a crippled balance sheet, TPG and KKR did in fact modernize a number of the facilities. Employment at Energy Future grew. From a broader perspective, the deal created within both firms a sense of the new world order for their business. TPG and KKR, largely because of Energy Future, now have established executives devoted to environmental and sustainability issues. The deal also precipitated the hiring of senior executives overseeing public affairs. Former Republican National Committee Chairman Kenneth Mehlman is at KKR; Adam Levine, who worked in the George W. Bush administration, is at TPG. Both worked as outside advisers before going in-house at their respective employers. Over at Carlyle, government relations falls under the purview of David Marchick, who worked in the Clinton administration and then as an outside lawyer to Carlyle before joining the firm.

Even before the TXU deal, Kravis and Roberts were becoming more and more aware of the increasingly public nature of the business. "If you want to own the Hiltons and the HCAs of the world, you're going to bring a lot of scrutiny," Mehlman said. "You're going to be the center of attention."

The process of negotiating for, buying, and winning regulatory approval for TXU only served to underscore all of that, he said. "That made us realize we had to do it in a methodical way." All of it speaks to a theme hammered on across the big firms. This is not the same business it was at the outset or even at the turn of the century.

Roberts said being public hasn't changed the firm much, or at least how he thinks about KKR. Gaining the ability to have a balance sheet, a credit rating that allows the firm to borrow more, and a currency with which to make acquisitions is worth the additional scrutiny and rigors of quarterly reporting. Roberts and Kravis intentionally don't participate in the public calls with analysts and investors around earnings releases, a choice Roberts pointed out was the same as at Goldman Sachs, where the chief financial officer handles those duties. Blackstone's Schwarzman and James do speak and answer questions on calls to announce earnings results.

But being public and being in the public eye are different, and Roberts conceded that the outside world has forced a change in his and his competitors' behavior. "It's gone from all that matters is shareholder value to being much more than that," he said, rattling off efforts around the environment, government relations, and outreach to unions. The firm has sought the advice of former U.S. House Majority Leader Richard Gephardt. Andy Stern, in the past decade the fiercest critic of private equity in the labor world, spoke at a KKR meeting in 2011.

"We have close to a million people working for our companies," Robert said. "We can't be tone deaf to that."

Chapter 6

Put on Your Boots

The Rise of "Ops"

Y ou'd never guess Deb Conklin is a native New Yorker. Her whole vibe is Southern, from her deep accent to her backslapping nature to her impressive knowledge of college football.

Three days before we met in something close to the geographically dead center of Pennsylvania, her team, Clemson, got clobbered by Georgia Tech and she was, as they say in the South, still spittin' mad. "I can't even talk about it yet," she said as we drove to lunch. Then she proceeded to talk about it extensively, and passionately, deconstructing her beloved Tigers' loss and the implications for their now-faded national championship hopes. Later, when the talk turned back to her work at the private-equity firm TPG, she used a couple of football analogies to explain what she actually does.

We chatted over sandwiches at Maria's, a small sandwich shop in Bellefonte, Pennsylvania. Our waitress told us the special was a meatball sub, and Conklin, tempted for a few seconds, opted for the Italian sandwich on bread we were assured was homemade.

"I just can't bring myself to order meatball anything," she said. Her mother's meatballs are just too good, and it feels like a combination of disloyal and foolhardy to the younger Conklin to eat them anywhere but at home. Certainly everyone's family history informs their own choices. Few more so than Conklin, whose career as an engineer and executive began with a life-changing accident. She was three years old, living in Ossining, New York, with her older brother and parents when her father dove into Conklin's uncle's pool and broke his neck, leaving her to watch as he was carted away in an ambulance. Doctors initially thought they wouldn't save him at all, then told him he wouldn't see 40 years old.

The resulting paralysis changed the entire course of the Conklin family's history and Deb's own life. They left Ossining and moved across the Hudson River to New Jersey to live near her grandparents. They stayed there until Deb was seven, when a trip to South Carolina to visit her aunt and uncle over Easter prompted her parents to buy a house in Lancaster, South Carolina, near the North Carolina border and a short drive to Charlotte.

Conklin became an apprentice of sorts to her wheelchair-bound father, an engineer who regained limited used of his arms and hands. They spent hours in the family's carport, Deb following his instructions about which wrench to use for various projects.

"I became his hands," she'd told me a year before we met in Pennsylvania.

I'd been introduced to Conklin originally as part of a *Bloomberg Businessweek* story on TPG's "ops" group. In the intervening year, she'd finished up an assignment in San Diego with another portofolio company and now was on loan to another TPG-backed firm, plastic bag maker Hilex Poly. Milesburg, Pennsylvania is the site of the company's second-biggest facility. Conklin is a member of the field operations group, a subset of the 60-person operations team inside TPG. She spends upwards of 45 weeks a year on the road, returning most weekends to her house on a lake in Charlotte. The Hilex Poly gig is a good one for several reasons. Initially seen as a "fly-by" assignment, she said, it morphed into her first COO role. Hilex's headquarters are in Hartsville, South Carolina, a couple of hours from her folks' house. That means most weeks she can head down on Sundays, stop in for dinner with her parents, and then on to Hartsville, and often she sees them on her way home on Thursdays. In October 2011, she attended her father's seventieth birthday party.

Once the money is deployed by a private-equity firm, it's up to people like Conklin to put it work. What she and people like her do, at TPG and beyond, stands as one of the biggest shifts in the private-equity equation during the past decade. That time period has seen the rise of "ops" as crucial to getting the money to generate the returns private-equity managers have promised their investors. Conklin and her ilk, many of whom are honest-to-goodness engineers, stand in contrast to the so-called financial engineers that earned private equity a nastier reputation. Financial engineering involves using leverage and creative balance sheet work to generate a return. With less debt available and higher prices, private-equity firms are focusing on actually changing companies' businesses to make money.

With rings and watches left back in the office, we grabbed clear safety glasses and disposable earplugs from a dispenser just inside the door to the factory. I reminded Deb that when we went to Bay City, Texas, the previous November to take a tour of a Valerus Compression plant that was part of her assignment at that time, we needed hard hats and steel caps strapped on our shoes. "I've spent more than any other person alive on various safety equipment," she said.

Part of TPG's theory for people like Conklin is that her skills as an engineer and expertise in a corporate philosophy called Lean manufacturing are ultimately transferable, not only across manufacturing operations but even in service businesses. Conklin, before Valerus and Hilex, was a vice president embedded at Caesars, running around the world figuring out ways to improve everything from check-in times at hotels to the efficiency of a cook in the kitchen, then working as a part of the senior management team to push Lean initiatives through the company.

Conklin led me through the creation of a plastic bag. There's the extruder that shoots a cylinder of 450-degree plastic 15 feet up to the next floor, where machines turn slowly to create rolls of plastic. As we descended to see what happens next, I asked Conklin whether she knew anything about plastic bags before she got this job. Over the din, and through my earplugs came the reply: "Heck no!"

TPG counts on the likes of Conklin to prove out the investment thesis here at Hilex and other companies where the firm has collectively decided they can somehow use their prowess around costs or revenue growth to make money. She and her cohorts take on senior roles inside the company, and are far from being occasional advisers. The ops component of TPG is overseen by Dick Boyce, a slight, serious looking fellow who came to the firm almost 15 years ago, recruited by Jim Coulter. The TPG founder had met Boyce a decade earlier when Coulter was a summer associate at consulting firm Bain & Co., where Boyce was a partner. Boyce went on to senior positions at companies including Pepsico, where he rose to oversee the soda giant's operations. Coulter came calling in 1997, only a handful of years after TPG, then called Texas Pacific Group, was born. Coulter and co-founder David Bonderman, emboldened by the huge profits from selling a once-broken Continental for more than 10 times their investment, wanted to build an operations capability within the firm to replicate that success.

Continental has emerged as one of the defining private-equity deals, by dint of its timing in the industry's evolution, as well as what it gave rise to. Coulter and Bonderman, who'd met investing money for the Bass family in Fort Worth, Texas, decided Continental was worth buying and fixing. The birth of TPG was for that deal; the funds came later. Continental required the men to bring in operational experts from the top of the executive ladder through the organization.

They were hooked, both on the tangible changes they could make, and on the financial rewards it could generate for them and their investors. The then 32-year-old Coulter, looking for ways to institutionalize an operations-centric approach, plumbed his network and came up with Boyce.

Boyce brings a Mr. Spock-like intensity and logic to the TPG process and tends to use diagrams and charts to explain an issue. The soft-spoken Boyce is a relentless networker and his assistant maps his travel schedule to his Rolodex, scheduling catch-up coffees and dinners with former colleagues and partners to keep up to date. One TPG operating partner, Vincenzo Morelli, met Boyce when the two were in business school at Stanford and played in a standing Saturday morning soccer game. Two decades later, he went to work for Boyce in Europe.

Boyce favors shirts with buttoned-down collars, and during one of our conversations at a partners meeting for the firm in New York, he made a point of showing me that he's in fact wearing a tie from J. Crew, which at that time TPG was buying. Again.

J. Crew, back in 1997, was one of the first deals Boyce worked on for TPG. The firm had bought the company for about $500 million from the family that had created it and quickly decided to fire the CEO before finding a suitable permanent replacement. Boyce, far from a fashionista, got the job and kept it until Coulter wooed Mickey Drexler, who runs the company to this day and who negotiated the second sale to TPG in 2011. The J. Crew deal, redux, brought TPG and private equity into a different sort of spotlight and triggered some uncomfortable questions from shareholders, some of whom sued over the buyout.

At issue was who knew what and when. Coulter had remained on the J. Crew board, even after TPG sold most of its investment after taking the company public in 2006, and he remained close to Drexler. According to public and court filings, Coulter approached Drexler about a new deal to buy J. Crew, noting the company's depressed share price. Drexler's delay in notifying the board caused shareholders to accuse him of trying to keep anyone from competing with TPG to buy the company. J. Crew ultimately settled the lawsuit, agreeing to pay the shareholders $16 million. The total value of the buyout was $3 billion.[1] Why buy the same company all over again? Coulter and Boyce said TPG has a whole series of things it can do, in concert with Drexler, to grow J. Crew in a new way, both geographically and through new products and brands. In the years since it bought and sold J. Crew the first time, TPG has pushed deep into emerging markets, especially China, a market where J. Crew had virtually no presence.

■ ■ ■

There are more and more Deb Conklins springing up around the world of leveraged buyouts, as private-equity managers, in the wake of the financial crisis, scramble to prove their operating bona fides. Showcasing a team dedicated to ops or a slate of proven managers from the corporate world became de rigueur in any investor and public presentations, and pitches to journalists, as buyout firms sought to burnish their image.

"It's completely, radically changed," Blackstone's Steve Schwarzman said. "It's no longer enough to buy a company and see how it does."

Firms like TPG, Clayton Dubilier & Rice, and Bain Capital all trace their lineage in operations back to their firms' inceptions. KKR has bulked up its Capstone unit (an internal consulting business that works with deal partners in the due diligence process as well as after the company is purchased) since its creation in 2000. Carlyle early on tapped what it originally called senior advisers—former executives of big companies brought in to help seal deals and consult—and now calls operating executives. Regardless of how they came to be, it's a key talking point for any firm trying to pitch an investor, or a target company.

The importance of operational expertise, and just the fact that it's talked about as much as it is, is revealing about the industry—those who have a stake in what private equity are demanding to unpack what's inside the black box. Investors especially are unwilling to settle for the bare minimum information about what the private-equity firms are actually doing with their money, and how they're getting to the profits they eventually distribute. A variation on that is true for another key constituency: the workers at the companies bought by private equity and, in some cases, the labor unions that represent them. Spooked by stories of massive job cuts and factory closures, they're demanding insights into what buyout firms do after the deal closes.

Another reason operations have come to the fore is due to what can generously be called enlightened self interest for buyout firms; simply leveraging up a balance sheet and flipping it rarely works anymore.

That's mainly because of the simple mechanics of any market, especially in modern times. The early private equity industry thrived in part because of imperfect information. That is, a firm could make a lot of money by buying something cheap, putting leverage on it, and selling it to someone else without doing much to it. In an age where there are few secrets, especially when it comes to companies that might be for sale, finding that unwanted, undervalued, and unknown company to buy is exceedingly difficult.

This gets to the heart of a private-equity fallacy, what in investment banker-speak is known as a "proprietary deal." Buyout managers, especially when they're pitching investors, love to talk about proprietary deals, and their ability to find them. A deal that no one outside of the

interested parties knows about until the deal is closed is at best endan-
gered. Any investment banker involved in a sale, or any executive
running a company, is going to do their best to ensure they attract the
best price from the market. Given the amount of money in private
equity alone chasing deals—the total "dry powder," or committed,
unspent capital in all types of private-equity funds was close to a trillion
dollars in 2011, with about 41 percent of that held in leveraged buyout
funds[2]—stiff competition for almost anything is a foregone conclusion.

■ ■ ■

How each of the big firms approaches operations ties back to their own
roots. TPG's Coulter, trained as an engineer, and Boyce, a veteran of
Pepsi and Bain, speak in reverent tones of this combination of consulting and, in Coulter's words, "academy companies," where executives get high-quality operations training and experience.

The management consulting thread runs strong through the
industry, nowhere more so than Bain Capital, which was born of that
business. Mitt Romney, has been well-documented during his U.S.
presidential run, was charged with taking the management consulting
playbook—dropping into a company and working with management to
fix what was broken—and turning it into an investment business.

Amid all the hubbub around Romney's candidacy, I talked with
Mark Nunnelly, a long-time Bain partner about the specific business of
applying those methods in the investment world. He pointed to Bain's
investment in Domino's Pizza, a deal Romney has cited as one that
turned out well for everyone involved.

Romney was deeply involved in winning over Domino's, which
was based in Michigan, where he grew up. Romney and Nunnelly were
among those invited to pitch founder Thomas Monaghan, who had
made it clear to his advisers that he wanted to sell the company and get
out of the business, not find a partner to keep growing the pizza chain
with him at the helm. Monaghan's strategy had the implicit endorsement of none other than the Pope. A devout Roman Catholic,
Monaghan was challenged by the Pontiff to do something to change the
world. He realized the only thing worth enough to fund his quest was
the pizza company he'd created with his brother.

Monaghan was a tough man to court, and Romney's attempt to bond over a shared Michigan lineage flopped when it turned out Romney's brother was running for office against one of Monaghan's close friends. As the clock on one of their meetings ran down, Romney noted a model of a 1957 Chevy on Monaghan's desk. The ice was finally broken as the men bonded over a love of cars. Bain eventually won the deal, paying $1.1 billion for Domino's.

With Monaghan out (he's gone on to devote the majority of his time to Catholic charities, including a new university), Nunnelly stepped in as the temporary CEO. More than a dozen Bain executives, split among deal guys and operating specialists, took on everything from uniforms to new products and promotions to pricing and expansion. They recruited a new CEO and revamped what had been a "siloed" management strategy, Nunnelly said. They reversed an effort overseas geared toward putting a small number of outlets in dozens of countries to focus on building bigger businesses and more substantial presences in six or seven key overseas markets.

Ultimately, Domino's doubled its sales across the chain and international sales increased by five times, Nunnelly said. The company went public in 2004 and has a market cap of about $2.4 billion. Through dividends and selling stock, Bain ultimately made about five times its money on Domino's over a 12-year period. "It demonstrated the full arsenal of our tools," he said.

■ ■ ■

Take as a given that very little is going to come empirically cheap and that these guys actually have to do something with the company. A private-equity manager few outside the business have ever heard of saw this in the late 1980s and was among the first to do something about it.

The view from Jay Jordan's office is actually better than Henry Kravis's down the street. He sits on the 48th floor of the General Motors building, the tower that's at the southeast corner of Central Park, across the street from the Plaza Hotel. Its first floor is home to FAO Schwartz—where Tom Hanks danced on the piano in the movie "Big"—and the CBS Early Show. The Fifth Avenue Apple Store plunges into the building's plaza, designated by a massive glass box with the lit Apple logo.

Tourists with Christmas lists were pouring into the Apple cube on a chilly afternoon when I met Jordan, who was dressed in a blue and white striped shirt and worsted wool slacks. Prompted by my comment about his view being superior to KKR's, he glanced in 9 West's direction and started talking about how KKR, specifically "Jerry and Henry," turned him on to the "bootstrap" business.

Jordan, working at investment bank Carl Marks in the late 1970s, heard through a friend about what Kohlberg and his young associates were doing in their post-Bear Stearns life so he convinced his bosses to let him do something similar. In 1982, he left and started his own firm, called The Jordan Company. Like KKR, he found insurance companies and pensions hungry for returns that would outdo the public markets. "There was definitely a market there," he said.

Like most entrepreneurs, he was insistent on doing things a certain way. To this day, the firm focuses its hiring almost exclusively on associates to ensure that employees learn the ways of the firm at an early stage of their career.

Jordan made an exception in 1988 when he saw that he needed to do something radically different with the business. There was a limited number of things to buy and growing competition. The returns he and his handful of competitors had achieved weren't going to last on this business model. "The whole industry was financial engineering," Jordan said. "I always thought the music would stop."

He called his former roommate at Notre Dame, Thomas Quinn, who at the time was an executive at the health care company Baxter International. Jordan convinced him to join the firm to run a new unit, the operations management group, or OMG. The underlying theory was relatively simple: a sharp focus on cutting costs to drive the bottom line through programs like streamlining factories, organic growth for the top line, and intense strategic planning to make smart acquisitions that built the business.

Two decades later, Quinn remains a partner at the firm and still runs OMG, which is thriving. The quest for lower costs for companies they already owned took the firm to China in the early 1990s, long before most other private-equity firms, and Jordan took his lumps in order to get comfortable in the economy many think will, and already may, dominate the world. "We lost some money but learned how to do business there," Jordan said.

After years of meeting local officials and giving to local charities, Jordan evolved his strategy in China from sourcing for his companies and selling to Chinese customers to actually buying a state-owned Chinese enterprise, a mining concern in the Heilongjiang Province called International Mining Machinery. The 2006 deal was the first such deal in that province and a rare buyout by a foreign investor in China, Jordan said.

■ ■ ■

The ops function and the executives it draws help dilute the recovering investment banker vibe at many private-equity firms, balancing the Ivy League pedigreed smooth-talkers with executives who have been in the proverbial trenches. True, many of them supplemented undergraduate degrees in science with MBAs and stints at management consulting firms, but many say their ability to apply their own experience gives them an advantage over someone who has just looked at Excel spreadsheets and case studies.

At KKR, Capstone was created in 2000 and is still run by Dean Nelson, a Purdue University-trained chemist who went on to get an MBA at the University of Chicago. He proceeded to work at Boston Consulting Group, considered along with McKinsey & Co. and Bain & Co. to be one of the top consulting shops, and Shell Oil.

KKR's initial ops effort several years before was to use a third-party consulting firm, headed by Steven Burd, who had worked at Arthur D. Little. Burd and a small staff acted as consultants, especially on KKR's string of grocery deals in the 1990s. He eventually went to Safeway as president and then CEO. In his absence, the operations consulting business faded away. As the decade wore on, Kravis and Roberts knew they needed to revisit the idea, as part of the broader effort to reinvent the firm. They set out to find someone to run a new operations group that would be an official part of KKR instead of an outside firm.

Nelson was living in Chicago and working for BCG when he got a call from a headhunter at search firm Spencer Stuart about a job at KKR. Nelson was intrigued, especially because his job in consulting had evolved into a lot of administration and new business generation, and little actual consulting. He also came to learn that KKR was serious, and came to appreciate the urgency. "The late 1990s were not a good time for the firm," he said. "Buying smart and making some basic changes to the operations of the company weren't going to be enough anymore."

KKR at the time was small, with a total of 14 partners. The firm had purposefully avoided hiring people in the middle of their careers. You either started at KKR and grew up there, or maybe got a job on the back end of your career as a senior adviser. Nelson went through two rounds with each of the partners, including a 90-minute meeting in November 1999 with Kravis in his library. Nelson returned to New York the next month during KKR's annual firm-wide meeting. He spent the day in 45-minute chunks with all 14 partners, starting with breakfast with Roberts, arguably the toughest audience in the firm. Nelson said it was hard to tell what Roberts thought because "he plays it very close to vest."

At the end of the day, KKR handed Nelson a case study of sorts—a deal they'd considered for Bic's pen business—and told him to give them thoughts on it by the next morning. Once he got the job, Nelson had to figure out how his group was going to operate. Kravis, Roberts, and Raether (the KKR senior partner charged with overseeing the operations effort) told Nelson they wanted it to be defined as different from pure dealmaking. "We were easing into the model," Nelson said. "We tried different approaches until we found the one that worked best for us."

Lacking any additional office space in 9 West, KKR set Nelson up in an office down Madison Avenue. The origin story stands as the exception to KKR's typical rigor. He came up with the name on his own, and said it doesn't really mean anything of significance. "I think I just got to the C's and got tired of thinking about it," he said. "I knew I couldn't use a Greek name because there were too many of those in private equity." He asked his sister, a graphic designer, to come up with a logo. While the firm's brass was supportive, close-knit KKR was institutionally skeptical of this new effort, just as they would be years later with Craig Farr's capital markets business. "It was a tough couple of years," Nelson said of 2000 and 2001. "We didn't do many deals in that period, and were still figuring out the right model."

The first deal Nelson got involved in turned out to be among KKR's worst in its history: movie chain Regal Cinemas. He and the rest of the KKR team were able to identify the problem—the company was effectively cannibalizing itself by opening too many theaters. But it was too late. The company was deemed unsalvageable. KKR lost almost $500 million on the deal.

KKR has never thought of itself as being in the distressed business—that is, targeting deeply broken businesses and making radical changes. Some of their deals ended up being worse than they'd thought, but KKR's general approach is to buy businesses that are undervalued or poorly managed. In describing where he wanted him to focus, Kravis told Nelson that KKR companies ran along a continuum of performance, from great to terrible, and neither of the extremes needed Capstone. The terrible companies were likely to be getting ample attention from the deal team, and the great companies probably just needed to be left alone. In recent times, the latter investments have often been in the energy sector, where KKR has made a bet on, say, shale deposits, where very little operational expertise is needed.

Somewhere between is where Capstone makes its bones, where pulling levers around things like procurement, pricing, or sales strategy can help generate an incremental 4 or 5 percentage points of return for KKR and its investors, which is often the difference between a decent and stellar investment.

While Capstone has a team working at a portfolio company, Nelson or another senior member of his group will sit on the board, a practice that seems somewhat symbolic, especially in cases where KKR is the sole owner (in those cases, KKR executives on the deal effectively *are* the board). It seems a way to show to the company, and to other parts of KKR, that the company in question is an operational work in progress. In Dollar General's case, Nelson sat on the company's board for two-and-a-half years, until shortly before the retailer went public. Being on the board can be of more use in a consortium deal, where there are multiple private-equity owners. KKR's joint ownership of US Foodservice has put it alongside a firm that's defined itself around its operational prowess almost since the beginning, Clayton Dubilier & Rice. That group's heritage dates back to the 1970s as well, and its story has several interesting intersections with KKR through those decades.

The first office of what was then called Clayton & Dubilier was space borrowed from Kohlberg Kravis & Roberts. The arrangement was a product of a relationship between Martin Dubilier and Jerry Kohlberg, who'd known each other since growing up together in Westchester County, just north of New York City. While what became CD&R didn't cohabitate with KKR for long, the two firms tracked each other through the early 1980s and, along with the likes of Forstmann Little and Wes Ray, formed the foundation for the modern LBO industry. CD&R was among the first firms to do a large-scale deal for an unwanted division of a big company, through its deal in the early 1990s to buy part of IBM.

The deal for the office products division was not a straight-ahead "carve-out"—hiving off a unit and running it as a separate business. What became Lexmark was a collection of office products units buried across IBM's empire. CD&R paid $1.5 billion for the business and eventually took it public in 1995.

CD&R has largely stuck with the business of carve-outs, buying Hertz with Carlyle from Ford and US Foods from Royal Ahold in well-timed deals, and the contractor supply business from Home Depot (called HD Supply), in a very poorly timed deal at the onset of the financial and housing crisis.

In its modern iteration, CD&R has become a full- or part-time home for some of the highest-profile former chief executives of global companies, including Jack Welch, arguably the most famous CEO of all time. After Welch joined as a senior advisor in 2001, CD&R added A.G. Lafley, who ran Procter & Gamble, and former Tesco CEO Terence Leahy. Paul Pressler, the former Gap CEO, is a partner, as is Edward Liddy, who ran Allstate. CD&R showcased many of them at its annual meeting for investors in October 2011, when it gathered at Cipriani, situated across the street from Grand Central Terminal in midtown Manhattan. For a day and a half, CD&R went into excruciating detail about each company in its portfolio, usually bringing up several executives from the firm and the company to discuss the latest numbers and projections. To underscore its long history and successful succession planning—a rarity in the private-equity world—CD&R showed a video interview of founder Joseph Rice by Charlie Rose, which was followed by Rose's live, on-stage interview with current CD&R CEO Don Gogel.

These meetings, closed to the general public, are part information dissemination and part sales pitch for the private-equity firms. These days, very little is glossed over, and firms like CD&R arm their investors with printed PowerPoint presentations and electronic versions on flash-memory drives to take back to their offices and digest. They have a much more collegial feel than shareholder meetings for public companies, where votes for the board of directors and various shareholder proposals are the centerpiece. Proving operational chops and sharing more data and strategy about the underlying investments are increasingly important to limited partners, and Gogel said they're becoming more vocal about those desires. "There are a lot of demands from our investor base," he said during the on-stage conversation with Charlie Rose. "That's probably overdue."

■ ■ ■

One way private-equity firms are making noticeable operational changes to their companies is by a different kind of leverage, the kind that comes when you control massive budgets and huge employee bases. In that regard, they're reviving a corporate concept largely abandoned in the 1980s: the conglomerate.

The notion of the conglomerate—a holding company controlling a sprawling set of companies in disparate industries largely went the way of the dinosaur as companies found it difficult to convince investors that there was value that was even equal to the sum of the parts. A few have hung on, including the Tisch family's Loews Corporation, which owns everything from hotels to oil fields to insurance companies. And the most famous remains Warren Buffett's Berkshire Hathaway.

Private equity in its early days was in part a conglomerate dismantler, a solution for those wanting to disassemble empires. The firms were willing to buy unwanted companies and run them as independent concerns. Yet the size and scale of private equity during the past decade has turned them into conglomerates in their own right, each of the biggest firms owning a wide range of companies from toy makers to refineries to amusement parks. Surely there must be a way to take advantage of that.

Blackstone's answer is a pair of programs designed to exploit the fact that they own companies with $117 billion in aggregate annual revenue and 680,000 employees, more in headcount than General Electric or Home Depot. The programs are managed under the auspices of the

Portfolio Operations Group, run by James Quellos. By using a company called CoreTrust, Blackstone goes out and shops for everything from overnight delivery services to computers, using the heft of what it owns to negotiate big bulk discounts. Companies participating in the program can keep with it even after Blackstone doesn't own them anymore.

One little-discussed fact that serves to underscore how deeply entrenched private-equity-backed companies are: CoreTrust is a part of HCA, the hospital company owned by KKR and Bain. The CoreTrust business was created in 2006 as a way to give HCA more leverage in negotiating contracts for its sprawling number of hospitals. While Core-Trust doesn't hide its affiliation with HCA, it doesn't exactly flaunt it.

Blackstone has a similar effort for medical benefits, called Equity Healthcare, which it created in 2008 and covers about 300,000 members throughout the companies it owns. The effort has extended to portfolio companies of other private-equity managers, and employees from TPG's J. Crew and Univision are among those that participate in Equity Healthcare, according to its website.[3]

A harder-to-quantify element of operations that's related to the conglomerate effect is the family of chief executives, financial officers, and other senior level executives who Blackstone and TPG bring together on at least an annual basis to share ideas and insights gleaned from running their companies. Blackstone has additionally put on meetings for its chief technology officers and the finance heads of its companies. This is part of the pitch, along with big potential payouts, that the firms make the would-be top executives: access to their peers and to the network of titans the buyout shops are plugged into. At TPG's annual CEO meeting one year, the guest speaker was JPMorgan Chase CEO Jamie Dimon.

All of this adds up to an approach that the practitioners say is much more focused on buying companies and making them better, not just playing with their balance sheets long enough to turn a profit and move on to the next deal. Conklin, though a road warrior, said she keeps in close touch with most of the executives she works with at her various assignments. Part of it is her adopted Southern nature, part of it's the nature of the modern LBO business. Either way, holding a company's guts in your hands tends to help form a bond.

Chapter 7

Aura of Cool

Inside TPG

T he Phoenician resort in Scottsdale, Arizona, sits snugly up against Camelback Mountain, a manicured golf course sprinkled with rocks and cacti winding through the complex. Every October TPG and its investors descend on these posh environs for two days of meetings.

The centerpiece of the meeting is a state of the union of sorts by Jim Coulter, the firm's 50-year-old co-founder. He's little known outside of the industry, younger and less visible than his fellow private-equity chiefs, including his partner David Bonderman, who while fervently press-shy has cultivated an air of diffidence and authority through an occasional industry speech or well-placed memorable remark. Coulter, long content to work behind the scenes and on deals, has begun to inch into the public eye. Coulter's relative youth came through in his presentation, an energetic 90 minutes sprinkled with a video clip of a

YouTube lip-syncher, an overarching investment theory gleaned from a decade of coaching his kids' suburban soccer teams, an illustration citing the popularity of "Gilligan's Island," and even a Trotsky quote: "War is the locomotive of history."

Wearing an open-collared shirt with the sleeves rolled up and sporting a tiny wireless microphone that could've been lifted from the Lady Gaga tour, Coulter paced the blue-lit stage set between a pair of two giant screens showing his slides and videos. Speaking without notes, he moved between nerdy analysis—including a three-dimensional matrix representation of his view of TPG's strengths—and industry crystal-balling, laying out his predictions for what he referred to as "Private Equity 5.0."

"This is probably the most interesting structural time in the industry during my 25 years doing this," Coulter said. By 2020 sovereign wealth funds will pull even with public pensions as the biggest contributors to private-equity funds. The number of funds of more than $1 billion, which jumped to about 400 as of 2011 from about two dozen in 1995, could reach 900 or so within a decade.

Coulter's valedictory of sorts capped a morning of presentations including one by Bonderman, who set out the strategy for emerging markets, predicting that when it settled out, TPG would invest about half of its money in North America and half around the world. He travels in excess of 200 days a year, ferried across the globe on his own plane. He recently upgraded from a Falcon 900 he bought used from CSX.

Bonderman, clad in loose grey slacks and a maroon pullover, then sat with Coulter and chief investment officer Jonathan Coslet for a rapid-fire panel session on a handful of issues bubbled up from a list of 40 topics they'd polled the audience on the previous day, from European debt to residential real estate. After a break, the stage was Coulter's, save for 15 minutes he ceded to ops chief Dick Boyce. Among the most forceful parts of Coulter's presentation was his explanation of the firm's decision to stay private for the time being, even as three of its largest competitors were publicly traded (at the time, Carlyle's IPO was pending). Coulter said he wasn't convinced that a private-equity firm can simultaneously satisfy the limited partners in its funds and public shareholders.

He conceded that the publicly traded firms can more easily make acquisitions. Blackstone used stock as part of its 2008 purchase of GSO Capital Partners; Carlyle snapped up fund-of-funds manager AlpInvest ahead of its IPO. Public firms have touted stock as a way to recruit and retain talent. The latter hasn't yet proven out, Coulter said. Still, he expressed his worry about the decision. "We are taking a risk that we got this wrong, but it is not clear you have to be early," he told his investors.

The going-public issue has been far from an open-and-shut discussion for TPG. Among the biggest benefits of an IPO is providing a means by which founders can cash out part or all of their stakes, just as Blackstone's Peterson, who sold almost all of his portion, and Schwarzman, who sold a small portion of his, did in 2007. Rubenstein said IPOs are a way for founders of firms like his to "liquefy" what they've built, in part to free up money for charitable giving.[1]

Nearing 70, Bonderman has been the stronger external proponent of an IPO as a means of selling some shares and has had private conversations with acquaintances and bankers to that effect. As early as 2007, he told an audience in Dubai that the firm would likely, eventually, go public if the rest of the industry's biggest names did. "Five years from now, I think all the major guys will be public. We would like to be on the tail end of that," he said.

"Being public isn't my favorite thing, but who remembers Brown Brothers Harriman," he said in Dubai, referring to one of the investment banks that chose to remain private after Goldman Sachs and Morgan Stanley finally chose to sell shares through IPOs.[2] TPG, people inside the firm say, wouldn't mind being the Goldman in this parade.

In 2012, Bonderman updated his theory, telling an audience in San Francisco: "We have no current plans but to sit and watch and see what happens." He noted that at the investor meeting, an overwhelming number of limited partners in a survey had expressed disapproval about general partners going public, but that there was little evidence they were doing anything to change their behavior. "If there turns out to be no negative consequence, we'll see happen in our industry what happened in investment banking."[3]

Coulter's aforementioned youth benefits TPG's timing. Almost two decades Bonderman's junior and far from anything resembling retirement, he's said he'd rather go public only if there's a strong business case. If it's simply about getting Bonderman some money, there are other ways to achieve that, either by borrowing money or selling a larger stake to a big investor. TPG sold small stakes to government funds run by Singapore and Kuwait in mid-2011. Carlyle, Apollo, and Blackstone all pursued similar strategies as fund-raising methods ahead of their IPOs. The choice to stay put, at least for now, is a differentiator Coulter seems comfortable with, giving him additional time to grow TPG outside of the public eye, and to some extent letting his competitors take the slings, and suffer the depressed stock prices that have been a fixture of private-equity firms listed on the New York Stock Exchange.

TPG revels in being different. Its location, its appetite for risk, and the quirky chemistry of the founders all support that ethos. It was a theme I heard constantly from people inside and outside the firm. At a theoretical Thanksgiving family dinner, TPG is the cool bachelor uncle you want to sit next to. He's always got great stories, and you never know quite what he's going to say. That's largely a tribute to Bonderman, but it's an element Coulter has sought to meticulously sew into the fabric of the firm they've built.

Coulter's knack for putting finance into everyday analogies and metaphors—he used the Whopper hamburger to illustrate a point about pricing power (TPG once owned Burger King), and compared institutional investors' allocation choices to his kitchen pantry—gives him at times the air of a folksy business school professor (to wit, he also cited the 1982 book, *Megatrends*).

In person he is intense but friendly, favoring simple white shirts and monochrome ties most days, almost always with the sleeves rolled up, but just so. Rarely is a hair out of place or his tie even slightly askew. He drives himself to work and coached the soccer teams for his two daughters and son. The culture of TPG and those who work there tends to reflect the mix of Coulter's smart-kids-can-be-cool ethos and Bonderman's straight-up eccentricity. The latter has an absentminded professor vibe that has managed to engender a deep loyalty from those who've worked with and for him. He collects people and nurtures relationships, largely by relentlessly circling the globe. While omnipresent via e-mail and telephone, he's rarely in one place for more than a few days. "Nobody is smarter than Bonderman," said Tom Barrack, who met Bonderman in the 1980s working for the Robert M. Bass Group in Texas. "He is the No. 1 cerebrally smartest guy. He's like a retriever, cutting across themes and cultures."

Because of the older founder's tendency and desire to be constantly on the road (he's been known to fly to China for a lunch appointment), much of the day-to-day vibe defaults largely to a Coulter ethos. He obsessively thinks about culture and process improvement; to make himself more effective, in 2011 he opted to hire a chief of staff to help manage the ever-growing TPG empire. Barrack said of Coulter, "He was a great complement to him because David is peripatetic and Coulter can sit down and build an organization."

The chemistry between the two unlikely partners is the defining element of TPG. While KKR's Kravis and Roberts have distinct styles, they are at their core more alike than different. Not so Bonderman and Coulter. "You put them together and you've got a really interesting blend of risk-taking and risk-aversion, of 'Let's go for it' and 'Well, wait a minute,'" said Coslet, who was the first non-founder employee of TPG. "They bring out the best in each other." Coulter said it occasionally works the other way, as well, with Bonderman "tapping the brake while I push the accelerator. It's the ability to have different skill sets and coexist." That was the case when TPG engineered a complicated deal to buy a stake in Chinese computer maker Lenovo to fund its purchase of IBM's personal computer division. Coulter's analysis ultimately overrode Bonderman's instinct that it wasn't a good deal.

Being outside of New York seems to help distinguish TPG. TPG's offices, with jaw-dropping views of San Francisco Bay, sweeping from the Golden Gate Bridge, past Alcatraz over to the Bay Bridge, make fancy art on the wall irrelevant. (The pithy line I heard inside TPG: "God is our decorator.") Walking a line between Wall Street perks and California sensibilities, the firm provides lunch for all employees, but opts to bring in burritos or soups on most days, often served on paper plates, instead of keeping a working kitchen staff on site. That TPG ended up in San Francisco is a tribute mostly to the partners just liking the place. What was settled early was that they wouldn't be in New York. "We didn't want to be like everyone else," Coslet said of the reasons to be outside of Manhattan. "We wanted to avoid being 'Wall Street' guys. . . . We knew it."

Coulter is fond of using a white board—in its absence, he'll grab a piece of paper to scratch out a diagram—and the partners' conference room adjacent to his office has a well-used board. During one conversation with me, he sketched out his vision of the private-equity world: the "three box model" divided among stock-pickers, deal guys, and portfolio managers. In that view of the world, stock-pickers choose what to buy like a public investor does, analyzing the merits of value and potential for growth. TPG's expertise, he says, falls between the latter two—scouting transactions in unlikely places and then figuring out how to save them or make them substantially better through radical change. That, he said, is "the secret sauce."

He pointed out that about 70 percent of the firm's deals aren't substantially different from its brethren in private equity, with the balance being in situations that are seen as unworkable or undesirable to everyone else. Since that latter 30 percent brings a disproportionate amount of attention, it's become a defining characteristic of TPG in the eyes of the public and in the media, Coulter said. Coslet described private equity in general, and TPG specifically, at its best as "fringe capital."

"It's got to be situations where the mainstream money says, 'I don't want to do that.' It's J. Crew when the founding family wants to sell it and can't find the public markets to buy it. It's Continental," Coslet said. "You have to do the stuff that's hard. When you forget that, you do what a lot of us did at the top of the bubble. That's a loss of recognition. You've got to get back to what we're here for."

Coslet conceded that approach inherently comes with more risk. "If really smart people think when they get to a fork in the road they should go left, it's probably the correct thing to do," he said. "But we've always said, let's figure out when to go right."

TPG has had misadventures, usually by veering into stock-picking. One deal, a stake in Washington Mutual that came and went within months, blew up practically before anyone knew what happened. The other is lingering. By dint of sheer size and profile, the record-setting takeover of TXU may stand as the final word on the buyout boom of 2007.

In both cases, TPG appears to have simply bet wrong, and with disastrous financial consequences. Certainly that was the case with Washington

Mutual. The bank was struggling as so many of its kind were in the financial crisis, and TPG bought a minority, non-controlling stake for $7 billion. The premise was that the financial crisis had bottomed out and TPG would reap a huge profit as WaMu, as it was known, got healthier. This wasn't a deal where ops expertise could help. TPG was basically operating on an educated hunch. It went exactly the other way. The government ultimately seized WaMu and sold part of it to JPMorgan, wiping out TPG's equity completely in the process. TPG and its co-investors lost about $2 billion (the balance was borrowed), with the firm's fund taking a $1.3 billion hit, the worst single loss in its history.

Betting big is part of the ethos of TPG, even if to Coulter's point, it isn't the only thing. A senior partner at a competing buyout firm told me: "When Bonderman is coming up to the plate, he's looking to hit it over the fence." Another rival put it more succinctly: "TPG has the biggest balls in the industry."

■ ■ ■

While its executive nerve center resides in San Francisco today, its technical headquarters is Fort Worth, Texas, and the roots of what was initially known as Texas Pacific Group—later shortened to TPG, presumably to make the increasingly global firm not sound regional—are there. The story began, oddly, with a fight over an interstate highway extension in Fort Worth that was opposed by a number of prominent residents, including Robert Bass, a scion of a wealthy Texas oil family. Casting about for a lawyer, Bass was pointed to Bonderman, a Washington attorney with the firm of Arnold & Porter. While his main area of expertise was complex bankruptcies (he'd worked as the trustee on the Braniff Airlines bankruptcy in the early 1980s), Bonderman devoted his pro bono work to historical preservation. He successfully fought a plan to demolish Grand Central Terminal in the late 1970s. A 1992 story described Bonderman as "a facile negotiator and deal maker with a finely honed sense of moral outrage and persuasion."[4]

His persuasion worked to great effect in Fort Worth. Bonderman helped prevent the freeway project, winning the admiration of Robert Bass, who was mulling a way to turn his inherited fortune into something even bigger, following the model of his older brother, Sid, who'd created a family office of his own, working with an investor named Richard Rainwater. Bonderman joined Robert Bass, eventually becoming the chief operating officer of the Robert M. Bass Group.

As Bonderman and Bass began to assemble a team to sniff out deals, Bonderman was introduced to a young investment banker named Jim Coulter. Not yet 30, Coulter was a farm boy who earned an engineering degree at Dartmouth and went on to get an MBA from Stanford. He'd done a brief stint on Wall Street before moving into the world of investments. He jumped at the chance to work for Bass.

Bass became a de facto incubator of sorts for the modern private-equity and real estate investment business. "The Basses had an incredible judgment about horseflesh, the talent," said Clive Bode, a lawyer who worked for the family, counseled Bonderman, and eventually served as TPG's general counsel.

In addition to the founding partners of TPG, Bass employed Barrack, a University of Southern California-educated native Angeleno whose early career wound from lawyering in Los Angeles to counseling members of the Saudi royal family on investments to a post in the Reagan administration. When the Bass band broke up, Barrack went on to create Colony Capital, an LA-based firm that has picked up distressed real estate across the globe, including the nearby Neverland Ranch, once the home of pop star Michael Jackson. Fellow Bass investor Kelvin Davis was a co-founder of Colony; he's now a partner at TPG. The Bass ethos, which dated back to Sid Bass and Rainwater, influenced the firms that it effectively gave birth to, Barrack said. "Everyone who came to Fort Worth felt paid attention to," he said. "It was cordial not hostile, non-Wall Street, non-aggravating." Another Bass investor, John Grayken, went on to create Lone Star Funds, a Texas-based investment firm focused mostly on distressed real estate. Others included hedge fund manager Marc Lasry, the founder of Avenue Capital.

A main area of focus during the Bass years was sifting through the detritus of the savings and loan crisis during the late 1980s, when more than 740 thrifts failed. Bass's boys deftly parlayed cash, debt, and government assistance into huge gains. For Bonderman and Coulter, the Bass milieu was what they constantly sought to create at what became TPG. "Our formative years were with family money, where we could walk down the hall and make the case for an investment," Bonderman told me during a chat in TPG's partners' conference room, where the couch and coffee table serve as his office when he stops by TPG San Francisco.

"People try and re-create where they come from. We're trying to recreate the best attributes of a family investment office, and in our case, one that was chaotic and quirky," Coulter said in a separate conversation. Comfort with chaos informed where the Bass group was trained to look for deals in unlikely places. Bonderman and Coulter identified a potential target nearby: the bankrupt, for the second time in a decade, Continental Airlines.

The two men, convinced they could make money buying and fixing it, were eager to do the deal. Bass wasn't interested under the auspices of the existing organization, but blessed Bonderman, Coulter, and another Bass partner, Bill Price, pursuing it on their own. The group scrounged together about $65 million of their own money, some from their partners at Bass, and Bass himself. They became the owners of Continental Airlines in 1993. They pursued a relentless strategy to overhaul the company, zeroing in on issues like baggage handling and food service. No detail was too small to be overlooked or commented on.

During the first year they owned the airline, Bonderman and Coulter were on a Continental flight, sitting in coach class. When the hot meal arrived, they were horrified at what lay before them and asked a perplexed flight attendant if they could keep one. Upon arriving, they slid the meal into an overnight-mail envelope and sent it back to the airline's Houston headquarters, to the attention of the CEO. Included with the meal was a handwritten note from Bonderman: "It didn't look much better on the flight."

The food improved along with the rest of the airline. The investment group made more than 10 times their investment as it sold shares over the subsequent years. "It was a harrowing and hugely empowering experience for them," said Kelvin Davis. "It set in place a core part of our foundation, cementing in their minds the value of operating capabilities." For the Continental deal, there was no firm, per se, just a limited partnership, called Air Partners, that owned the airline. As the deal progressed, the two partners faced a decision. They could work with little or no staff, taking it deal-by-deal, raising money as they went.

Or they could try and build a small infrastructure to pursue a handful of deals at multiple times.

It wasn't a slam-dunk decision, and while the two men agreed they weren't wild about going the seat-of-the-pants route, Bonderman at least had no intention of building something that would become the size of what TPG stood at two decades later. "We never thought it would be what it is now," he said. "We just set out to do a few deals." Coulter brought a slightly different perspective. At 32, he'd decided this was exactly what he wanted to do for the rest of his career. "My time horizon was a little bit different," he said. He'd also seen the power of the Bass confederation of brains and wanted to harness more than just what he and Bonderman could bring to the table. "If David and I just hung out a shingle, we might make more money in the short term, but we couldn't attract the talent to build a long-term business."

With the Bass ties strong, the Texas Pacific guys kept in close touch with their former partners Barrack and Davis, who'd started Colony in 1991. Starting in 1994, the handful of partners working at Texas Pacific and Colony would gather annually at Bonderman's home in Montana, and later in Aspen, where Bonderman moved and still has a home today. The multiday sessions were meant as strategy salons for the nascent investment groups. By 1996, Coulter was showing Power-Point presentations about expanding TPG. "He was talking about it like a guy who was trying to build a real business," Davis said.

■ ■ ■

TPG, by virtue of the size of its funds, its deals, and historical returns, belongs in the top ranks of the big global private-equity firms. Like its slightly larger brethren, it has pushed, albeit somewhat more tentatively, into areas beyond leveraged buyouts. The firm backed a hedge fund, called TPG-Axon, but does not control it. Rather than setting up a separate real estate business with dedicated funds as a number of larger competitors did, TPG chose to pursue those deals through its existing buyout funds. There have been internal discussions about raising a dedicated real estate pool, under the auspices of Davis, who left Colony and joined TPG in 2000.

TPG therefore straddles the worlds of pure private-equity investing and the broader, alternative asset strategy pursued more vigorously by Blackstone and Carlyle, and to some extent, KKR. That potentially makes TPG more vulnerable, at least in the short term, in so far as a series of bad deals, or a bad fund that spooks a herd of investors, could radically change the future of the firm. TPG's chemistry has so far allowed it to endure. Bonderman and Coulter have cultivated an air of quirky hip—at least as quirky and hip as you can be in the investment business. An executive at a rival firm told me: "TPG has an aura of cool that transcends performance."

Like Kravis and Roberts, Coulter obsesses over his firm's culture. He loves to talk about it and analyze it. When I even mentioned the word during one interview, he lit up, leaning forward into the table between us to emphasize certain points. "As you go through a career, you start worrying for other people and looking for the satisfaction not just of the next deal, but of building something," he said. "David and I always took the position it was not about us and that someday we wanted to leave with no one noticing. I want to be able to look at the 27-year-old who wants to work at TPG and say, 'You can make a career here.' "

Coulter keeps a sheet of paper in his office where he jots down important elements about the firm's culture and he and Bonderman give speeches, sometimes via video, to new hires that join the firm. "You instill the culture on long airplane flights," Coulter said. "You tell stories and legends and model the behavior." He noted that a small firm with a lot of money at its disposal places great trust in the people it hires. "If somebody some place makes a bad decision, it could bring the whole place down."

When talking about the firm, TPG partners are quick to mention Coulter's "No assholes" rule. Another way Coulter and Bonderman said they stressed togetherness and transparency is open meetings: any person at any level of the firm can register to listen in and participate in any investment committee meeting across TPG's funds. "We want to let the young people talk and have a voice," Bonderman said.

TPG faces a variation on a couple of themes when it comes to succession. Unlike the firms where the founders are all in their sixties or above, Coulter's age means there's less discussion about who will replace the men who started it all. Bonderman, like Schwarzman at Blackstone, has embraced some of the statesman-like trappings of the job. "He's an artist and this is his palette," Coslet said. "He's at a point where he's getting an invitation from Vladimir Putin to advise on how Russia should think about investing."

Beyond the founders, Coslet is a key voice in the direction of the firm by virtue of chairing the investment committee and the private-equity management committee, as well as a tenure that matches the founders'. Then there's Davis, the fellow Bass alumnus who reunited with Coulter and Bonderman after founding Colony. He's charged now with building up the firm's real estate efforts and has the trust of the founders dating back more than two decades to the Bass experience. Another more recent senior addition to the firm is Alan Waxman, a former Goldman executive who joined TPG in 2009 and helps run the special situations group. Waxman set out to raise TPG's first dedicated distressed debt fund in 2011, and his profile is notable given that he's not a leveraged buyout guy in the classic sense.

That serves to underscore how TPG, though less broadly diversified than some of its larger peers, responded to the same forces of the market, and its investors, by reaching beyond takeovers. "We'll all have a cafeteria," Clive Bode said. "You can take the soup, but not the entrée. Private equity, energy, real estate, pure credit. It's all going to be there. PE's not going to die, but in the overall structure, it will be smaller."

Bonderman's contribution was set early on, from the Continental deal and the ethos he cultivated at Bass. His combination of intellectual horsepower, appetite for risk, and appreciation for the eclectic are impossible to replicate in a single person. Coulter won't find Bonderman's like, even in his disciples, and it will be up to him to figure out what combination of people adds up to something resembling a Bonderman. To that end, TPG's place in private equity's future landscape rests squarely on Coulter and his ability to bottle the firm's secret sauce, a blend of traditional investments with a heavy dose of deals no one else will touch.

Chapter 8

Hundreds and Billions

Workers and Owners

T he numbers speak for themselves. U.S.-based private-equity firms employ 8.1 million people by one estimate,[1] out of a total workforce of roughly 154 million. That's one in 20 workers, meaning at a cocktail party, kegger, or family reunion, there's a good chance at least one person ultimately works for private equity.

KKR and Blackstone together, through the companies they own, count more than 1.5 million workers between them, based on data they post on their websites. That makes the firms huge employers on a global scale. Walmart had about 2.2 million employees at the end of 2012, according to Bloomberg data.

To be clear, all of the people who work at Blackstone companies don't wear Blackstone name tags or even get a paycheck signed by Steve Schwarzman. The firms, and especially their lobbyists in Washington, have gone to great lengths to point out that a ride operator at Legoland has no direct connection to a housekeeper at Hilton. That's especially important in the eyes of regulators and the government, who are rightly wary of situations where one company's failure can have a domino effect. Were Legoland to struggle financially, it would have no impact on Hilton, despite their common ownership. Each company is technically owned by a distinct partnership created by Blackstone, a partnership that shares nothing other than a common owner.

Still, any concentration of companies that have a lot of debt is worrisome to people who watched an overleveraged global financial system come to the brink of collapse in 2008 and 2009. When the subject of regulation was being debated in mid-2011, I talked with a senior investment advisor at the AFL-CIO named Heather Slavkin. "If we learned nothing from the financial crisis, highly leveraged opaque pools are breeding grounds for systemic risk," she said.[2]

And as demonstrated in the discussion around operations, controlling all those companies does make for an influential owner. Look at it another way. KKR companies together had annual revenues in 2010 of $210 billion. That's more than $50 billion more than General Electric had that same year.

Setting aside the pay of the founders and top executives of the firm, private equity is on average, a very lucrative business. The data are hard to come by; except for the small clutch of publicly traded firms, these are closely held partnerships. One researcher pegged the average cash earnings for a private-equity executive at $248,000 in 2011, a 6 percent increase from a year earlier.[3] That's roughly five times the median household income at the end of 2010 in the United States of $50,046, according to Bloomberg data.

The dollars involved are at the root of private equity's biggest issue: the perception, real or imagined, that they are making huge amounts of money on the backs of people who are paid a tremendous amount less. A similar gulf certainly exists between the top managers of publicly traded corporations and the vast majority of employees at those companies.

In defending their record to me, and characterizing the public misperceptions of them as unfair, private-equity executives several times sought to draw a comparison between what they do and the chief executives of big companies like General Electric in terms of rationalizing what lines of business they should be in, how many employees they should have, and where geographically a company should expand or contract.

What does separate private equity from a public company—and this is a key part of the pitch buyout managers give for their existence and the superiority of their business model—is the speed, and some would say the ferocity, with which they go about making those decisions. Because the clock is ticking on their investment from the moment they make it, they are highly motivated to do something, and do it fast.

■ ■ ■

So in our journey following the money through the private-equity cycle, we arrive at another crucial, simple question that of course doesn't have an easy answer: Should you be thrilled or terrified when private equity arrives on your company's doorstep? More to the point, are you likely to lose your job?

As a nerdy financial journalist, my first instinct is to retreat to the data, which bring a lack of clarity and ultimately disappointment. The most comprehensive study to date, updated in 2011, was conducted by Steven J. Davis, John Haltiwanger, Ron S. Jarmin, Josh Lerner, and Javier Miranda. Titled "Private Equity and Employment," it comes to a maddening conclusion for those looking for an easy answer: It depends. Overall, the study says, private equity is neither a massive job creator nor a massive job destroyer.[4]

The research drills deep into the companies it studies, taking into account not only employment for each company, but at each individual facility (plants, field offices, and so on). Several interesting nuggets emerge. The researchers were able to divide firms into three sectors— manufacturing, retail, and service—and the results are varied among those, with manufacturing coming out at essentially a wash. Service companies see some initial job growth in the first couple of years, then a slowdown. Retail companies experience the most dramatic overall job loss. The result "serves as a caution against painting with an overly broad brush when characterizing employment outcomes in the wake of private-equity buyouts," the authors wrote.

The findings about which sectors face the most job destruction in the wake of an LBO is particularly interesting. It may help explain the reputation that private equity has earned in the wider world. Public-to-private deals are ones involving a company that is listed on the New York Stock Exchange or other such stock market, and those comprise the vast majority of the biggest deals in history, from Caesars to Hilton to RJR. Firms in those types of transactions experienced job loss of 10 percent versus comparable companies. Those companies also experienced less job creation at what the researchers call "establishment births," or the opening of new offices, factories, or branches. The authors summed it up: "Along with the high visibility of public-to-private deals, these results help to understand concerns about job loss related to private-equity buyouts."[5]

Here's the interesting twist that underscores that finding: The data show the opposite result for private-to-private deals, or transactions where a buyout firm buys an already closely held company. There, employment *grows* by 10 percent during the first two years, a factor the authors chalk up to the buyers' tendency to expand rapidly through acquisition.

Perhaps not surprisingly, the study also found that disruption is almost guaranteed at companies that go through an LBO, and job losses occur disproportionately in the months immediately following the takeover. In other words, if you work for a company headed for a buyout, buckle up.

■ ■ ■

Jobs have become a centerpiece question in the private equity industry in large part because one of their own is running for president: Bain Capital founder Mitt Romney. The former Massachusetts governor made the economy and job creation a centerpiece of his campaign, touting his skills honed in the private sector to win over voters.

The Romney candidacy inserted private equity into the broader national conversation in an unprecedented way, as voters and the press began examining his personal and business record anew. A stream of stories told tales of Romney and Bain deals gone bad and focused mostly on a handful of companies, including American Pad & Paper, KB Toys, and Dade International, a medical company. Romney took a huge amount of criticism for each of these deals, largely because they portrayed him and Bain as overseeing a system whereby they essentially guaranteed they and their investors got paid regardless of what happened to the company.

Political opponents seized on that narrative. Former U.S. House Speaker Newt Gingrich's campaign experienced a surge in late 2011 as he took aim at Romney on a variety of fronts, including his Bain tenure. After Romney suggested that Gingrich return the $1.6 million he was paid as a consultant to mortgage provider Freddie Mac, Gingrich parried: "I would just say that if Governor Romney would like to give back all the money he's earned from bankrupting companies and laying off employees over his years at Bain that I would be glad to then listen to him."[6]

During that same period, Romney's campaign got a taste of what they'd face during the general election, when President Obama's surrogates took aim at his private-equity career, as well. David Axelrod, the president's chief campaign strategist, took aim at Romney within days of Gingrich's comment. Keying off an ill-advised debate quip where Romney offered to bet Texas Governor Rick Perry $10,000, Axelrod said: "What was startling to me was that generally his practice has been to bet other people's money, not his own." He continued: "That's the way he ran his leveraged buyout business. They closed down hundreds of factories. They outsourced thousands of jobs. They took a lot of companies to bankruptcy and made a fortune off of those bankruptcies."[7]

One unhappy former worker at a company bought by Bain was credited in part with Romney's failing to unseat the late U.S. Senator Edward Kennedy in 1994. The most potent symbol then was a man named Randy Johnson, who worked at a factory that had been acquired by Bain-owned American Pad & Paper. Johnson was among those who lost his job when the factory was shuttered.

The American Pad & Paper saga became part of an advertising campaign against Romney in the Senate campaign and is credited in part for leading to Romney's defeat by the incumbent. Johnson himself traveled to Massachusetts to campaign against Romney. Johnson, who subsequently relocated to Pittsburgh and now is a member of the United Steelworkers, re-emerged in late 2011 to again campaign against Romney. In an interview with ABC News, he framed the question in stark terms: "I was stunned by the amount of wealth he created in a short amount of time," Johnson said. "He definitely got the money, but was it the right thing to do? Was it the moral thing to do with workers and people?"[8]

In late 2011, as the nomination contest was narrowing, the *New York Times* analyzed how Romney had continued to earn money from Bain deals, even after his departure in 1999. The article cited layoffs at companies including KB Toys, a retailer that eventually went bankrupt, as well as job cuts at Clear Channel Communications, the broadcast company Bain and Thomas H. Lee Partners bought in 2007. Romney's campaign repeatedly asserted that during his time at Bain, the firm created more than 100,000 jobs through the companies it invested in, including Domino's and Staples. After months of staying mostly quiet, Bain sent a letter to its investors in March 2012 that in part addressed the jobs issue. "While experts agree that calculating net job growth across a portfolio of companies is difficult to do with precision, the revenue growth in our companies has created hundreds of thousands of jobs over our 28-year history," the partners wrote.[9] The firm said the companies it had invested in had increased revenue by more than $105 billion.

■ ■ ■

The jobs question had broader consequences and was the subject of consternation in the halls of private-equity firms beyond Bain. Top executives within Blackstone, Carlyle, and KKR spoke repeatedly about how a Romney nomination would manifest itself for the industry in the context of a nasty, well-financed presidential campaign. The Private Equity Growth Capital Council and the individual firms scrambled to gather employment data to try and stem the inevitable flow of stories that portrayed private equity as job destroyers.

There was a certain fatalism in many of the discussions and a number of them conveyed that to me when the topic came up, which it inevitably did during any meaningful discussion of what was happening in the industry. Most of the firms were assembling information from their own portfolios to try and distinguish themselves, either from Romney, or Bain, or their peers, all while understanding that they would help the broader business put on a brave face.

The reality, they said, was that they needed to prepare themselves and, more importantly, their investors, for a storm that was coming. It's hard to imagine any limited partner would be surprised to learn that Romney once worked in private equity. It's also hard to imagine that having Mitt Romney as a presidential nominee will have an actual impact on deals getting done. Capitalism tends to trump politics, especially once the stump speeches cease and the hot lights of the campaign dim. One private-equity executive said to me, with a sigh, when I brought up the topic of Romney, "This too shall pass."

■ ■ ■

But the Romney candidacy and the inevitable flood of questions from voters and reporters, along with the dozens and dozens of political ads, do lead to another larger private-equity question: Should the industry, or individual firms, ultimately be judged on how many jobs they create or destroy?

In the context of Romney drawing a line between his private-equity experience and skill growing employment, one sentiment I heard repeatedly from managers in the buyout business was: We never said we were out to create jobs. Steve Murray, the CEO of CCMP Capital, told me jobs could be a by-product of good investing. "The payoff on growing the business is better than the payoff from cutting it," he said. "Adding jobs is usually in our interest, but I don't think private equity alone can solve the overall unemployment issue."

It's an idea that some who've studied the industry agree with. Oliver Gottschalg, a professor at HEC in Paris, told me: "It shouldn't be based exclusively on jobs. For me the question is whether the company is better positioned versus its competitors. That's what will drive employment in the longer-term as well." He's far from an industry cheerleader and is among those pushing for more data to actually prove, or disprove, a lot of the things that people assume about private equity. In his estimation, private equity has an easy analogy.

"I see it as a fitness camp. You do a few things that may not be fun while you're doing it, but beneficial in the long term," he says. Some cases, he contends, are beyond saving. "For some it's beneficial. For some the fitness camp was inappropriate or hopeless."

Gottschalg circles back to the lack of data. It points largely to the immaturity, and potentially the arrogance, of the industry and the individual firms. For years they took incoming fire around their activities without responding and developed a reputation as "strip and flip" artists. Yet they never produced any evidence to the contrary, which looked to those on the outside like at best, pleading the Fifth Amendment—invoking the right not to incriminate one's self.

The reality in several cases seemed to be that the data didn't exist, at least in an easily accessible way. There also were questions around what constituted creating a job. Private-equity firms wrestled with whether they could or should count jobs where they were a minority investor, and whether jobs created after they sold their stake in the company should count. Echoing the political calculation used by the Obama administration, they also wondered aloud whether they should get credit for "saving" jobs, that is, employment in cases where they bought a company that was likely to go out of business without their investment.

In political and public relations terms, the venture capital industry rather brilliantly outflanked private equity by positioning itself as a job creation engine. The industry's chief lobbyist in Washington, the National Venture Capital Association, said that as of 2010, venture-backed companies accounted for 11.87 million jobs and over $3.1 trillion in revenue, citing a study produced by IHS Global Insight.[10]

Said one private-equity executive: "That's tiny compared to PE. And you're talking about companies out in Silicon Valley that are hiring computer engineers from Berkeley and Stanford. They create wealth, not jobs. It's private equity that buys old line industrial companies, companies where we can make a difference."

Blackstone pressed its companies in 2010 and 2011 for data that it could use to tell its story to Washington and to the press. Synthesizing what it got back, Schwarzman and James told anyone who'd listen that their companies had cumulatively grown employment. Blackstone posted on its website that U.S. companies in which it held a majority ownership grew jobs at 4.6 percent, versus 1.1 percent for the broader economy in 2010. The other firms were conducting similar exercises, asking the portfolio for employment information.

■ ■ ■

One place where two sides of the private-equity equation collide is with labor unions, which can find themselves as both beneficiaries of the profits generated by private-equity funds and at their mercy as employees after their company is bought out. There's also this less examined but important piece: Some number of labor union members rely on the private-equity managers for a piece of their own retirement through their pension funds.

Slavkin of the AFL-CIO participated in a session at the Brookings Institution, the Washington think tank, in November 2011 and talked about that conundrum and how members of the unions affiliated with her organization dealt with it. The event was co-sponsored by the Private Capital Research Institute, a non-profit group that aims to foster the independent academic study of private capital. The PCRI is headed by Harvard's Josh Lerner and its backers include CD&R founder Joe Rice. Slavkin described a situation where private equity has a mixed track record with labor, citing Blackstone's mostly positive interactions vis-à-vis hotel workers at Hilton, as well as other, less positive situations where buyout firms had taken over casinos.

The unions, she said, are happiest and best served, not surprisingly, when they're at the table and participating in the decisions around the deal and the future of the company. "These are people that oftentimes have been working for a company, that know the business better than the private-equity fund coming in to purchase the company, and hope to stay there for a long time into the future," she said. When shut out of the process, though, things can turn ugly. "If the workers are seen as the enemy, it can cause some major headaches," Slavkin said. "It can become a big expense for the private-equity fund."[12]

■ ■ ■

KKR and Clayton, Dubilier & Rice had a flare-up with the Teamsters in late 2011, one of a handful of times in recent years when a private equity versus labor dispute bubbled into the public eye, albeit briefly. Teamsters at US Foods, which the two firms bought in 2007, went on strike at the company's Streator, Illinois, facility as the union negotiated a new contract. The action brought sympathy pickets at other US Foodservice locations. The sides ultimately finalized a new contract in December 2011.

The showdowns at US Foods were not the first time the Teamsters had clashed with KKR specifically. Teamsters General President James Hoffa in April 2010 wrote a column for the Huffington Post to urge Congress to increase the tax rate on carried interest. "The Teamsters have had plenty of experience with private-equity firms, and it hasn't been pretty," Hoffa wrote. "Time and again, private-equity firms have bought good, profitable Teamster employers only to devour their cash."

He continued: "Kohlberg Kravis Roberts & Co.'s history with Teamster employers is one of underinvestment, stretching workers and equipment to the breaking point. KKR's pattern has been to kick to the curb the carcasses of what were once productive enterprises."[13]

■ ■ ■

The Service Employees International Union, or the SEIU, was probably the most vocal and visible critic of private equity at the height of the leveraged buyout boom. Under the guidance of Andy Stern, the Washington-based union took aim at a handful of the largest firms, especially Carlyle. The centerpiece of the SEIU's campaign was a 42-page report, released in April 2007, called "Beyond the Buyouts," which underlined the scope of private equity's ownership and question some of its methods, particularly in light of the workers at private-equity-owned companies.

The tone was sweeping and focused largely on the wealth gap that would several years later become the centerpiece of the Occupy Wall Street movement. "These profits come during a period of historic income inequality in America, at a time when millions of Americans are working harder and harder for less, with less health care, less retirement security, and less time to spend with their children," according to the report.[14]

The report went on to give a primer on the LBO business and provided snapshots of five of the biggest firms. It also provided five separate narratives of private-equity deals where it determined the owners made choices detrimental to workers, through job cuts or decisions like dividend recapitalizations. It concluded with a list of proposed principles for the private equity industry, pushing for more representation of workers at the outset of a deal being negotiated, more transparency of information from the firms, and more involvement in the communities where managers bought companies.

The SEIU was just getting started. In July, the union sponsored a double-decker bus tour of New York's Times Square, where it pointed out private equity's presence throughout. By the SEIU's count, within 50 blocks encompassing the square famous for its billboards and New Year's Eve celebration, there were 53 locations of 28 companies owned in part or wholly by private-equity firms. That included KKR and Bain's Toys "R" Us, whose flagship store sits near the center of Times Square.

The union's effort hammered home the income question in the context of the toy retailer, describing how the firms had already earned fees from the takeover while laying off workers. "A handful of private-equity executives are personally making millions of dollars in buyout deals but workers are being left behind," Stephen Lerner, who led the SEIU's private-equity effort, said at the time.[15]

"They never saw themselves as conglomerates, and we were forcing them to think about that," Stern told me. "I don't think they were ready to be out in the public like that."

Through 2007, as Carlyle was seeking approval for its takeover of nursing home chain Manor Care, SEIU protesters were a fixture on Carlyle co-founder David Rubenstein's public speaking schedule. They routinely showed up at speeches, sometimes picketing outside, other times making their way into the events to chant or unroll banners. Chants included: "Better staffing, better care/No more money for billionaires."[16] The SEIU also targeted Carlyle at its headquarters in Washington. In October 2007, members of the union rolled wheelbarrows full of fake money from the offices of the Internal Revenue Service to Carlyle's Pennsylvania Avenue offices and dumped them in front of a person dressed up as a "fat cat." A banner with Rubenstein's picture on it said, "Caution: Carlyle Deal in Progress, Taxpayer Money Moving to David Rubenstein's Pockets."[17]

Stern wasn't afraid to venture into the lion's den. In early 2008, he turned up on a panel at Columbia Business School's annual private-equity conference, where he sparred with buyout executives on a panel in front of a standing-room-only crowd of B-school students, journalists, and industry executives. There was even undercover security in the audience and the moderator, the *New York Times* columnist and author Andrew Ross Sorkin, later described it: "If Jerry Springer had a show about business, this might have been an early episode."[18]

Then a funny thing happened: The SEIU, at least publicly, seemed to lose interest in private equity. The union turned its focus to the more traditional banks as the financial crisis deepened, creating a campaign that helped oust Bank of America CEO Kenneth Lewis. The SEIU also spent a lot of its time and resources on healthcare reform. Stern himself was a frequent visitor to the White House after Obama was elected.

The SEIU leaders had envisioned a type of global settlement, whereby all the big firms agreed to sign on to a set of principles that would govern their behavior in leveraged buyouts. That never happened. Instead, the union won smaller victories, like when Blackstone agreed in August 2007 to provide health insurance to janitors in the Boston area who worked for Equity Office Properties.[19]

What appeared to be a mellowing toward Stern's private-equity foes bubbled into public view in mid-2011. In a Bloomberg Television interview, Stern said: "I was awfully tough on . . . private equity and the banks. Some of it was totally appropriate; other of it probably was a little bit out of hand."[20] He turned up around the same time as a speaker at a meeting of KKR's limited partners. After working as a fellow at Georgetown University, he accepted a fellowship at Columbia Business School. That's where I found him in 2012 to ask him about what appeared to be a conversion, or at least a change of heart.

A couple of funny things struck me as I walked to Stern's office, tucked in a warren of small workspaces in the school's Uris Hall. I'd last seen him in full throat steps from here, at the aforementioned conference four years earlier. The second was that if Stern continued this gig at Columbia for a few more years, the most vocal agitator of private equity was likely to be working at a building named for Henry Kravis. Kravis's $100 million gift to the school included the honor of having a building at the new business school campus in East Harlem named for him.

It turns out Stern was not so much a changed man, but a slightly more contemplative one, maybe by virtue of having a post in the relatively cozier world of academia and some distance from the hand-to-microphone combat of running a union day in and day out. During a relaxed conversation in a quiet conference room, he showed how he retained some of his fiery rhetoric about private equity.

"We have every right to criticize business practices, but not business," he said. "This is a way that people invest money and we can't be too coarse. We need to attack the practices and not the vehicles."

The vitriol Stern once directed at the private-equity firms was redirected at the sources of their money, namely the public pensions. "There's a contradiction of values and practices," he said. "It's a loss of opportunity because it's their money being used against their interests."

The investors have an obligation to force the issue of what Stern calls "secondary returns," that is, proof that what the private-equity managers are doing to companies and economies has some benefit to society at large. Just as the investors have pushed for more favorable economic terms through efforts like ILPA, they need to press managers to prove their social worth. "If you want to make change, have money," Stern said. "That's what I've learned."

The idea of the investors pressing for social change was described to me in a slightly different way by another labor leader with private-equity experience. Marty Leary is a long-time labor man, having started his career in the late 1980s organizing state workers in Mississippi. At Unite Here, the hospitality workers union, he's run across private equity through acquisitions of hotels and casinos. What he's found, and he has an obvious affinity for unions, is that when an industry is already organized, it does better in the context of a takeover because the buyer is more likely to include the workers in the earlier conversations. "If you're in an industry that's not organized and you're suddenly part of a huge conglomerate that's all about cutting costs and making the nut in terms of the debt load, it's going to be a rough ride," Leary said.

His clear-eyed view of private equity echoed a sentiment of Stern's: Ultimately the private-equity guys are not ideologically in favor of or opposed to unions. "They're in to get their carry and get out," Leary said. "If workers can position themselves so their cause is at least not counterproductive to PE managers' goals, it's possible they can find an opportunity to win collective bargaining rights that might not have been otherwise possible."

Also like Stern, he put the onus on the pensions to affect real change in private equity: "It's a little bit like saying, 'Are bosses good or bad?'

It's here, we're not going to stuff the genie back in the bottle," Leary said. "The question is, How do we create some rules that allow these guys to do what they do without wreaking havoc and devastation?"

"The real owners are way too timid, that's the problem," he said of the big limited partners. "They are letting the private-equity owners use our own money to devastate our communities. They are the only ones who can rein these guys in." Leary's version of Stern's secondary returns is a "double bottom line," where investors demand of the private-equity firms that they generate not only good financial returns, but essentially good social returns, as well. It's here that Leary has a nuanced view of private equity and job creation—mainly, that it's not just about the numbers.

"The issue is really are those jobs going to be good jobs or crappy jobs," he said, noting that this is especially important when you're talking about workers who want to work at one place for an extended period, not a one-off construction job. "It's the long-term jobs that matter over time. The people who work in the facility are the ones who live in the town."

■ ■ ■

Where the relationship between unions and private equity goes from here isn't clear. Some inside the big buyout firms worry that while it was relatively quiet from 2009 on, that didn't signify a meaningful evolution in the dynamic. Rather, the distractions of the financial crisis and the fight for Obama's healthcare plan had diverted resources away from criticizing LBO firms. One executive characterized it to me as simply a "lull."

The unions, too, represent an increasingly small part of the work-force, especially within the private sector. Government employees, though they may have money invested with private-equity firms, aren't likely to be a party to a leveraged buyout. According to the Bureau of Labor Statistics, the union membership rate for U.S. workers was 11.9 percent in 2010, down from 20.1 percent in 1983, the first year when comparable data were available. Breaking it down by public and private sector: 36.2 percent of public workers were members of a union, while only 6.9 percent of private-sector workers were unionized.[21]

Unions, though, have managed to become a bigger part of the perception equation as private-equity firms contend with the broader implications of being big, visible institutions.

A lot of my project was about finding where the rubber meets the road for private equity—for the firms, for their investors, for the companies they buy, and for the people who work for their companies. I kept asking the question, what difference private equity makes for all of those pieces of the equation. For George Sterba, it meant 100 bucks less a month in retirement.

Sterba is a retired truck driver from Chicago. He worked for Ashland Distribution until he retired in July 2011. We met in San Francisco in 2012, when he was part of a protest against TPG. We sat on a short stone wall outside the Fairmont Hotel on a picture-perfect San Francisco winter day, breezy and sunny, just cool enough to make the black hat on Sterba's head necessary.

While TPG co-founder David Bonderman spoke on a panel at a conference inside the hotel, Sterba and other members of the Teamsters Local 705 were outside. They handed out flyers, one of which said "TPG Capital = Pension Fund Buster" and asked people to call Bonderman's office to "ask him to stop TPG's anti-worker practices."

In Sterba's case, his retirement plan shifted after Nexeo Solutions, an affiliate of TPG, bought Ashland's distribution business in early 2011. After the transaction, the new management switched to a 401(k) from the pension plan the company previously had. For him, the switch meant that he didn't get credit for the last few months of his service in pension terms. Since he'd reached 25 years, he was entitled to $2500 per month, and then $100 a month for each subsequent year. Retiring in July meant he'd reach 27 years, or $2700. but the switch away from the pension meant those months between April and July didn't count and he didn't get credit for that last year.

Sterba, a guy with two kids and two grandkids, and whose own dad was a member of Local 705, struck me as more resigned than angry. "I try to understand both sides, but part of the case for the workers is the light at the end of the tunnel," he said. We talked about the conundrum of private-equity firms including TPG investing on behalf of pensions while simultaneously taking actions that affect the very people for whom those pensions are a promise. It's a case the private-equity managers make more and more—that they are a vital participant in the retirement system for millions of U.S. workers. The Teamsters, in the flyer, put it this way: "The reality is these pension plans are helping to fund TPG's anti-worker investments."

Sterba said, "It's like cutting off your nose to spite your face. You gotta give the incentives for the workforce to stay with you." For him, the upshot was that seemingly small difference in his monthly check. "I'm missing a hundred bucks a month. It may not seem like a lot, but to someone on a fixed income, it sure feels like it."

Officials at TPG and Nexio declined to comment about the situation. A person familiar with the transaction said that Nexeo had in fact gone to great lengths to ensure that those who switched from pensions to the defined benefits plan got a deal that ultimately would have similar benefits and without the risk of an underfunded pension.

■ ■ ■

One way unions and others have sought to ensure private-equity firms act responsibly is through programs like the United Nations Principles for Responsible Investing, which ask investors to sign on and follow certain guidelines around environmental social and corporate governance (known as ESG).

Like the principles created by the Institutional Limited Partners Association, the UNPRI has become a way to keep an eye on private-equity firms and either encourage or require them to meet certain agreed-upon standards or explain why they didn't. KKR in 2011 released a companion report to its annual report focused exclusively on ESG issues. Carlyle in 2012 issued its second detailed report on corporate responsibility. The move toward proving they are good environmental stewards has been an especially interesting one to watch, in part because of the personalities involved and in part because of some of their investments, including TXU. There, the company has shuttered a number of coal-fired plants in the wake of the LBO.

Bonderman has been an active environmentalist for decades, and moving in those circles spurred a friendship with a fellow named Ed Norton, a former deputy director of the Nature Conservancy and the founding president of the Grand Canyon Trust. Norton (father of the actor Edward Norton) was living in Indonesia in 2007 when Bonderman, whom he'd met through the Grand Canyon Trust two decades previous, called and asked to get together during one of Bonderman's frequent trips to Asia to ask how the firm and companies it owned could improve their environmental performance and how TPG could integrate those issues into due diligence. That meeting led to the elder Norton joining TPG as a senior adviser on environmental issues, where his group develops sustainability policies and strategies, as well as metrics to cut costs and reduce environmental impacts.

KKR has undertaken an ambitious effort, dubbed the Green Portfolio, created in partnership with the Environmental Defense Fund. Through that program, KKR has pushed the companies it owns to cut costs and improve profits through energy efficiency and waste handling measures. The firm said in late 2011 the participating companies had avoided costs totaling $365 million since 2008.[22] KKR's Mehlman, the former Republican National Committee chairman, is fond of using the term "stakeholders" to talk about the various parties who have an interest in private equity. He has aggressively built out a global unit focused on those issues, prodding companies KKR owns to think about everything from the environment to wellness, all with an eye toward the bottom line. Synthesizing the move to KKR in 2007 with the rest of his career—he also ran George W. Bush's 2004 reelection campaign— he said, "I'm a mission guy."

Stern argued to me that this is the template to use for pushing private equity to think more holistically about ultimately being better employers. Their ideology is to make money. They have proven—as KKR has done with their environmental efforts—that they're open to doing business in such a way that allows them to both do good and do well. Whether the tycoons ultimately agree with that approach remains to be seen.

Chapter 9

Take This Exit

Payouts, Dividends, and Consequences

T he founders of private-equity firms aren't usually thought to be cheeky, but that's just what the trio behind Carlyle went for in its 2011 corporate holiday greetings. In a video message sent in mid-December to the firm's investors, Conway, D'Aniello, and Rubenstein "imagined" what would have happened had they not created Carlyle two decades earlier.[1]

Rubenstein turns up perched behind a lemonade stand, pitching kids on an opportunity to forego a simple cup in favor of becoming a limited partner in the stand. Conway sits in a telephone call center (a nod to his previous job at MCI), and D'Aniello sells pastries and coffee at Carlyle-owned Dunkin' Donuts. While investors likely chuckled at the self-directed send-up, they were much more interested in another private message from Carlyle that arrived a few days later. And they got the evidence of why Carlyle was especially feeling its oats at the moment.

The investor letter is a staple of the private equity industry, one of the few ways that managers communicate in detail on a regular basis. They are meant to be confidential missives, in part because they often disclose private information about closely held companies and reveal the strategy of the firm. The four-page letter, dated December 21st and signed by the three founders, was a technical rundown of the year, with the numbers investors needed to best judge Carlyle's performance. In the third paragraph was the money shot. The founders disclosed that for the year, they expected to distribute $17.8 billion to their investors, a record for the firm, and to their knowledge the most any "alternative asset" firm had ever paid out in a single year. The announcement came as welcome news to Carlyle's clients.

Private equity only works if the money actually gets back to the investors who committed it in the first place, in a reasonable time frame and with a healthy return. That's why private-equity managers justify their enormous fees at the end of the day: because they can deliver returns investors can't find anywhere else. When and how the money comes home to roost is one of the most contentious running arguments in and around the industry and provides the most fodder for critics.

A private-equity fund usually has a life of about 10 years, and during that period investors expect to put money in and get it back on a regular basis. Most companies bought by a fund aren't held for the duration of the fund, but bought and sold within five to seven years, sometimes less. Even though a holding period is measured in years rather than months, weeks, or days for some mutual funds (or minutes or seconds or fractions of seconds, as it is with some hedge funds), the clock is ticking from the moment a private-equity fund buys a company.

The goal is an "exit," an event that leads to a distribution of profits to the investors, with a cut going to the manager. The investors get 80 percent of those profits, and the private-equity firm gets 20 percent, the piece known as carried interest. Those exits can be accomplished in a number of ways, and we'll get to them. But let's talk first about how the buyers can reap fees and profits while they still own the company.

■ ■ ■

The sheer volume of money that flows to the private-equity managers is at the heart of most every criticism they face—from employees, unions, executives, and politicians—and in their honest moments, the buyout managers themselves concede this. It is undeniably an extraordinarily lucrative business and the amount of wealth makes for a skeptical world at large. One of the areas that became increasingly hard to defend as the industry matured, and the mechanics of the business became more apparent, were the fees beyond management and carried interest.

The main targets were transaction fees and monitoring fees, both fairly descriptive terms. The former is a fee levied by the firm on the company when the deal happens; the latter is for providing usually unspecified advice to the company. Investors were especially incensed by this practice when they realized that the managers were charging these fees and not sharing them with the limited partners. In the Institutional Limited Partners Association guidelines that helped galvanize investors in 2010 and 2011, the authors took aim at these sorts of fees directly. "[W]ealth creation from excessive management, transaction or other fees and income sources . . . reduces alignment of interest," according to the second version of ILPA's private-equity principles, released in early 2011.[2] The ILPA guidelines called for such fees to accrue to the fund rather than go directly to the private-equity managers. That way, if the managers insisted on charging them, they'd at least get the traditional breakdown of 20 percent to the private-equity firm, with 80 percent going to the limited partners.

A study by researcher Preqin and law firm Dechert in late 2011 showed that increased scrutiny and criticism around the fees had done little to slow their use. The researchers mined data around deals over multiple years and found that while monitoring fees and transaction fees dropped off during the financial crisis, they came roaring back during the recovery. They also found that of the 72 firms they surveyed, about 20 percent of respondents said that all or a substantial portion of the fees went to the private-equity manager.[3]

There's another way to take money off the table before a manager actually buys or sells a company. A dividend recap is something akin to a second mortgage, and in a lot of ways just as potentially treacherous. When a family opts for a second mortgage, sometimes they have a compelling reason; it may be the only way to pay for college or medical bills. But sometimes it's for a new car or flat-screen TV or fancy vacation.

Either way, it's more debt, and that's how it is for a company, too. Through a dividend recapitalization, the owner of the firm is changing its balance sheet (recapitalizing) in order to create a payout (dividend). In all the talk about alignment of interests, this is one place where the argument seems to break down. The investors in the private-equity fund are generally happy with a dividend recap on paper. After all, this is one of a handful of ways they get a profit distribution. The managers of the private-equity fund are happy. They'll likely get either closer to earning their carried interest, or if the fund is far enough along, 20 percent of the dividend will go right to them. So far, so good.

But what about the company? Debt has to be paid back. Thus more cash has to be diverted from hiring new employees and expanding business lines and opening new factories toward paying off loans.

Then there's a philosophical point. Private-equity firms often can recoup their initial investment, and more, through a dividend recap, and continue to own the company. While casino analogies are generally both provocative and insufficient when it comes to describing investing, it seems fitting in this case. They are at the blackjack table and have won a few hands. They can take back the initial stake and put in their proverbial pocket. Any gains from here on out are essentially won playing with house money.

Kenneth Hackel, whose Connecticut firm advises institutional investors, has been a vocal critic of dividend recaps. In his estimation, the main problem is that it redirects more free cash flow to debt payments rather than something that could actually improve the business. "This is all about greed," he said. "This does not improve the company on any metric that really counts."

In an article on Forbes.com in late 2010, Hackel laid it out this way: "By virtue of leveraging of the balance sheet while getting nothing in return, both investors and employees are much worse-off. No jobs in research, no machinery, technology, or productive plant were put in place as multibillion-dollar checks were mailed out."[4]

Private-equity managers, not surprisingly, disagree with the criticism over dividend recaps. They argue they are being good stewards of their investors' capital and have a responsibility to return their money, with a profit, to those backers in a timely manner. They also shoot down the implication that their alignment of interest chain is broken since they are not selling any equity in such a transaction. Blackstone's Tony James put it this way to me: "It's not a gimmick. Investments do mature at times when the market doesn't give you a way out." He said lenders won't do a recap deal if the sponsor doesn't have a significant portion of equity remaining in the company. "In that sense it's no different than an IPO. They are exactly the same, exactly the same emotional alignment."

While it's logical, it still makes folks uncomfortable, probably because a dividend recap usually means *additional* debt, and making money by borrowing money simply doesn't feel right. Romney's presidential candidacy spurred a flurry of stories that included details about dividend recaps in 2011. In at least one example of a Bain deal gone bad tied to Romney's tenure, the recap apparently was what helped push the company into bankruptcy.

The company in question was Dade International, which Bain bought in 1994. Michael Barbaro of the *New York Times* in 2011 analyzed the deal, showing how Bain essentially saved the company, then did very well by its investors through the Dade transaction by making eight times its original investment. Yet the company eventually filed for bankruptcy, after Bain engineered a $242 million dividend for itself and its investors. The *Times* story quoted the former president of Dade, who earned $1 million from the dividend, questioning the practice in retrospect.[5]

The story of that takeover achieved meta-status in December 2011, when *Times* columnist Andrew Ross Sorkin noted that the company was one of the ones most often mentioned in profiles of Romney. Sorkin pointed out that the Dade deal was in fact one where Bain saved the company from bankruptcy and set it on a path to health, only to cripple it with more debt via a recap.[6] *Fortune* writer Dan Primack, one of the most-followed voices writing about the industry and a frequent critic of dividend recaps, took it a step further, arguing that Sorkin shouldn't grant Romney any quarter just because Bain initially did some good at Dade. He drew a stark analogy whereby someone fed and clothed a homeless person, only to later rob him when he begins to earn money again, and watch him die of starvation.

"Was my action morally acceptable because he would have starved years ago without my help? Dividend recaps often are the worst of private equity, contributing to the industry's reputation as destructive financial engineers," Primack wrote.[7]

Siding with Hackel and Primack as a dividend recap doubter suggests that just because an investor can do something doesn't mean he should. In other words, as managers' ownership of the broader economy deepens, so too does their responsibility to think beyond purely financial returns.

■ ■ ■

Dividends are one way that private-equity managers take their money off the table, distributing it to their investors while keeping their proscribed cut. That's just an interim step in most cases. There's still the matter of exiting the investment completely. There are three general ways to do that, with slight variations: selling the investment to another company, selling it to another investor like a fellow private-equity firm, or taking it public. All have their pros and cons. How pro or con you are probably depends on where you sit at the table.

Selling out for cash seems to be the cleanest way to get out. You agree to a price, you get the money, the company gets a new owner. Your limited partners get their money back and, hopefully, a profit. Carried interest flows to the private-equity firm.

Like dividend recaps, the strategy of selling to another private-equity firm comes with some baggage, though more for the buyer than the seller, and for the buyer's backers. The seller is generally happy to get out. Investors, though, sometimes have some questions. These "pass the parcel" deals have the danger of being a game of financial hot potato, whereby somebody is going to be left holding on to something that's not worth as much as they thought. There's a fear that there's a greater fool theory at work here.

"You either have a superior insight, specialization, an angle that helps you pay a little more than the others, or you nudge the debt package and pay a higher price because you need to invest," Neil Harper, managing director at Morgan Stanley's private-equity fund-of-funds unit in Europe, told Bloomberg in 2010. "The concern is that you have more of the latter than the former. This will affect returns."[8]

Investors also worry because there are fees involved in every transaction, and those are ultimately paid mostly by the backers of private-equity funds. At one point in late 2010, almost half of the buyouts by value in Europe involved this type of deal, known technically as a secondary buyout. One investor estimated that the cost of buying and selling a company amounts to 2 percent to 5 percent of the purchase price. Using that math the $35.3 billion in global secondary deals during that period in 2010 cost as much as $1.8 billion.[9]

While taking a company public may not be the fastest way to get money back and passed on to investors, there's an argument that it's the most equitable and sensible, when done right. It also seems to align the investor with the company and its future shareholders, since they have a stake in the company going forward for some period of time.

Let's go back to Dollar General. KKR had a heavy incentive to take the company public at a time and a price where the company could continue to grow its earnings and, therefore, its stock price. If the stock price continued to go up, KKR and its co-investors could methodically sell their shares for more and more money down the line, a theory that played out for the first two years after Dollar General's IPO.

That would seem to be ideal for everyone across the private-equity equation. The money goes in, is put to work, and in a reasonable amount of time starts to come back, in measured amounts that add up to a hefty return for the investors. Meanwhile, the company has a chance to thrive in the public markets, giving other investors the chance to participate in its growth by buying and selling the public shares. The original investors retain a large enough stake in the firm for a time that they have an incentive to encourage the company to keep performing.

■ ■ ■

A crucial element of the entire conversation around private equity is not just the ultimate returns, but how they are measured and, ultimately, how they are judged. One way that argument has played out in recent years is a nerdy debate on evaluating a firm on percentage returns versus cash returns. Call it the "You can't eat IRR" debate.

The measuring stick for private equity has long been internal rate of return, or IRR, and you can't have a conversation with any manager without talking about that metric, or being told unprompted if it's especially good. We all measure investments in terms of returns, whether we're talking about our 401(k) or the appreciation of our house or how much stock in Home Depot has gained or lost in a week, a month, or a year.

What private equity's backers learned the hard way is that looking at performance purely on that basis isn't going to cut it. Internal rate of return is basically a fancy way of saying how much your money appreciated, on average, over the time that it was invested. What's important to note is the time element. That is, the quicker the gains are booked, the higher the IRR and the better the manager looks when he goes to market his next fund.

Here's the issue: Pensions can't use IRR to fund a retirement plan. A university endowment can't give financial aid or pay a maintenance worker in IRR. They need cash, real money that can be deposited in a bank. For a private-equity fund to really be of use to its investors, it needs to deliver those returns in the form of money coming back, in healthy multiples of what the pension or endowment put in. An analysis by Bloomberg News in 2009 showed how much a handful of public pensions had at stake in private equity. From the beginning of the decade, three big pensions in California, Washington state, and Oregon had together committed at least $53.8 billion to private-equity funds. As of the end of 2008, they'd only gotten $22.1 billion back.[10]

A thawed IPO market and overall stabilizing economy helped jumpstart distributions in 2010 and 2011, leading to the record Carlyle number. KKR distributed $5.6 billion that same period.[11] Still, the gap that emerged during the first decade of the century showed just how much pensions and other investors had on the line with private-equity funds, and how a nasty couple of years could derail the gravy train. Staff at the plans made it clear that they were growing more and more interested in the actual cash returns, not just IRR numbers. Gary Bruebaker, whose Washington State Investment Board has been one of the biggest contributors to private-equity funds, put it bluntly.

"I work for over 400,000 employees, and they can't eat IRRs," he said in 2009. "At the end of the day, I care about how much do I give you, and how much money do I get back."[12]

As it is with jobs, the academic research around performance of private-equity firms is far from voluminous, and therefore it's difficult to get a definitive answer on how we should think about how private equity does vis-à-vis the public markets. After all, one of the simplest questions should be: Given the chance to put money in private equity or stocks, what should a person or institution do?

It's worth reiterating here that this is a purely theoretical exercise for the average person, who can't in fact invest in a typical private-equity fund. They are by design limited to accredited investors, which means meeting a threshold of net worth of $1 million in liquid assets or $200,000 in annual income for a single person. This, of course, cuts both ways. It protects the retail investor from putting her money at undue risk. It also prevents her from participating in the lush profits that can be generated through these vehicles.

Returns, of course, are at the very core of how private-equity firms pitch their services to investors. The most-frequently heard characterization is that a fund is "top quartile," meaning it's in the top 25 percent of its peers, better than three-quarters of the rest. The frequency of the claim has become a running joke in the industry, like the contention on the radio show "A Prairie Home Companion" that all the kids in the fictional Lake Wobegon are above average. In other words, it's mathematically impossible.

Oliver Gottschalg, the HEC professor, and colleagues conducted an exercise in 2009 that illustrated this very point and underscored how much leeway the managers have in representing their performance. What they found is that private-equity funds rank themselves according to so-called vintage years. But a fund usually takes several years to raise, giving them a range of years to choose from. In addition, there are a couple of different benchmarks to select; the researchers identified both Preqin and VentureXpert. Those benchmarks varied wildly as well, sometimes more than 10 percentage points for a given year. Factoring in that variability to the spread of years and the choice of benchmarks, the researchers identified 500 funds raised during a proscribed number of years. The result: 66 percent of them could justifiably boast of being top quartile on some basis.[13] Yet the larger question of how private equity stacks up as an investment on average remains. Investors ultimately need to justify paying fees to these managers far in excess of what they'd pay to stick the money in a mutual fund.

Steven Kaplan is one of that small cadre of academics who spend their time almost exclusively thinking about and researching private equity. A professor at the University of Chicago Booth School of Business, he's a widely quoted expert on the industry, and when I checked in with him in early 2012, he was inundated with calls about Mitt Romney and this mysterious club known as private equity. His research on returns is seen as the most rigorous and comprehensive.

In 2011, he released a new study that surprised some people, largely because it partially contradicted some of his previous work. At issue was a 2005 study by Kaplan and Antoinette Schoar of the Massachusetts Institute of Technology that found average net returns for buyout funds were roughly equal to the S&P 500 Index. That was disheartening, to say the least, for private equity and its investors. The study did point out that the data showed a wide range of performance and "persistence," that is, that a successful fund tended to spawn more successful funds by the same manager, as well as draw more money for later pools. Still, the main takeaway—private equity was a wash with public stocks on average—was troubling to say the least for the industry's participants and proponents.

In the intervening years, Kaplan and others found a problem with his original data set, which was culled from Venture Economics (the basic issue was that Venture Economics appeared to understate returns). In the new paper, written with Robert Harris of the University of Virgina's Darden School and Tim Jenkinson of Oxford University's Said School, the researchers used a broader data set, relying primarily on a commercial database from Burgiss that gathered information from limited partners. They used several other sources, including Preqin, Cambridge Associates, and Venture Economics again.

The result was markedly different: "[I]t seems very likely that buyout funds have outperformed public markets in the 1980s, 1990s, and 2000s," they wrote. Specifically, they found that between 1984 and 2008 across nearly 600 funds, $1 invested in private equity returned 1.2 times a dollar invested in the S&P.[14]

"The bottom line," Kaplan told me, "is that until 2005 the returns were terrific. For 2006 and 2007 and 2008 it's probably not going to be as good. It's too soon to tell."

That last thought goes to a couple of other findings beyond the major revelation that returns weren't so middling after all. One is that as commitments spiked from investors, returns tended to go down.

This was bad news for the megafunds spawned in the middle of the first decade of the century. The study also found that multiples of invested capital, not IRR, were a better measure of performance relative to the public markets, more evidence that Bruebaker's "can't eat IRR" approach was sound.

In the quest for simplicity, there is one element of the private-equity conversation that seems clear: Returns are going down. The data bear this out, both in the aggregate and anecdotally, especially at the larger firms. Take CalPERS, whose commitment to private equity is well demonstrated: Over the years, it has committed $66 billion to its alternatives program. Examining the last decade's worth of performance bears out the theory of falling returns. CalPERS concedes that it's unfair to judge a fund before it is four to five years old, so it has a chance to make investments and start returning money, or at least pegging a value to what it owns.

Funds raised in 2003 delivered a 24.3 percent IRR for CalPERS, and 2.1 times its money, right in the range of what most private-equity managers promise. Every year since then, through 2006 when the CalPERS data end, that performance has dropped, to 16 percent, 8.1 percent, and 2 percent, respectively. The multiples, too, have fallen, to 1.5, 1.3, and 1.1.[15]

What's most worrisome for those following CalPERS and other big pensions is the sheer volume of money directed to private equity since then. For 2007 vintage funds, CalPERS committed $14.8 billion to various funds, roughly the same amount the pension committed in the three previous years *combined*. As of September 2011 (the most recent data available at the end of the year), it was too soon to tell how well those investments would do in the aggregate. Of the $14.8 billion, about $10.8 had been called by the private-equity managers. The cash out and remaining value (the total of realized and unrealized gains, taking into account the current value of the investments) stood at $12.4 billion.

Dig into the individual funds' performance, also made available by CalPERS and a handful of other pensions like Washington State and Oregon, and the same trend of declining performance is there. Take KKR's results at Oregon. The firm delivered undeniably amazing results during the 1980s, when it was the only private-equity manager Oregon invested in. The 1986 fund ultimately returned Oregon $918 million on a $201.8 million investment; Oregon calculates the IRR at 26.3 percent.

Fast-forward almost two decades. KKR's Millennium Fund, raised in 2002, won a huge commitment from Oregon; the pension ultimately gave KKR more than $1.3 billion. As of late 2011, about eight years into the fund, the performance was merely respectable. Oregon estimated the IRR at about 17 percent. For Oregon's $1.31 billion, the pension had thus far gotten $1.33 billion back. Oregon estimated that the remaining value of the investments was around $748 million.[16]

Looking at the Oregon list, which is organized by year committed, is an interesting lens to view the incredible growth of the private equity industry, both in terms of the size of the commitments and therefore the size of private-equity funds and the sheer number of funds being raised. After committing money to a total of 27 funds in the 13 years ending in 1994, Oregon committed to 29 funds in 2006 alone.

The competition for deals surely has hurt returns, according to most experts, and that's a simple product of a maturing market. The best returns come from investments where there is an information advantage—in other words, I win because I simply know something you don't or before you do. You never even have a chance to play the game, or my understanding is so far superior that it's not a contest. A shrinking world and the Internet have helped accelerate that phenomenon; almost nothing is for sale without multiple parties knowing about it and getting a chance to bid, either formally or informally.

The sheer number of private-equity firms plays a related role. A business this lucrative for its practitioners and its investors can't stay secret, despite their best efforts. Competition drives up the price buyers have to pay to win an auction; that's Economics 101. Higher prices on the front end often lead to lower returns. If the ultimate value of what I own is static, my profit from buying it and selling it hinges on how good a deal I can get to begin with.

This leads to one of the more uncomfortable conversations for private-equity managers, who have long defined themselves in terms of absolute returns—that is, delivering upwards of 20 percent a year no matter what. That may be an egotistical, misguided approach, more and more managers argue. What they should really care about is returns that are good for their investors relative to the public markets.

Jay Jordan, in addition to running his eponymous investment firm in New York, is the chairman of the endowment at Notre Dame, his undergraduate alma mater. He contends that limited partners ultimately want to put significant amounts of money to work and get a predictable return over a prescribed period of time. As long as that return is several percentage points above their target return (in most cases 8 percent), they are happy. "All they really need to go for is 12 to 15 percent," he said. "Everyone was so focused on IRRs and not as much on multiples of invested capital. Ultimately, this is about matching to their liabilities."

Focusing on lower, less risky returns is something of a radical concept in private equity, but Jordan argues that the most consistent returns come from less risk. "We place a higher premium on losing no money," he says.

Big investors' appetite for predictable returns, even at the risk of bypassing outsized gains, was at the core of the discussions in 2011 that led to the deals between the Teacher Retirement System of Texas and Apollo and KKR, as well as the tie-up between Blackstone and New Jersey's pension. It is not a coincidence that big pensions are lining up with big private-equity managers, and a number of smart people in the industry predict this represents an inflection point for the buyout industry that will help define the business going forward. It's a phenomenon that dominates any big conversation about private equity and its future.

It's the barbell theory of private equity. On one end there are the bulge bracket names best known on Wall Street and in the world at large: Blackstone, KKR, Apollo, Bain, Carlyle, and TPG. These firms measure their total assets under management in tens of billions, or in some cases hundreds of billions. It's highly unlikely that they limit their business to private equity. Blackstone is the most extreme example, with about 28 percent of its assets and less than 20 percent of its 2011 revenue coming from private equity. But even Bain and TPG, probably the least diversified of that set of firms, have some combination of hedge funds, real estate, and credit investments in various stages of development.

On the other end of the barbell are the mono-line private-equity firms, those who have actively chosen, or passively accepted, that they'll focus almost exclusively on the buyout business. This is where firms like CCMP Capital, the private-equity firm that spun out of JPMorgan Chase; Clayton Dubilier & Rice, Permira, and hundreds of other much smaller firms live. The Private Equity Growth Capital Council, the industry's chief lobbyist, estimated in 2011 that there were roughly 2,400 private-equity firms headquartered in the United States.[17] "As we've seen what's happened in the market, the model has changed, and you have two kinds of players: public and diversified and private and focused," Colony's Tom Barrack said. Managers at the firms where private equity remains the main, or only, business argue that they're the only ones who can generate the sort of returns that the industry originally delivered and has promised ever since. "This asset class is not going away," said Thomas Lister, co-managing partner of Permira. "There will be people who continue to make 20 percent IRRs off a reasonable pool of capital. I'm not a believer in just making 5 points over the S&P. I believe in 2.5 times your money and 25 percent returns."

Private-equity guys talk a lot about alpha, a Greek letter that's taken on many meanings in the modern world, especially in finance. It's a given that private equity, as an adjunct to Wall Street, has its share of alpha males, fellows who strive to be the leader of any pack. But in investment terms, alpha generally means a return that's achieved beyond what can be generated by the market at large. It's based on some amount of skill or ability to see something different. Investopedia defined it this way: "Simply stated, alpha is often considered to represent the value that a portfolio manager adds to or subtracts from a fund's return."

Alpha is where private equity made its bones and how it convinced pensions and endowments and others to pay the big fees that they've earned over the years. At the Tuck School of Business at Dartmouth, they say it even cleaner: "Alpha is a proxy for manager skill."[18]

One of the lurking existential questions in private equity, especially as its largest practitioners expand beyond doing leveraged buyout deals into real estate, funds-of-funds, and capital markets, is whether alpha—those outsized returns that gave the industry its raison d'être, its right to charge more than any other type of manager, and its staying power for three decades—is still the top priority. "This will become a smaller, more concentrated business, mainly because the funders need to buy in bulk," said Howard Newman, the founder of Pine Brook Partners and the former vice chairman of Warburg Pincus. "The big firms will get bigger, investors will look to smaller and specialized firms for alpha, and the super returns will go away except for the very best funds."

Chapter 10

The Taxman Cometh

As Occupy Wall Street reached a fever pitch in early November 2011, I went downtown to check it out for myself, having seen spin-off protests in both central Phoenix and outside the U.S. Post Office in Chapel Hill, North Carolina.

Despite the ire being aimed broadly at Wall Street and corporate America, private equity has never been directly in the crosshairs of the protests. Schwarzman's residence was picketed in mid-October 2011 when a throng of protesters marched on various apartment buildings known to house billionaires. His Park Avenue place, the sprawling apartment once owned by John D. Rockefeller, Jr., was on the route. Still, private equity remains largely ignored, to the genuine surprise of some in the industry, who've seen unions and other political action groups occasionally protest takeovers and companies, from Carlyle's Manor Care to Bain and KKR's Toys "R" Us.

As I walked around Zuccotti Park—the protesters referred to it by its former name, Liberty Park—and marveled at the mini-tent city that would capture the nation's attention for nearly two months, I spotted the first evidence of private equity creeping into the conversation. There, printed on orange cardboard, were the words, "Carried Interest Loophole," with a circle-and-slash symbol in fluorescent marker around it. This admittedly less catchy sign (another read, "No Bulls, No Bears, Just Pigs") explained exactly why private equity was avoiding the negative press: the complexity. It would take a Republican candidate from a private-equity firm and the more digestible and volatile issues of class warfare to garner national headlines. The porcine insults were then directed mostly at the leaders of the big-name banks, from Bank of America to Goldman Sachs. Those institutions, vilified in the public imagination as well as on Capitol Hill, bore the vast brunt of the criticism about causing the financial crisis.

Within weeks of my Occupy visit, private equity was very much back in the national conversation, perhaps on a level where it never had been before, thanks to Mitt Romney. In early 2012, the tax question that had lingered in the background for five years became a defining issue for Romney and, by extension, the industry he helped create. As we've seen, carried interest is the portion of the private-equity equation that creates the extraordinary wealth for the industry's practitioners. Normally, any discussion of taxes leaves most of us desperate for a change in subject. In this case, the private-equity tax question became a touchstone for a broader debate about income inequality and class, viewed in the hothouse of a presidential election year. How the question is ultimately answered touches on some of the basic economics of how the private-equity money flows back to its most successful players.

The question dates back decades, to the earliest days of the industry. The so-called "2 and 20 structure" of a typical fund gives, by most accounts, a clear incentive for managers to deliver profits to their investors. The 2 percent annual fee pays the bills, and most established managers charge less than 2 percent since they have more substantial cash flow from previous successful funds. The 20 percent, carried interest, is the real money. That buys the second and third houses and the jets and means you have the coin to get your name on a building at your alma mater or a symphony hall somewhere.

Most institutional investors, for the most part, seem okay with this, as long as they're getting the returns they were promised and so long as the managers get rich on the carry and not from the management fee or other assorted fees. This was an area where Texas's Steve LeBlanc and others in the ILPA principles movement directed some of their fire.

Here's the catch on the tax side and what the protesters, and others including the Obama administration, characterize as a loophole: Carried interest is considered investment income and therefore taxed at a capital gains rate, which in 2012 stood at 15 percent, versus the top ordinary income rate of about 35 percent. For years, this practice was noted by some in Washington, and there were half-hearted efforts to change it. Then Victor Fleischer, a young law professor who blogs, wrote a paper. He later told a reporter he hoped it would help him secure tenure at the University of Illinois College of Law, where he was teaching at the time.[1] Now he's at the University of Colorado, and he was hailed by Politico in 2007 as the then-36-year-old "this season's academic It Boy."[2]

Fleischer wrote a refreshingly straightforward paper that started making the rounds of key offices on Capitol Hill in early 2007. The introduction to the 59-page article, eventually published in the *New York University Law Review*, says it all: "This quirk in the tax law allows some of the richest workers in the country to pay tax on their labor income at a low rate. Changes in the investment world . . . suggest that reconsideration of the partnership profits puzzle is overdue." He goes even further, asserting he will prove "that the status quo is an untenable position as a matter of tax policy."[3]

Fleischer's paper was exceptionally well timed because in 2007, the year of megadeals, mega-birthday parties, and Blackstone's IPO, political will coalesced, and suddenly Washington was primed to take up the issue. Politicians saw an easy target—the ultra-rich getting away with something that could be remedied. The *New York Times* editorial page, citing Fleischer, eventually called on Congress to act.

The political establishment had another advantage. Private equity as an industry had barely paid attention to Washington for essentially all of its history, beyond personal relationships (read: donations to candidates) and occasional calls to testify before a subcommittee about a deal gone bad in a powerful member's district. In part anticipating this fight and a broader need to engage more openly in public discussions, a handful of the largest firms had decided in 2006 to form an industry association, decades after their peers in real estate and venture capital had set up similar lobbying shops. In early 2007, the Private Equity Council opened its doors.

The group, and its members—comprising the founders of KKR, Carlyle, Blackstone, TPG, and those firms' respective public affairs heads, among others—imagined they would spend the early days educating lawmakers about an industry that was already, at best, unknown, often mistrusted or misunderstood, and in some cases, loathed. Whatever honeymoon it had could be measured in weeks.

The argument that private-equity managers make, at least in public and through their lobbyists, is that the tax treatment—"founded on sound and settled tax policies"—is designed to encourage entrepreneurial activities and risk-taking. The group also points to the fact that real estate partnerships and venture capitalists enjoy the same tax benefits. Those other industries, both of which are well-represented in Washington, did in fact initially give the private equity industry cover and ultimately helped delay any action on carried interest by the Congress. The emergence of a vocal Republican faction that had literally sworn not to raise taxes also helped stave off any changes.

The bigger story around carried interest for private equity, though, may be what might be considered the political opportunity cost. The decision to make carried interest tax such a major issue right out of the gate meant that "Don't you dare raise taxes on us billionaires" became the defining issue for an industry. It didn't help that the initial make-up of the Private Equity Council was limited to a handful of the biggest firms run by the most visible titans of the industry, including Kravis, Bonderman, Rubenstein, and Schwarzman. The storyline was too easy: Wall Street firms, along with Washington's most politically connected investors, are trying to keep a loophole open so they can pay less taxes than the average Joe.

And yet, the member firms were united in their opposition throughout. The movement to change the tax treatment struck at the heart of the business model. Their staunch defense dominated their Washington agenda, pushing any plans about broader initiatives to educate lawmakers to the fringes.

■ ■ ■

The Private Equity Council in March 2007 set about dealing with carried interest largely as a tax issue. The group sought out meetings with tax-focused staffers to make their case.

The story burst beyond the tax geeks on March 22, 2007, when Blackstone filed to go public on the New York Stock Exchange. The public started to get a sense of how much the firm was generating in profits and later, when the firm filed details of Schwarzman's and Peterson's compensation and the implied value of their stakes, it deepened still. Suddenly, carried interest wasn't a nerdy tax question of abstractions. It was about these specific billionaires and their taxes.

Washington went a step further. Senator Max Baucus and Senator Chuck Grassley wrote a bill aimed squarely at taxing publicly traded partnerships, a move so clearly aimed at one firm that it became known as "the Blackstone bill." While distinct from a bill in the House introduced by Representative Sander Levin to treat carried interest as ordinary income, the two pieces of legislation converged in the collective Beltway mind.

At the Private Equity Council, the staff and members realized that only a small handful of firms would go public, limiting the impact of the Blackstone bill. (In an only-in-Washington twist, the bill that unofficially bore its name had a grandfather clause that would have exempted Blackstone, effectively giving Steve Schwarzman's firm a competitive advantage and reward for getting out first.)

The Blackstone bill also served to muddy the broader issues, and some members begin to question what the driving principles were. On carried interest, the venture capital industry especially argued that it should be carved out from carried interest, positioning itself as a growth engine versus the leveraged buyout firms. The real estate business negotiated an amendment in the House bill for similar treatment that was defeated, and talk of carve outs served to take steam out of the debate. During the election year of 2008, little happened, and as the credit crisis dominated the headlines and talk turned to massive bailouts and Lehman-sized bankruptcies, private equity inched further out of the spotlight.

With Obama's arrival in early 2009, the industry assumed it was mostly a matter of when, not if treatment of carried interest would change. Talk began to bubble about cutting a deal, specifically a "blended" rate that would raise the taxes on some portion of carried interest, or peg a rate somewhere between capital gains and ordinary income. The debate over health care reform served to sideline the issue once again, and while there was some talk of using carried interest as a way to pay for Obama's health plan, the architects of that legislation ultimately decided not to use any non-health care revenue as sources of money. Private equity coasted for the rest of 2009.

What appeared to be the final push came in the spring of 2010, when Baucus called representatives of the private equity real estate, hedge fund, and venture capital industries and said he was planning to use carried interest as a revenue generator that year. He and Levin negotiated a deal whereby 75 percent of carried interest would be treated as ordinary income, with the balance taxed as capital gains. What ultimately helped undo that effort—along with a growing anti-tax sentiment promoted by the Tea Party—was an element, shorthanded as the "enterprise tax," that was designed to prevent private-equity executives from moving their carried interest into the firm itself and paying the lower rate when they eventually sold their interest in the firm (aka the enterprise). Private equity and its lobbyists, many of whom had resigned themselves to a higher carried interest rate, seized on this maneuver and used legislative jujitsu.

This would affect not only billionaire private-equity managers, but restaurant owners and other small businesses, they argued. Legislators listened and enough ultimately balked that the broad package that included carried interest and enterprise failed to pass.

The debate returned to the fore, and fiercely, in 2012, when Romney's taxes became the big story. After weeks of resisting, despite near-constant attacks from his opponents, Romney released his 2010 and estimated 2011 tax returns in late January 2012. While political journalists set aside hours to comb through the returns to glean their impact on the campaign, so too folks who follow private equity tucked in for a rare look at a buyout maven's finances. Some of the private-equity-related elements weren't new. In separate financial disclosure forms released the previous year, Romney laid out his investments, including the fact that he, his wife, or trusts managed on their behalf, had some financial interest in 31 different Bain-related funds. They also had investments in funds managed by Goldman Sachs, as well as Golden Gate Capital, a San Francisco-based manager of buyout and credit funds. Golden Gate's better-known investments included jewelry retailer Zales and outdoor clothier Eddie Bauer.[4]

There was nothing especially controversial in Romney's returns from a private-equity perspective, though it was a stark reminder of how much money can be generated from investments that are only available to a small number of participants. Beyond Bain, Romney had investments in vehicles open only to qualified investors. The day after the returns were released, Carlyle's Rubenstein spoke at the World Economic Forum in Davos, where he was asked about Romney and taxes. "You change the law and they'll pay the taxes," Rubenstein said. "Romney said, and I'm not his defender, he's paying whatever the law required. If you change the law, change the law, but don't criticize him for paying the taxes that the law requires him to pay."[5]

While Rubenstein's logic is sound, private equity seems to have lost the argument. Long quiet about this issue, the industry's biggest investors started making their opinions known in 2012, shifting the discussion. Joseph Dear, the chief investment officer of CalPERS, was blunt at a meeting of his $234 billion pension in February 2012. "General partners should recognize that tax treatment of their income has become indefensible," Dear said. "The tax treatment is incomprehensible to ordinary taxpayers and citizens. . . . If people come to believe that private-equity general partners are reaping giant returns, while paying less in taxes than wage earners do, their support for those policies that enable private equity to work will be withdrawn."[6] Dear's strong words have the benefit of being true, and they make an even larger point as to why private-equity managers should concede the point on taxes when given a chance. If the industry's biggest investors won't abide something, the entire private-equity system is at some level of danger. While paying a higher tax rate may dent the economics of individual men and women, in private equity, the possibility, however remote, that big investors will balk at future commitments over the tax rate is too great a risk to run.

Then there's the impact that transcends dollars and cents and gets to common sense. The prolonged fight obscured nearly every other issue that private equity needed to bring to Washington's attention. Friendly visits to Capitol Hill to talk about private equity's benefit to local and state economies were derailed by discussions around carried interest. The hubbub deepened mistrust around other initiatives, including a burst of interest by private-equity firms in buying struggling banks during 2009. After allowing a small handful of deals including IndyMac and Bank-United, federal regulators quickly damped enthusiasm for more deals through tightened regulations aimed squarely at private equity.

Private equity is far from out of the woods in terms of Congress. When President Obama unveiled his framework for tax reform ahead of the 2012 election, he proposed not only changing the tax treatment for carried interest, but eliminating the deductibility of interest. In Washington, the renamed Private Equity Growth Capital Council, having chased carried interest from its inception, already was assembling its arguments around that issue. The strategy was part of a broader effort to expand the industry's reach that began with the group expanding its membership beyond the handful of largest firms to a growing body of research around employment and economic benefits it ascribed to private equity.

While Washington was reluctant to let buyout firms be part of the banking solution, its actions around financial reform have clearly not identified the industry as part of the problem. To the contrary: Lawmakers and regulators have so far pursued a new regulatory regime that allows private-equity firms with grander ambitions to accelerate those plans.

The industry has found perhaps an unlikely ally in Paul Volcker. The former chairman of the Federal Reserve lent his name to a key piece of reform, the Volcker Rule, a central tenet of the Dodd-Frank legislation aimed at preventing another financial meltdown and series of bailouts.

The Volcker Rule at its most basic seeks to limit what big banks can do with their money, thereby diminishing the risk they can take as federally insured, deposit taking institutions. That means strict limits on what's known as proprietary trading and principal investments. During the early part of this century, a number of banks, most notably Goldman Sachs, grew their investing arms into massive institutions in their own right. Goldman's 2007 private-equity fund totaled about $20 billion, second only in history to Blackstone's $21.7 billion raised that same year. Under Volcker, Goldman is effectively out of that business, at least to anything close to the extent that it was. The same goes for Morgan Stanley, JPMorgan, and Bank of America.

If they're losing, who's winning? Blackstone, Carlyle, and KKR. Not only are the firms losing major competitors, they have an opportunity to snap up the profitable units the banks have to shed, or the teams that run those strategies. KKR in early 2011 hired a team of ex-Goldman traders led by Robert Howard to start Kravis's and Roberts's first-ever long/short hedge fund.

Blackstone is on the constant hunt for acquisitions, albeit selectively. Through purchases like GSO Capital in 2008, it has bulked up its credit unit. With Wall Street in disarray, Blackstone's hedge fund solutions unit, which finds hedge funds for clients to invest in, has become the biggest such business in the world. Schwarzman is bolstering his restructuring and M&A advice division, seeking to feed a broader need for unbiased counsel amid lingering questions about Wall Street banks. Says an executive at a competitor: "Blackstone wants to be Goldman Jr."

Chapter 11

It's a Steve, Steve, Steve World

Inside Blackstone

My first official day on the private-equity beat coincided with Blackstone's annual media dinner, which in 2007 was held at Daniel, a posh restaurant on New York's Upper East Side. The off-the-record gathering was meant to mix the reporters who wrote about the firm on a regular basis with Blackstone's top managers in a more relaxed setting than a conference room.

For me, it was more like sensory overload. I'd barely begun to recognize the names of the big firms, who ran them, and what they owned. I barely knew who Steve Schwarzman was. Being the newest guy on the beat, I didn't rate a seat at his table, but a Blackstone rep was nice enough to provide an introduction after dinner. Told I was the new Bloomberg reporter and it was in fact my first day, he looked at me, looked around the lavish party, and said with a twinkle in his eye and a subversive humor I'd come to learn was a signature, "Every day is like this."

In a nod to the new frugality, Blackstone in 2009 switched the dinners to the Waldorf-Astoria, which it clearly pointed out on the invitation was a "Blackstone portfolio company" through its ownership of Hilton. In 2011, the firm opted to have a series of smaller dinners at its headquarters to give meaningful access to more Blackstone executives across its lines of business.

The Daniel dinners had a nice symbolism for Schwarzman. He and Blackstone co-founder Peter G. Peterson held some of the seminal conversations related to the firm in the space that now belongs to Daniel, long before it was among Manhattan's fanciest dining spots. In the mid-1980s, it was the cafeteria of the former Mayfair Hotel. The two men met there most mornings for breakfast to discuss plans for the new firm.[1]

The name itself came from a Schwarzman brainstorm. Given that each of their names was too long, he proposed putting together English translations of each of their names, black for Schwarz, stone for Peter, or *petra*.

David Carey and John Morris's book on the firm, *King of Capital*, provides an excellent and thorough history of Blackstone, chronicling the trials and tribulations of the early days as Schwarzman and Peterson found it difficult to translate their earlier success at Lehman into a hybrid advisor/investor through its emergence into the massive firm it is today.

Peterson is now retired from Blackstone and working full-time on his foundation, which is focused on increasing public awareness of what he describes as the country's urgent long-term fiscal challenges, a long-standing passion. During a conversation, he recalled those early difficulties. "One of the hardest periods of my life was raising the money for the first fund," he said, describing how he plumbed his bulging Rolodex for connections, "there was nearly always a personal relationship."

That translated to deals, as well. Blackstone's initial approach was to team with a well-known corporation, tapping that Rolodex cultivated when Peterson was the chief executive of Bell & Howell, the U.S. Secretary of Commerce and the head of Lehman Brothers. Going in with a company had a couple of benefits: Would-be sellers took the offer more seriously, and it also helped assuage worries that Blackstone was a corporate raider looking to dismantle what it bought for a quick buck. "By aligning yourself with blue-chip firms, you were instantly the white knight," JPMorgan's Jimmy Lee said. Blackstone also offered the chance at times to hang on to a slice of the unit being divested, helping the selling CEO avoid potential embarrassment of selling too cheap and watching Blackstone reap huge profits down the line.

It's undeniable that the biggest private-equity firms today stand as financial behemoths given what they own and their expansion into areas beyond buying companies with borrowed money. Blackstone is the furthest along in that regard, and it was a strategy in part born of fear.

Diversification is Blackstone's long-term business plan, executives there say, in part because of the terror of watching Lehman Brothers collapse around them—the first time, in the mid-1980s. Peterson, who had come to hold various positions at Lehman Brothers including the top job, had lost a series of nasty battles with Lew Glucksman over the future of the firm that ultimately led to Peterson's departure. After Lehman limped into a sale to American Express, a white-knight scenario that Lehman hotshot Schwarzman helped engineer, the younger banker reunited with Peterson.

The two men, scarred by their experience at Lehman, were determined that no one would ever be able to stage a coup of any sort at their new firm. They consolidated power between the two of them, power that now rests firmly with Schwarzman alone, following Peterson's retirement after the IPO. They also were unwilling to rely too much on any one business for profits and ultimately for the firm's existence. "There is a real refugee mentality," says J. Tomilson Hill, the firm's vice chairman who now runs the hedge fund solutions business, Blackstone's biggest unit by assets under management. A former top Lehman executive himself, he joined Blackstone in 1993. "There's a feeling it could all go away at any moment, and that's because of the experience at Lehman."

Peterson, who'd become CEO of Lehman only to watch it flirt with extinction three weeks into his tenure because of a series of bad trades, said, "There are certain lessons from an experience like that. One of them is we had to be risk averse, particularly given our very limited equity capital."

Private equity made Blackstone famous and its founders and many other senior executives very rich. Based on several measures, from assets under management to profit, private equity is no longer what Blackstone mostly does. The ethos of that drive ties to a man who has come to symbolize all the superlatives, good and bad, of the industry.

Every discussion of Blackstone still begins and ends with Schwarzman. He remains the face of Blackstone and arguably the defining figure for the entire industry at the moment. What Kravis was in the late 1980s and early 1990s, by virtue of the RJR Nabisco deal, *Barbarians at the Gate*, and his high-profile social and charitable life in Manhattan, Schwarzman was for the first decade of this century, and remains so. What has separated Schwarzman from his peers in part is the ambition to create a long-lasting firm, with private equity as but a piece. "Steve first and foremost thinks of himself as a businessman, while others would say they are first and foremost deal guys or private-equity guys," Hill said.

■ ■ ■

Even peers who roll their eyes at his occasional eyebrow-raising public remarks concede he has built the single most powerful company in the business. "There's Blackstone, and then there's everyone else," one manager told me.

In the era of Twitter, blogs, and constant instant commentary, Schwarzman is shorthand for the private equity industry and its excesses, real and perceived. A posting in the online magazine *Salon* in September 2011 referred to him as "a living symbol of post-industrial late capitalism's gaudy depravity."[2] Later in 2011, no less than Matt Taibbi, the *Rolling Stone* writer who famously described Goldman Sachs as "a great vampire squid wrapped around the face of humanity" characterized Schwarzman thusly: "one of the more uniquely abhorrent, self-congratulating jerks in the entire world."[3]

What perpetuates Schwarzman's profile is his tendency to go off script. At a meeting in July 2010 for a nonprofit organization, he drew an unfortunate comparison between private equity's fight with Washington over tax policy and World War II. "It's war," *Newsweek* reported him saying. "It's like when Hitler invaded Poland in 1939."[4] Schwarzman later apologized.

Gaffes like that make it more difficult for Schwarzman to achieve the statesman-like role he's told people around him he aspires to.

Schwarzman grew up with his parents and two younger twin brothers in the Philadelphia suburb of Abington. In high school he was a basketball player as well as a star runner. He told the *New Yorker*'s James B. Stewart about a time he slipped during a cross-country race, broke his wrist, finished in record-setting time, then went to the hospital. The football stadium at the school is named after him.[5]

Since then he has built a sprawling global empire with more than $190 billion in assets from a $400,000 investment, in a matter of a couple of decades. He lives in a Park Avenue apartment once occupied by Rockefellers. He has achieved enough wealth to have the nation's most famous library—the Main Branch of the New York Public Library—renamed the Stephen A. Schwarzman Building in honor of his contribution of $100 million toward the building's renovation and expansion.

■ ■ ■

Companies Blackstone owns directly, as well as insights gleaned from real estate, credit, and equity markets by its various arms, give the firm the potential to analyze the global economy as well as just about anyone. The chairman and CEO of such a firm has the potential to be an important voice.

To that end, Schwarzman has taken to writing the occasional op-ed piece to share his views of the world, including a piece in the *Financial Times* in September 2011 under the headline, "An olive branch to Obama: I will share the pain." Schwarzman, while criticizing politicians for portraying financial firms as "villains" in the wake of the economic crisis, preached a message of shared sacrifice in pursuit of smaller deficits and job growth.[6]

Since he derives at least part of his importance from his professional perch, burnishing Blackstone's reputation and appearance becomes that much more important. Part of Blackstone President Tony James's role, in addition to growing the firm and taking it public, has been to professionalize it, a key element in the evolution of all the private-equity firms.

Blackstone, once a cult-of-personality partnership, now has the trappings and constrictions of a grown-up corporation. During 2010 and 2011, Blackstone renovated its headquarters, upgrading its surprisingly worn offices. Many a visitor had scratched his head at the seeming inconsistency of Schwarzman's lavish shows of personal wealth and the holes in Blackstone's carpet.

Now visitors to Blackstone bypass the general public's security desk for an enclosed Blackstone-only reception area with its own couches and dedicated attendants. The firm's main lobby on the 43rd floor has lovely views looking north over Manhattan's Upper East Side stretching into Harlem and the Bronx. Down the hall is the "lunch room," where Blackstone employees gather each day for complimentary food made in-house.

The jewel of the new headquarters, though, is the boardroom, which for a private-equity firm is far from ceremonial. This is where everyone of any importance spends some or most of their Mondays, taking part in the weekly rundown of what deals stand where and any other pressing matters.

The senior members of the firm sit at the table, which has built in, voice-activated microphones jutting up at every seat. Junior executives sit on settees against the two long walls. The real innovation is what might be called "Steve Vision," the screens that emerge from the ceiling all around the room to pull in the other offices from around the world via videoconference.

■ ■ ■

On a mid-October evening in 2011, hours removed from a quarterly conference call with investors, Schwarzman was at the Waldorf-Astoria, two blocks south of his office, clad in tails and a white tie, schmoozing Catholic priests, politicians, and bank executives ahead of a very different kind of speech for him.

This event was an odd confluence of Schwarzman's worlds. The Alfred E. Smith Foundation Dinner is an annual gathering meant to raise money for Catholic children's charities and honor the late governor of New York, who had been, back in 1928, the first Catholic nominee for U.S. president. Schwarzman has directed a surprising amount of his philanthropy toward Catholic charities in New York, so here was a Jewish guy from Philadelphia giving a speech whose past orators have included almost every major party's Presidential candidate, plus Bob Hope and Beverly Sills. In an additional twist, the standing venue for the dinner, the Waldorf-Astoria, is a Blackstone property. Surely, this was the first time the owner of the hotel was the headliner.

Mayor Michael Bloomberg, New York Governor Andrew Cuomo, Bank of America CEO Brian Moynihan, JPMorgan's Jimmy Lee, and two dozen other religious, financial, and political luminaries sat alongside Schwarzman and his wife Christine, who is Catholic. The whole event had a throwback feel, from the multi-tiered dais on the stage to the dress code (the important men wore tails, while the rank-and-file guests were in black tie) to the opulent room, with its balconies overlooking the ballroom. Waiters, whose average age suggested they may have served Al Smith himself, smoothly delivered hunks of medium-rare beef tenderloin and filled glasses with red wine.

The Smith dinner has evolved into a New York institution with a Washington edge, especially in an election year (which this was not, giving Schwarzman an opportunity to take center stage; the previous year, he'd also sat on the dais, within chatting distance of both Barack Obama and John McCain). In a town that sees a dozen such dinners a night in midtown alone, this one feels different, in part because of its eclectic draw and long history.

The traditions of the Smith dinner call for the speaker to deliver a humorous talk, roasting some of the luminaries in the room, including the guest of honor. Schwarzman, who'd worked with his staff, an outside speechwriter, and his wife to draft his remarks, didn't disappoint. He skewered Moynihan by equating Bank of America with his brother's orphanage in Haiti ("Their parents must be so proud to have two sons each running an underfunded non-profit institution"); referenced disgraced Governor Eliot Spitzer's sexual indiscretions; and proposed a merger between Catholicism and Judaism.

He referenced his own philanthropy, alluding to his New York Public Library donation. "Through Blackstone's growth and successes, I've remained a regular, down-to-earth, guy," he said. "For example, like a lot of folks, if I want a book, I'll go to my local library, check out the book, and leave my name . . . carved into marble at the entrances to the building."

He didn't spare himself, making a well-received joke at the outset about his much-talked about sixtieth birthday party, "I look around at this audience: hundreds of New York's most powerful people, dressed to the nines, all in one room—and I think to myself: Is it my birthday again already?" The audience largely missed some of the wonkier private-equity and hedge fund jokes—Schwarzman attempted a joke that equated breaking bread with breaking up underperforming companies—but roared at the broader Wall Street-focused humor, including a timely reference to the protesters gathered just a few miles downtown, who had marched outside a number of high-powered apartment buildings including Schwarzman's, under the aegis of the Occupy Wall Street movement. He went through the necessary thanks and recognitions about the dinner, then quipped, "or as I call it, Occupy Waldorf."

After the speech, Schwarzman stepped down into the ballroom from the stage to chat with well-wishers and receive congratulations. While most of the dignitaries departed quickly (the titular host of the evening, New York Archbishop Timothy Dolan, gave a quick bene-diction to close the ceremony and excused himself to catch the end of a game featuring his beloved St. Louis Cardinals in the World Series), Schwarzman stayed until the room was almost empty, basking in the afterglow of what he knew was a successful speech.

Congratulated on the Moynihan joke, which as the comedians say, killed, he said he might have to place an apologetic call the following day. "I'm going to pay for that," he joked, noting that Blackstone is a large customer of Bank of America.

This is Schwarzman. He has a devilish streak to him and gives the distinct impression that he sometimes just can't help himself. He carries himself with the demeanor of a man who can't quite believe this is all happening and, to Hill's point, that it could all disappear. The joke on himself about the birthday party was something of a seminal moment, showing that he finally was able to publicly laugh about it. For several years after the actual event, he was alternately befuddled by the attendant hoopla and defiant about his choice to throw the party in the first place.

He told Stewart in the New Yorker profile titled "The Birthday Party" that part of what drove him, including throwing the bash, was a rare protein deficiency that's potentially fatal, and for which he's tested every few weeks. "We have limited time, and we have to maximize it. Live life intensely—I've always believed in that," he was quoted as saying. "I'm happy to be here. I was happy to make it to 60. That's the simple reason for the birthday party."[7]

Much to Schwarzman and Blackstone's public relations team's chagrin, the party has become an emblem for excess, shorthand for what's wrong with private equity and Wall Street and its highest-profile and best-paid practitioners. It is difficult to have a conversation about the LBO boom, or the perception of private equity, without someone uttering the phrase "the birthday party," with something ranging from a smirk to a scowl. Most people don't even mention Schwarzman's name, but the details—a black-tie affair at the Park Avenue Armory in midtown Manhattan, replicating part of his apartment in the cavernous space, including a portrait of himself; the performances by Rod Stewart, Patti LaBelle, and Marvin Hamlisch—all are well-documented. What rankles Schwarzman and his defenders is that it's far from the only party of its type in the annals of private equity. TPG's Bonderman had thrown himself a sixtieth birthday blowout five years earlier, in Las Vegas, with the Rolling Stones as the entertainment. In 2011, Apollo's Leon Black threw a lavish sixtieth in the Hamptons featuring Elton John. A *New York Times* article about that event in part presented the party as a compare-and-contrast to Schwarzman's.[8] It seems all private-equity sixtieths, before and after, will be judged against Steve Schwarzman's.

■ ■ ■

While Schwarzman remains inextricably tied to the firm in economics and the public imagination, he did something few of his peers were willing or able to do: He began the process of replacing himself. Tony James's arrival in 2002 portended a radical acceleration in Blackstone's business.

James practically oozes the languid confidence of a modern Wall Street man, with the requisite dark suit and expensive shoes. His lanky frame and his relaxed demeanor are a counterpoint to the shorter and wired Schwarzman. Part of Schwarzman's charm is the uncertainty about what may come out of his mouth next. James gives the appearance of being almost preternaturally controlled. He inspires fierce loyalty among those around him, an admiration that comes with a healthy dose of fear, according to those who've worked with him before. He is an unrelenting worker himself, as evidenced by his habits. Leaving the office after a dinner one night at 9 P.M. with a bagful of reading material, he admitted that he would go home and read until he fell asleep, then naturally wake up around 3A.M. to continue reading and responding to e-mail. After an hour or so of that, he'd catch another few hours, then head into the office.

One striking thing about James's work habits and his drive at Blackstone is the fact that he was already rich and accomplished before Schwarzman came calling. James worked at Donaldson, Lufkin & Jenrette for more than a decade, ultimately running that firm's investment banking operations and helping engineer its sale to what was then known as Credit Suisse First Boston in 2000.

"Wall Street doesn't have a surplus of people with a sophisticated understanding of financial markets who are also good managers," Peterson said. "This is because investment bankers often tend to be high on the short-term chase of getting deals and not to be focused on building the firm and its culture over the long term. Finding Tony and hiring him was a seminal moment."

With Schwarzman plying him with a chunk of Blackstone (James owns about 5 percent of the firm) and the chance for an encore on a potentially even bigger stage, James jumped. Within Blackstone, he emphasized some elements of DLJ's near-legendary and increasingly foreign to Wall Street focus on culture and teamwork. He didn't initially find fertile ground, given Blackstone's heritage as a deal shop with lots of egos and competing interests. James brought in elements like 360-degree feedback and formalized reporting structures.

To replicate the DLJ culture, he hired people he knew from there, including Garrett Moran, who served for a time as Blackstone's chief administrative officer, and Joan Solotar, a former DLJ research analyst who had gone on to run research at Bank of America. As the head of all of Blackstone's public markets activities and a member of the executive committee, she is among the highest-ranking woman in private equity. A DLJ founder, Richard Jenrette, sits on Blackstone's board, one of four independent directors on a board that also includes Harvard Business

School's Jay Light, former Canadian Prime Minister Brian Mulroney, and former Deloitte Touche Tohmatusu CEO William Parrett. Schwarzman, James, Tom Hill, and Jonathan Gray are the four Blackstone directors.

James's biggest DLJ alumni recruitment doubled as Blackstone's biggest bet during the last decade, and it was not leveraged buyout but a deal for itself. In early 2008, James convinced a skeptical Schwarzman that the best way to grow Blackstone's then-small credit business—the unit that bought debt and provided so-called mezzanine loans to companies—was to make an acquisition, something Blackstone had never done in any sort of scale. The world was a mess. The leveraged buyout boom had collapsed in the summer of 2007 and Blackstone and its peers were staring nervously at both deals that hadn't been closed, and maybe more nervously at the ones that had. Blackstone had, after all, agreed to buy Hilton the previous June for $20 billion, weeks ahead of the credit markets freezing.

This was the best time, James argued, to boost the firm's ability to invest in and around troubled credit. He proposed an acquisition of GSO Capital, an independent firm that had spun out of CSFB after the DLJ acquisition. Bennett Goodman, Tripp Smith, and Douglas Ostrover (the G, S, and O) agreed to be bought for upwards of $900 million, instantly adding about $10 billion in assets to Blackstone's credit portfolio.

James, while overseeing the likes of GSO, the advisory business that includes both mergers and restructuring advice, real estate, and the hedge fund group, remained a private-equity guy at heart. Until 2011, he was the de facto head of that business. That year, he installed Chinh Chu and David Blitzer as co-chairmen of private equity. James's willingness to delegate more of the private-equity oversight may signal how much Blackstone has evolved from a dealmaking firm that does some other things to a much more broadly based asset management firm.

James is officially designated as Schwarzman's successor, a point spelled out for investors when the firm went public. The clear line gives both private and public investors some measure of comfort, especially in contrast to Carlyle and KKR, which have made no such designations. Still, it's possible that Schwarzman will last longer than James, in part because, as one observer says, "Blackstone is Steve's life."

Not so for James, who can't imagine going the Pete Peterson route and staying at Blackstone until he's 80, which Schwarzman is likely to do, in some form or another. That's in part due to Schwarzman's statesman ambitions. Blackstone gives him the infrastructure to both gather the intelligence he needs to form his opinions, and the stage from which to deliver those pronouncements. Having James run the show allows Schwarzman to experiment with things like his own geography. In late 2010, Schwarzman and his wife temporarily relocated to an apartment in Paris from New York, in part to deal with Schwarzman's Asia and Middle East–heavy travel schedule.

So who will eventually run the show?

■ ■ ■

Jon Gray was a young Blackstone analyst in the early 1990s, a freshly minted graduate from the University of Pennsylvania with bachelor's degrees in English literature and business. Blackstone was still relatively tiny then, with a couple of dozen employees, and while it had a small private-equity fund, working in that business was a mix of investment banking and investing as the firm split its time advising companies on deals and looking for its own.

Gray liked the looking for and doing deals part and was asked to work on the private placement memo for a new fund dedicated to real estate. Schwarzman and Peterson initially created real estate as a joint venture, its M.O. for businesses beyond M&A advice and LBOs in those days. The partner for real estate was a fellow named John Schreiber, an already-seasoned hand in the business who could help the nascent Blackstone with credibility.

A few analysts, including Gray and Blitzer, were summoned to assist Schreiber. The first fund was described as a $330 million pool, which technically overstated it by two-thirds. Only $110 million was committed to the discretionary pool. The balance was committed as co-investment dollars by investors in the fund, meaning they would have a say as to which deals they did and didn't commit to.

It was an unqualified success on a financial basis, with a net average annual return of 39.7 percent and a multiple of invested capital of 2.4 times, according to a document created to pitch the latest fund to pensions. Blackstone would go on to raise increasingly bigger funds every three to four years until 2006 and 2007, when it raised a fund each year.

There at the creation, Gray two decades later is the head of Blackstone's real estate business and has led the firm's two largest deals of all time, the purchases of Equity Office Properties and Hilton Hotels. The renovation of Blackstone's offices in 2010 and 2011 elevated Gray literally and figuratively. He occupies a corner office with northwestern views of Manhattan, pictures of his wife and four daughters lining the windowsills. He holds meetings in an adjacent living-room–like setting with couches and chairs in place of the traditional conference table.

Unlike private equity, which proved in the LBO bust that it may be scalable only to a certain point, real estate appears to have room to grow, and Blackstone's ability to raise a new real estate fund bears that out. Unlike private equity, where Schwarzman's sixth fund was about 40 percent smaller than his fifth, the seventh real estate fund stands to collect more than its most recent $10 billion predecessor.

Blackstone's main brand of real estate investing has roughly the same economics as its private-equity business, which makes sense, since the leveraged buyout industry lifted its model from existing partnerships like real estate and oil and gas. While doing it well and lucratively is far from easy, the underlying premise is relatively simple. Just as in leveraged buyouts, borrowed money is the key to success. Blackstone's twist was to come at real estate in part from a private-equity perspective, using some tools in the financial arsenal to make even better deals on the front end to maximize profits.

The approach through the 1990s was relatively straightforward. Blackstone would pool money and use some of the fund's cash, along with bank loans and bonds, to buy real estate assets they had decided were undervalued, do some amount of work to them, and sell them as real estate values rose. The breakthrough started right after the turn of the century, when Gray and his group started investing in the so-called extended stay hotel business. These are hotels designed as "suites" for longer-duration visits, often for traveling sales reps. Blackstone bought Homestead Studio Suites, one such chain, right after the September 11 terrorist attacks.

As that investment gained in value, Blackstone looked around for more, and some key things happened. First, Gray's team took advantage of an increasingly friendly and more creative debt financing market. They sought bigger targets by using forms of debt not typically used in these types of deals, specifically commercial mortgage backed securities (CMBS) and so-called mezzanine loans, a riskier type of borrowing.

Blackstone was willing to put additional risk on the deals because of the second realization tied to its extended stay forays. Big publicly listed hospitality companies were trading at values Gray believed were less than the sum of their parts. With that in mind, Blackstone bought Prime Hospitality for $790 million in 2004, then turned around and sold Prime's AmeriSuites hotels for $600 million to Hyatt later that same year. "I'd bought a fruit basket," Gray said. "Then I sold the pears to the guys who really wanted pears, and so on."

The template was set: Gray tapped banks for CMBS and started shopping for fruit baskets. Blackstone went on to create the same trade, with minor variations, almost a dozen times over the next three years. The strategy culminated with the then record-setting $40 billion purchase of Equity Office Properties in 2007, when Gray basically bought the fruit basket and started hawking fruit almost instantly. Deals for pieces of the sprawling Equity Office empire were announced within days—all told, Blackstone sold $27 billion worth of properties.

The Equity Office transaction stands as Blackstone's biggest in its history. The second-biggest also belongs to Gray: the $20 billion takeover of Hilton Hotels announced just as the credit markets seized. Announced on July 3, 2007 (within hours of KKR's first filing for its long-delayed IPO), the Hilton deal in retrospect marked the end of an era. Given its profile and timing, it may stand as a defining deal for Gray and Blackstone.

While the price tag in 2007 was borderline pedestrian (after all, it stands as only the eleventh-biggest LBO in history). It involved a huge bet by Blackstone with an equity check of $5.7 billion, split between real estate and private-equity funds; Blackstone added $800 million more around Hilton's debt restructuring. Beyond that, the timing of the purchase and the notoriety of the target ensured that it would be a high-profile deal.

In the intervening years, Gray told anyone who'd listen that Hilton would turn out to not just be a good deal, but a great one, and he presses the case that it proves private equity can grow a business. Chris Nassetta, who was recruited by Gray to run Hilton after the purchase, is an unabashed fan of both Gray and Blackstone. Nassetta, a longtime hotel executive, had met Gray on his second day at Blackstone, back in the early 1990s. He knew John Schreiber from the board of directors of Host Marriott, where Nassetta served as CEO prior to being recruited to Hilton. "You want to keep up with them," Nassetta said. "You want to run with the horses."

Gray wooed Nassetta to Hilton on the basis of the opportunity. "It was a sleeping giant," Nassetta told me. "This sort of deal allows you to reboot the company's hard drive, to really ask yourself what it should be."

Nassetta replaced more than half of the company's top 100 managers and turned his focus to the international markets, where the Hilton brand was known, but without having a significant number of actual hotels. The percentage of Hilton's hotels under construction that are outside the U.S. increased to almost 80 percent in 2012 from roughly 11 percent at the time of acquisition.

The growth of the real estate business within Blackstone seems instructive as to the mindset of the firm—Schwarzman's idea, relentlessly executed. Timing and luck played a role. After growing steadily for 15 years, Blackstone was able to seize on the financial crisis to its great advantage, exploiting the relative weakness of its biggest competitors—in-house real estate arms of investment banks—to create what in 2011 looked like an insurmountable lead over its private-equity competitors, at least in terms of assets under management and scope of the business. Asked on a 2011 investor call about the chances a competitor could raise a $10 billion real estate fund in 2011, James said: "I think the only one who has a shot at it is us."

By the first quarter of 2012, Blackstone had already raised $10 billion, and had set its sights on $2 billion more.[9] As the size of private-equity funds contracted, real estate was expanding.

That boded well for Gray's stature within the firm and he has emerged as a likely heir to Schwarzman's seat. Already a member of the management committee, he was named to Blackstone's board of directors in 2012.

■ ■ ■

Credit was a business Blackstone had dabbled in, but it took the GSO deal, the first acquisition for the firm after the IPO, to cement it as a legitimate leg of the strategy. Probably because it was not born of

Blackstone, GSO feels the most distinct in terms of style and culture. By some combination of circumstance and desire, GSO was able to keep its offices a couple of buildings down Park Avenue from head-quarters for several years. The differences were subtle, but the kind that end up feeling important—GSO executives only put on ties when they have a meeting with Tony or Steve. They relished their relative independence.

GSO has emerged as one of the most acquisitive branches of Blackstone, growing both by attracting new investors as well as snapping up CLOs (credit loan obligation funds) cast off by other asset managers. Goodman, given his longstanding relationship with James and the success of the business before and after the acquisition, has taken on a prominent role within the firm. His name is mentioned along with Gray's as a potential someday CEO.

If growth in credit and real estate were somewhat predictable, less so was the rise of Tom Hill's group. Now formally known as Hedge Fund Solutions, what began as a side project to invest partners' money has grown into Blackstone's largest business by assets and the biggest business of its kind in the world. Hill bristles at the term fund-of-funds because he says it understates what his group actually does for its clients, which is a more bespoke approach to hedge funds.

That Hill should be in this position is remarkable, or at least unlikely. His relationship with Schwarzman dates back to before their days working at Lehman together. As very young men, the two were assigned to the same Army reserves unit in New York, a dentistry detail. After earning an undergraduate degree and an MBA from Harvard, Hill was an early mover in the mergers and acquisitions business, helping create the M&A department at First Boston. His path crossed more meaningfully with Schwarzman and Peterson when he joined Lehman in 1982 as a partner, later rising to run investment banking there and serve as co-CEO. After the firm was sold (and Peterson and Schwarzman left), Hill was the co-president and co-chief operating officer of the new Shearson Lehman Holding Company.

After he was ousted from the firm, Hill continued his investment banking career by reuniting with his two former partners at Blackstone in 1993, serving as the co-head of the corporate and M&A advisory business through the balance of that decade. Then Schwarzman asked him to step in to figure out the then-tiny hedge fund business. During a call with investors in 2011, Schwarzman noted that the business had grown by about 80 times since he asked Hill to take it over in 2001.

Initially, Schwarzman asked Hill to conduct a search for a new person to run what was then known as Blackstone Alternative Asset Management, or BAAM. He gave him six months. After three, Hill realized it could be a big business and told his boss so. Schwarzman asked Hill if he wanted to just run it himself.

Hill, with his Harvard credentials and Lehman pedigree, looks the part of an investment banker. There's long been a rumor on Wall Street that at least the physical elements of the Gordon Gekko character in the seminal movie *Wall Street* were based on Hill, who is an impeccable dresser and slicks his hair back to this day. He has built a similarly pedigreed group—seeing them in a room is like walking into a living Brooks Brothers calendar—that is charged with taking big slugs of money for clients and picking hedge funds based on their appetite for risk. Blackstone has access to managers across the spectrum of hedge funds, from so-called macro funds to those who describe themselves as "event driven," that is, focused on trades around something like a merger or acquisition.

Blackstone's hedge fund group has achieved such scale that it got into the business of helping start, or "seed," other hedge funds. In those cases, Blackstone will give a new fund enough money to get started, in exchange for a cut of the fees and an equity stake in the management company of the fund. Blackstone then goes on to invest its clients' money with those new funds.

And then there's the smallest Blackstone business, which happens to be the firm's oldest: giving advice. Once headed by Tom Hill, it's now run by former Morgan Stanley and HSBC banker John Studzinski, a colorful character (known within the firm and on Wall Street simply as "Studz") who's well known in London for his patronage of the arts and connections around the worlds of both finance and culture.

While small relative to the massive investment banking operations of big Wall Street firms, Blackstone's advisory group has managed to pull off some big assignments, including a key role advising insurer AIG on the disposal of its assets in the wake of the financial crisis.

Within the context of the advisory business is another Blackstone effort that's become a signature of the firm, the restructuring group headed by Timothy Coleman. The creation of that group was another hedge of sorts on Schwarzman and Peterson's part and help put Blackstone in a business that blossomed in the wake of the credit meltdown. The group was created in the early 1990s by the late Arthur Newman, whom Schwarzman and Peterson had recruited as an early effort at diversifying what the firm could do for clients. Newman recruited Coleman, who later became his co-head and eventually took over the group upon Newman's retirement (Coleman serves on the firm's executive committee, an indication of its growing importance in the broader context of Blackstone).

The group specializes in one of the more rough-and-tumble corners of Wall Street dealmaking: the fights between debtors and creditors as a company wrestles with how to fix a business or pursue bankruptcy. Blackstone's team has emerged as one of a handful of specialty groups adept at these hairy situations, along with Houlihan Lokey, Moelis & Company, and Alvarez & Marsal. Coleman's group has found a number of niches, including newspaper companies, gambling firms and, in 2011, began working with the Los Angeles Dodgers baseball team as it entered bankruptcy, triggered by the divorce of the McCourts, its then-owners. Coleman advised on the sale process, which culminated in a group led by former basketball star Magic Johnson buying the Dodgers for more than $2 billion.

While parts of Blackstone, especially real estate and private equity, and Tom Hill, are strikingly similar in terms of personnel to what they were two decades ago, the firm also has the highest-profile alumni of any of its private-equity brethren. Blackstone is rare among the largest private-equity firms for having endured the departure of a founder and the hiring of a high-profile second-in-command as well as a host of notable departures. The turnover rate is cited by competitors as evidence that Blackstone is a tough place to work and Schwarzman an especially demanding boss. One person familiar with Blackstone told me it wasn't a place you go for hugs. Firm insiders characterize turnover as evidence that Blackstone is a mature company.

The "black" in BlackRock, the multi-trillion-dollar asset manager, is not a coincidence. That firm, run by Laurence Fink, started as an "affiliate" similar to John Schreiber's real estate joint venture. Blackstone in 1988 staked what was then known as the Financial Management Group with a $5 million line of credit and office space in return for a 40 percent stake in the company. Six years later, after Fink and Schwarzman disagreed over how new hires at what became BlackRock should be given equity, the group spun out. PNC Bank bought Black-Rock for $240 million.[10] As of March 2012, the now-public BlackRock had $3.67 trillion in assets and a market capitalization of $30 billion, more than twice that of Blackstone.

Roger Altman, the investment banker who has shuttled between jobs on Wall Street and in Washington and worked at Lehman Brothers with Peterson and Schwarzman, joined the pair in 1987 as vice chairman. He headed the firm's advisory efforts and served on the investment committee until 1993, when he left to serve as President Clinton's deputy Treasury secretary. Upon returning to New York, he created the investment banking boutique, Evercore.

Mark Gallogly was an early Blackstone partner—he conducted Jon Gray's on-campus interview at Penn—and left in 2005 to create Centerbridge Partners. That firm, which specializes in distressed financial and real estate deals, has remained close enough to Blackstone to partner on deals including BankUnited. Another partner, Chip Schorr, left in 2011 after overseeing the firm's technology investments. He created a new firm as well, called Augusta Columbia Capital Group. Another tech specialist, Jamie Kiggen, departed in 2012 to become the president of Riverside Co., a private-equity firm that specializes in buying companies worth less than $200 million and describes itself as "more Gandhi than Gekko" on its website.

Real estate, credit, and hedge funds at Blackstone dwarf private equity by most measures. Describing Blackstone as a buyout firm is insufficient. For marketing purposes, Blackstone refers to itself as "one of the world's leading investment and advisory firms." That lack of dependence on leveraged buyouts draws the most criticism from Blackstone's private-equity brethren, who decry the firm as "asset collectors."

Inside Blackstone, from Schwarzman down, they tend to greet that moniker with some combination of a shrug and a chuckle. A *Fortune* story in 2011 was titled "The Triumph of Blackstone on Wall Street," evidence that there's a growing sense Blackstone got it right by downplaying private equity, or at least treating it as but one of a number of just-as-important businesses.

One thing is clear: If this particular diversified model is the future of what began as private equity, Schwarzman got there first. In 2011, he tried to exploit his advantage, synthesizing Blackstone's head start in diversifying with a drumbeat that was growing louder from investors. The deal with New Jersey's pension plan, which came on the heels of the Texas teachers' new arrangement with KKR and Apollo, was the first public indication of something that had been brewing inside Blackstone for much of that year, spurred largely by Schwarzman himself.

Earlier that year, Schwarzman called a meeting of the entire firm and pressed each piece to talk about what they were seeing in the markets. He realized he was getting detailed analysis, the kind of insights the likes of Goldman Sachs had used to create its powerful and lucrative proprietary trading desk. Schwarzman was faced with a decision: use the firm's money to trade on these ideas, or set up a new sort of business, or set of products, and start selling it to the biggest pools of capital in the world.

The pitch to them is akin to what New Jersey is getting—the ability to more easily move money around to whatever Blackstone, in consultation with the client, decides is the best strategy for the current market or return expectation. In May 2012, CalPERS agreed to a similar separate account arrangement totaling $500 million.

Since Blackstone wasn't organized to manage big relationships in quite that way, Schwarzman and James appointed Blitzer, the private-equity co-chairman, to play the role of point man for the New Jersey deal.

The set-up, Schwarzman said, has an added benefit for Blackstone: continuing to groom the younger partners and his and James's successors. "In terms of integrated investors, that's really been limited to me and Tony," he said. No one else needed to think about what all the different pieces of the firm were doing unless they were directly involved. A real estate partner might tap a GSO executive for an insight into credit, and was encouraged to do so, but it was ad hoc. "This takes the next generation and gets them working together in a different way."

For his part, Schwarzman attributes his quest for the next product line to his investment banking days—the overall competitiveness among firms and the need to keep coming up with new products and services to offer corporate clients, whether it was stock and bond underwriting, merger advice, or the increasingly complex debt that defined Wall Street during the last two decades. He also saw waves of wanna-be bankers hang out shingles and be successful. "When you start out working in investment banking, you learn there are no barriers to entry in this business," he said.

Chapter 12

Not-So-Private Equity

Out of the Shadows

With the weight of its own secretive history bearing down, private equity is finally stepping out of the shadows. That's how I ended up in Delaware City, Delaware, watching Tony James surrounded by politicians and workers in jumpsuits. It was October 2011, and the occasion was reopening a refinery owned by PBF Energy, a venture created and funded by Blackstone with private-equity energy specialist firm First Reserve. PBF bought the closed refinery in June 2010 from Valero, which had shuttered it a year earlier.

The biggest private-equity firms are now very much in the public eye, and seeing James that day in Delaware was notable not so much for what he said, but that he or any top Blackstone or private-equity executive was even there.

James was in charming PR mode, showing up for a Bloomberg Television interview scheduled around the reopening with a *Fortune* reporter in tow. The morning was well-scripted, evoking a stop on a campaign tour, a feeling enhanced by the half-dozen senior elected officials on the program. Under a white tent in the back parking lot, plant workers in jumpsuits and local executives munched on mini-quiches and cinnamon rolls. Small banners proclaiming "A New Beginning" and "Congratulations on a Job Well Done!" hung from one side of the tent.

Blackstone and First Reserve pumped $450 million into updating the Delaware City facility and reopening it, returning 500 full-time jobs and 250 contract workers to the processing plant. This was big news for the area, and politician after politician took the stage to make sweeping pronouncements. "When a place like this shuts down," said Chris Combs, Delaware's junior U.S. Senator, "it leaves a hole. It's like a punch in the gut to families." Then he went even bigger. "We face a question: 'Are we a great nation?'"

Once James took the stage, after Coons, U.S. Senator Thomas Carper, and Governor Jack Markell, the Blackstone president echoed their grand sentiments and used the opportunity to make the case for private equity to the assembled media, refinery workers, and government officials with similarly elevated language. "This is the sort of partnership that should be a model for America," he said, a winning applause line for the crowd that had dutifully given every speaker a standing ovation. "It takes a lot of money to save America's industrial base."

After the speeches and the ribbon cutting, set on a patch of grass so as to use the soaring towers of the refinery as a backdrop, James milled about chatting with the plant bosses and politicians, as well as the designated union representative from the United Steelworkers. That friendly encounter was another twist in the day. Organized labor has long been a critic of private equity and remains one, given the industry's reputation for cutting jobs, but here was a senior labor guy who'd flown all the way from Texas not to bury private equity, but to praise it.

Gary Beevers, a Steelworkers vice president, was there because 350 of his "brothers and sisters in Steelworker blue" had been put back to work. During his brief speech, his gruff Texas baritone was a striking departure from the well-cadenced remarks of the politicians and moneymen, and he pointed out that private equity was, in this case, a good friend to organized labor. After the speech and the ceremonial ribbon cutting captured by a dozen local-media cameras, Beevers and I stepped to the side for a chat. When I asked if he wanted to sit down, he said he'd prefer to stand. He looked around and, with some relief, plucked a piece of Copenhagen from the round can in his pocket and talked private equity. He repeated what James had said during his remarks—that big oil had announced three refinery closures that very week, days away from this facility being officially reopened. At the end of the day, getting his members back to work was what he cared most about. "They got the financing for this when no one else could. What we worry about is long-term jobs. This is a group that provided them," he said, pointing to the handful of workers still milling around after the event, "an opportunity to get back to work."

This was part of private equity's new public push, and an event like this one simply would not have taken place before. These firms were largely content to let their story be told without them, even if it meant effectively ceding the narrative to those who would focus on the jobs lost. Being in the public eye is only enhanced by a listing on a major stock exchange. Blackstone's 2007 IPO, of which James was a primary architect, helped reshape the industry and effectively separate Blackstone and a small handful of its peers into a distinct class apart from the rest of the private-equity business. The money's journey, once tucked safely out of view, now goes through the New York Stock Exchange and Nasdaq, radically changing the nature of how the industry's biggest players operate.

The choice of whether to go public, when, and how stands as a way to explore the cultures, motives, and founders' personalities at each of the largest private-equity firms. There is a standard set of talking points around why a firm would choose to sell shares to the public and open itself up to far greater scrutiny than it would have to otherwise endure. True, it gives the firm a way to raise "permanent capital"—money that can remain on its balance sheet indefinitely rather than funds that are committed by investors for a finite period. True, it gives firms a currency by which to make acquisitions beyond whatever cash they have set aside for those purposes. Still, a major, if not *the* major, reason to go public is so that the founders and senior executives of the firms can get paid for what they built, as was the case with Peterson at Blackstone and as Carlyle's Rubenstein has expressed publicly. Cashing out smooths the transition to the next generation.

Some firms have managed to stay private while allowing their founders to move on. Warburg Pincus, one of the oldest private-equity managers (it was created in 1966) handed the keys to a younger pair of leaders in 2000. Charles Kaye and Joseph Landy took over that year from Lionel Pincus and John Vogelstein. Warburg has stayed firmly in the private-equity business and invests from one global fund; it has total assets of about $30 billion.[1]

Bain Capital, too, chose to stay private, even when its founding CEO decided to leave to pursue a life in government and politics. In 1999, when Romney left the firm he created, in favor of running the Salt Lake City Olympics, his partners negotiated a severance agreement with him that allowed for his ownership of the firm to be spread among the partners, helping avoid a sale to an outside investor or a public offering. In return, Romney continued to participate in some of the economics of Bain. Unlike rivals where one or two founders have remained in tight control of the firm, Bain took an approach more akin to that of a law or consulting firm. A nine-member committee is the primary decision-making body of Bain. The investment vetting process is similarly spread among a number of individuals. "By staying more focused on the pie than the slice, we've created an organization that's truly sustainable," Mark Nunnelly said.

The dispersion of ownership has allowed Bain to stay private and yet it's grow the business dramatically since Romney's departure; it has more than $60 billion globally in assets under management, versus $4 billion when he retired. Bain also has opted to pursue growth by growing new businesses organically and with homegrown talent rather than by buying them.

At Blackstone, Schwarzman and James were building a different type of firm, and going public was a means not only to transition the founders, but to give the firm a currency to expand the business rapidly. While a Blackstone IPO may have been inevitable, its completion was far from certain in 2007. When the time came to actually sell the shares to the public, in the middle of 2007, Schwarzman knew he had to hurry.

The year had been going exceedingly well. In addition to the birthday party, he'd been on the cover of *Fortune* ("Wall Street's Man of the Moment")[2] and pulled off what was for at least a few weeks the biggest leveraged buyout in history (Equity Office Properties). In

March, Blackstone had become the most prominent private-equity firm to file for an initial public offering, though not the first. Fortress Investment Group, which manages private-equity and hedge funds, along with real estate, had gone out in February.

But Blackstone's S-1 filing with the U.S. Securities and Exchange Commission was a whole different matter. For the first time, public investors—not to mention Wall Street rubberneckers and curious students of the financial markets —would have a peek inside a buyout machine and get at least a taste of the secret sauce. Not to mention that they could find out how much Schwarzman and other Blackstone executives were actually worth. Journalists, me included, tracked every twist in the path to going public, scouring each new amended filing with the SEC for additional nuggets. Early one June Monday morning came the jackpot: the filing that detailed ownership and compensation. The previous year, Schwarzman had earned $398.3 million at Blackstone, a staggering figure, especially compared with the $54 million Lloyd Blankfein had been paid to run Goldman Sachs, then the world's most profitable securities firm.

What we learned that day was that Schwarzman's stake in the company he created would be worth almost $8 billion at the predicted IPO price. As planned, the 80-year-old Pete Peterson would cash out the vast bulk of his ownership and set up a foundation. Schwarzman would hang on to the bulk of his stock and keep ownership worth 24 percent of the total firm, but sell shares in the offering for a total of $684 million. The chattering classes were awed. The story about pay was among the handful of most-read Bloomberg News stories for the entire week.

Yet even as Blackstone's bankers, led by Goldman Sachs and Citigroup, forged ahead with the road show, the leveraged buyout market was showing signs of strain. Word of record subprime mortgage defaults in the United States were rippling through the credit markets, causing banks to worry about financing new deals. On June 21, Blackstone sold 133 million shares at $31 apiece, at the high end of the predicted range. The investment bankers opted to sell additional shares, the so-called green shoe, or additional shares set aside for heavy demand. The following day, when it began trading, the stock rose to $38 before closing at $35.06. That remains Blackstone stock's all-time high. It has yet to come close to that mark in the intervening five years and has at times dipped below five dollars a share.

Had they waited more than a few days, they simply might not have done the offering, potentially for several years. That was the case for KKR, which filed its own S-1 on the evening of July 3, and ended up getting public in the U.S. three years later through the complicated merger with its European fund. Carlyle put off its own IPO contemplations and debuted almost five years later.

As the stock market digested an increasingly bleak outlook for private equity, Blackstone shares foundered. While Schwarzman and James touted Blackstone's ability to weather slow LBO times through their growing non-buyout businesses like hedge funds and real estate, the overall gloom was too much to overcome. Blackstone continued to trade largely on the perception of the private-equity business.

One nagging element from the beginning of the going-public trend was the concept of a publicly traded private-equity firm, which seems to be a contradiction in terms. There's the whole notion that these are the guys who spend a good chunk of their time convincing boards and executives of public companies that the markets are inherently stupid and don't understand them and unfairly judge them on a quarter-to-quarter basis. Go private, they whisper, and you can do all the things you want to do without all those people watching. The managers have found all too well that everything they've said all along about being public may be true, as they wrestle with Wall Street over how to fairly value the firms. Another issue that's not been resolved to many people's satisfaction is the real or perceived conflicts between the two classes of private-equity investors: the pensions and endowments who comprise the limited partners in their funds, and the institutional shareholders who buy shares on the public market.

The conflict seems straightforward. Limited partners count on their private-equity managers to deliver their money back to them, with a healthy profit, in due course, but only when it makes sense. The only pressure they should feel is to deliver the best return to their limiteds, with whom they are theoretically aligned in terms of economics. After all, a private-equity manager only gets paid the super big bucks off carry. And carry only comes when the limited partners get paid first.

But what if all of a sudden you're part of a publicly traded company answering to shareholders looking for consistent profits, or at least some profits? The value of your stock is based in part on your ability to produce earnings. The clearest way to make money in the private-equity business is to sell what you own. Isn't there a natural pressure then, at least potentially, to look to sell something to make *those* investors happy, too? And to boost the price of the stock, which by the way, now constitutes the buyout manager's own stake in the firm?

Limited partners, while kvetching quietly behind the scenes, and to each other, have so far shown little appetite to avoid investing in funds managed by publicly traded firms. The firms themselves argue, loudly, that they are in fact all aligned and that public investors are getting a slice of the same profits that the managers themselves strive for. Blackstone laid out in its prospectus that it would favor the rights of its limited partners over that of its public shareholders if there was ever a question.

For their part, public investors seem to have decided that they can't find a coherent and consistent way to value private equity. The problem stems from one of the most fundamental elements of the business, and it goes back to private equity's core pitch. By the very nature of its ownership, private-equity owners don't have to sell the companies they own and, because the underlying companies are closely held, they aren't beholden to public shareholders. That's theoretically very good news for the private-equity managers themselves and the investors in their funds, who count on them, and pay huge fees for the expertise that determines the best times to buy and sell. The problem for a public investor in a private-equity firm is that it's basically impossible to gauge when a firm is going to sell a company and therefore reap the fees, or carry, from that deal. Public stock valuations are by their nature forward looking. Investors who buy stocks are betting the stock will gain in value in the short- or long-term, allowing the holder to profit by selling it at a later time. Or they may see that a company pays a predictable, generous dividend and hold it for that steady income stream, even if the stock doesn't rise dramatically in value. With that in mind, investors and analysts place a value on a stock that's usually based on a multiple of earnings. With private equity among the biggest questions is what actually constitutes those earnings and when investors will actually see evidence of them.

Blackstone, once effectively alone as a publicly traded private-equity firm, now has company, with Apollo and KKR listed on the NYSE, and Carlyle on the Nasdaq. More choices and comparisons may help raise the profiles of the private-equity managers in the eyes of would-be public investors, a fact that theoretically could boost some or all of the share prices. One obstacle arose from private-equity firms' attempts to be more transparent to public investors, or at least guide their analysts and investors to an accurate picture of their business at any given moment. Blackstone and others rely on a complicated measure called economic net income, or ENI, that's meant to more accurately reflect the earnings of the business without factoring in some costs associated with actions like going public. It has served to further confuse investors, in part because it swings wildly as companies held in private-equity funds get marked up and down in value.

The broad reaction from mutual funds and other institutional investors is to vote by just not showing up to buy the shares, despite a majority of research analysts who follow the firms posting "buy" recommendations. The lack of broad ownership is reflected in the relatively anemic volumes. In late 2011, Blackstone traded about 440,000 shares a day on average and KKR traded half that. Goldman Sachs traded, on average, about 860,000 shares during the same period.

Also, because the stocks aren't widely held, volatility can be fierce. One or several shareholders deciding to buy or sell can have a dramatic effect on the price rising or falling as they drive up the price by snapping up stock, or drive it down by flooding the market. Blackstone's stock especially can move on what could be called "the Steve effect." Blackstone usually releases its results at around 8:30 in the morning, holds an on-the-record public call where reporters ask questions an hour later, then a call for analysts and investors, which is open to the public and transmitted through its website at 11 A.M. The complexity of the quarterly earnings often leaves investors confused in the several hours between the release of the results and the conference call. A few well-placed words from Schwarzman can reverse a stock slide, giving the impression, perhaps rightly, that the stock is a barometer of his mood on the broader markets.

To wit, in October 2011, the morning of Schwarzman's Alfred E. Smith dinner address, Blackstone badly missed Wall Street's consensus estimate of a 1-cent-per-share profit, posting a 12-cent-per-share loss. That was triggered by the fact that the firm was forced to mark down the value it put on the companies it owns, despite its argument that those companies were likely to regain value in the subsequent quarters. The stock dropped more than 3 percent.

Enter Schwarzman, whose comments buoyed the shares. By the time the stock market closed, the stock had reversed its losses and gained more than 3 percent, following his remarks that despite the economic gloom, Blackstone's real estate group was poised to have one of its best periods ever and the firm had brought money into every one of its businesses during the quarter. The Steve effect that day was worth 6 percent.

■ ■ ■

The move away from private equity is among the most dominant and pressing questions facing the industry. A commonly held view is that there's a bulge bracket of sorts among firms who made their name in leveraged buyouts—Blackstone, KKR, Carlyle, Bain, Apollo, and TPG being the most often mentioned names—are and should be considered fundamentally different from what are essentially monoline private-equity firms. While the big firms bristle at the notion that they're somehow diminished as investors by expanding into non-buyout classes, their focus on growing assets is undeniable. Blackstone has more than doubled its assets under management since it went public, to $190 billion. The vast majority of that has come from bulking up credit funds and money invested for clients in hedge funds, along with new funds in private equity and real estate. Carlyle and Blackstone, especially, have engaged in what's effectively an AUM arms race. Carlyle bought a majority stake in AlpInvest, a fund-of-funds manager, in 2011 that brought the firm to within striking distance of Blackstone, at about $159 billion in total assets. It also puts the two firms well ahead of their closest competitors by that measure, since KKR has about $62 billion in assets. That's creating a more distinct rivalry between Blackstone and Carlyle, one that came up a number of times in discussions. One Carlyle executive equated it to great sports rivalries like Duke University and the University of North Carolina, or the New York Yankees and the Boston Red Sox.

With Carlyle public, it will become easier to judge who ultimately will win over shareholders, and many of the recent efforts to grow AUM involve businesses outside of private equity, underscoring Schwarzman's designs on creating the modern financial services powerhouse. The moves in large part tie back to the conundrum of valuing stocks of these firms, who now rely on public shareholders to determine their worth. Those investors can't get comfortable putting a value on carried interest, despite its outsized profitability for the managers and, at least theoretically, the shareholders of the firm. The fees from managing a fund-of-funds are much more predictable and therefore more attractive for public investors.

While public investors are increasingly important, and their support necessary if these firms are going to breed another generation of tycoons, private-equity firms still rely primarily on limited partners, the pensions and endowments whose money is the starting point for the industry. Ultimately, even as the founders contemplate making themselves emeritus, they are constantly on the road, solidifying those existing relationships and courting new partners. This is, after all, the heart of the business they started several decades ago.

Schwarzman is living proof. He's rarely in his office at headquarters, but he's almost never out of reach, or out of touch. Nor does he want to be. For one of our last interviews, I showed up at his office on Valentine's Day, which is also his birthday, and took a seat in the small room adjacent to his corner office. Soon, Schwarzman appeared on the screen, in high definition from Paris.

He was in the midst of a month on the road, a trip that would bring him briefly back to the United States for a meeting of CEO collective The Business Council but mostly involve forays into the Middle East, Europe, and Asia. The day before, he'd been in London, holding a town hall meeting of sorts aimed at ensuring that the Europeans were acting in concert with their U.S. and overseas counterparts. This is Statesman Schwarzman in all his glory, taking his peripatetic, always connected persona on the road. Over the course of two hours, we took a couple of 20-minute breaks so he could field other phone calls. While he mostly eschews e-mail, he's constantly on his cell phone and almost never can resist picking it up.

Schwarzman passionately made the case that he's worked hard to make himself redundant. "Even if I died, nothing would change," he said. "I'm irrelevant. I've done my job."

Within a few breaths, he partially undermined his own point. Talking excitedly, he described a town hall meeting the previous day in London, where he addressed 183 employees (he knew the exact number), many of whom had joined during the two years previous. "I went in and said, 'This is what we believe. I don't care what you've been told. This is how it is.' That's important. It's just a like a car getting a tune-up every once in a while."

He reflected on what it means to be the ultimate owner of dozens of companies that people know and use every day, noting that it fundamentally alters how people inside the firm think about what they do, even him. "When you own the world's largest hotel chain, that changes things," he said.

Schwarzman may be working hard to bulk up the bench, but his is a slow, noisy fade, just as it is and presumably will be for his biggest competitors. He has built a firm beneath him that allows him to press Blackstone's advantage. That means thinking about his biggest customers, staying ahead of the competition, and spending most of his time away from Park Avenue. Those billions aren't going to raise themselves.

Schwarzman has a habit of getting on a roll, oblivious to time constraints or schedules. But when he's done, he's done, and moving on to whatever is next. That was the case this day, when he finally realized his wife was waiting for him to celebrate his birthday. After dinner there would inevitably be calls to return to New York, as headquarters finished up its workday. When that was done, Asia would be waking up. He stood up and soon I was left staring at an empty chair.

I descended from the Blackstone offices down to Park Avenue. Somewhere in midtown, David Rubenstein was likely regaling a would-be owner of his stock about the virtues of Carlyle's impending public offering and his vision for Carlyle's continued growth. Kravis, fresh from a trip to the Middle East and Asia, was preparing a presentation to his own shareholders about Capstone and the specific levers KKR had pulled at the likes of beer purveyor Oriental Brewery and pill maker Capsugel. Coulter was adapting the speech he gave in Scottsdale as a state of the union of sorts for the industry's annual Super Return conference in Berlin.

They were all making their case, each with more than a passing glance at the other's strategy, and with an eye trained on their ultimate legacy as firms and as an industry. All this with more pressure from investors to perform, combined with the weight of their own ever bigger, ever more costly organizations. They had to keep the money coming in, keep buying, and keep building ever-growing empires.

Afterword

Almost a year to the day after visiting Legoland, I was walking with my wife and sons down a stretch of Broadway, just above Columbus Circle in Manhattan. We'd just spent the afternoon at the American Museum of Natural History looking at dinosaur bones and learning about the solar system. Now we were headed for dinner and I was pointing out various sites of personal significance—where their uncle had gone to law school; an outpost of my favorite burger place; the spot where the Big Apple Circus sets up every year. And there on Broadway, just north of West 62nd Street, was an entrance to the David Rubenstein Atrium at Lincoln Center. I pointed. My wife just shook her head.

Through the course of reporting and writing this book, I became even more annoying than usual to those around me, as I constantly discovered more evidence of private-equity ubiquity. I mused whether Blackstone and Bain pushed the Weather Channel to improve its iPad app. I wondered whether the private-equity owners had any say in casting Will Arnett for the commercials for Hulu that ran during the Super Bowl. At one person's suggestion, I briefly considered living for a

week or month using only private-equity products, a sort of Supersize
Me, private-equity style. Thankfully for my family, I chose not to.

As a journalist, I'm trained to look for the surprise. The omni-
presence of this industry did in fact surprise me, even as it was a major
premise of the book and a business I'd been reporting on for years.
I began to realize that companies that weren't owned by private-equity
firms could someday be, or that some enterprising analyst tucked in a
windowless cubicle at Blackstone or KKR probably built an Excel
spreadsheet about it. Somewhere, someone has run the numbers. Even
in a subdued, post-LBO boom age, it seemed there was nothing they
couldn't buy at least a piece of.

The intense focus on personal legacy on the part of the founders also
surprised me, though maybe it shouldn't have. After all, men in their
sixties and seventies are prone to think a lot about what they've done
and what they've left to do, especially when their names are literally or
figuratively on the door. They've made more money than most of them
could have ever imagined. Now it's about going out a hero, or at least
leaving something meaningful behind, as businessmen and as people.

Rubenstein's name jutting out from that building on Broadway
made me think of the most prominent local monument to private-
equity wealth and largesse, the Stephen A. Schwarzman Building. The
Main Branch of the New York Public Library had been a frequent
writing spot for me. It's an iconic and beautiful artifice, situated on a
parcel of land in the heart of Manhattan adjacent to Bryant Park, where
New Yorkers can ice skate in the winter and enjoy picnics while
watching outdoor movies in the summer.

One afternoon, while I was deep in the throes of book research,
I was walking up the stairs of the Schwarzman library behind some
tourists, one of whom was wearing a Jack Wolfskin jacket. The apparel
maker is owned by Blackstone. Resisting the temptation to point out
the connection to the unsuspecting visitor, I proceeded to find a spot to
plug in my laptop. The main reading room where I typically worked is
awe-inspiring and appropriately quiet, the silence punctuated only by
chairs being pushed and pulled on the tile floor and the vibration of
mobile phones. I spent many hours there, writing about Schwarzman
and his competitors in the building that is his monument.

Lest you forget it's *his*, Schwarzman's name is peppered throughout the library, on placards providing directions, and also inscribed on the ground just outside the main revolving door. In the lobby, there are other names inscribed in stone, names like Astor. The private equity barons are, truly, the new tycoons.

With this much money and this many people involved, the big questions loom and there aren't any easy answers. I can't give an unqualified endorsement of private equity as an industry or as a practice. Nor can I condemn it as across-the-board destructive. One person inside the industry told me along the way that private equity isn't good or bad—it just is.

Anyone who directly has say over that much money and can so deeply impact millions of lives has a big responsibility. Such people can't be judged solely on how much money they make for their investors or themselves. And they can't even be judged simply on how many jobs they create or destroy.

The institutions that give these men all that money share their burden. Even with their desperate need for the investment returns private equity promises to deliver, those big organizations—especially public pension funds—continue to influence how private-equity managers earn their rich rewards. The best managers will have to demonstrate with hard numbers that they are, on balance, improving the companies they buy for the long term.

And that's where it will ultimately matter to all of us. My kids don't especially care who David Rubenstein is, though maybe someday they'll enjoy Lincoln Center or marvel at the Magna Carta. Maybe they'll study in the Schwarzman library or enjoy the art in the Henry R. Kravis wing of the Metropolitan Museum of Art. Maybe one day they'll rely on investments made by KKR, Carlyle, or Blackstone for their retirement savings. In the meantime, my boys are ready to tell me what they want from Dunkin' Donuts.

Notes

The material in this book is largely the product of dozens of interviews with executives at a number of private equity firms, and many of the events described I witnessed first-hand. In cases where I wasn't present, I relied on the memories or recollections of at least one person who was there. Much of the data was derived from the Bloomberg Professional Service. I have relied on various other sources where noted.

Prologue

1. Paul Hodkinson, "Logjam Gives Buyout Firms $1.2 Trillion Hangover," *Financial News*, March 19, 2012. http://media.efinancialnews.com/story/2012-03-19/logjam-gives-buyout-firms-hangover
2. Katie Gilbert, "New Green Portfolio Program Could Change Private Equity," *Institutional Investor*, September 6, 2011. www.institutionalinvestor.com/Article/2895315/New-Green-Portfolio-Program-Could-Change-Private-Equity.html

Chapter 1: Find the Money

1. Jason Kelly, "Private Equity Finds the Easy Money Gone," *Bloomberg Businessweek*, August 26, 2010.
2. Hui-yong Yu, "Oregon Pledges $525 Million to KKR's New Buyout Fund," Bloomberg News, January 26, 2011.

3. Jason Kelly and Jonathan Keehner, "BCE Lenders May Sidestep C$10 Billion in Losses," Bloomberg News, December 8, 2008.

4. Jason Kelly, "Ontario Teachers' Gives Blackstone, KKR a Run for Their Money," *Bloomberg Businessweek*, March 1, 2010.

5. Michael Marois, "California Prison Physician Ranks Atop State Payroll Figures," Bloomberg News, July 6, 2011.

6. Robert Novy-Marx and Joshua Rauh, "The Crisis in Local Government Pensions in the United States," Northwestern University's Kellogg School of Business, 2011, Forthcoming in *Growing Old: Paying for Retirement and Institutional Money Management after the Financial Crisis*, Robert Litan and Richard Herring, eds., Brookings Institution, Washington, DC.

7. "Private Equity Principles 1.0," Institutional Limited Partners Association website. http://ilpa.org/principles-version-1-0/

8. "Private Equity Principles 2.0," Institutional Limited Partners Association website. http://ilpa.org/principles-version-2-0/

9. Jonathan Keehner and Jason Kelly, "The People vs. Private Equity," *Bloomberg Businessweek*, November 28, 2011.

10. Beth Jinks and Jason Kelly, "New York Pension's Schloss Raising Allocation to Private Equity," Bloomberg News, September 28, 2011.

11. Devin Banerjee and Sabrina Willmer, "Blackstone's Biggest Investment Shows Clients' Clout," Bloomberg News, December 9, 2011.

12. Dalton Conley, "Seeking SWF," *Democracy*, Issue 12, Spring 2009. www.democracyjournal.org/12/6674.php?page=all

Chapter 2: All the Money in the World

1. Georr Colvin, "Carlyle Chief: Opportunity Is Everywhere," *Fortune*, April 5, 2010. http://money.cnn.com/2010/03/31/news/companies/carlyle_group_rubenstein.fortune/index.htm

2. James Glassman, "Big Deals," *Washingtonian*, June 2006.

3. Ibid.

4. Henry Sender, "From a Carlyle Founder, a Warning Shot," *Wall Street Journal*, Deal Journal, March 1, 2007. http://blogs.wsj.com/deals/2007/03/01/from-a-carlyle-founder-a-warning-shot/

5. Glassman, "Big Deals."

6. Dan Primack, "Could Carlyle Reunite with the bin Ladens?" Fortune.com, May 2, 2011. http://finance.fortune.cnn.com/2011/05/02/how-long-until-carlyle-reunites-with-the-bin-ladens/

7. Jason Kelly and Katherine Burton, "Carlyle to Shutter Blue Wave Hedge Fund After Losses," Bloomberg News, July 31, 2008.

8. Jef Feeley and Miles Weiss, "Carlyle Group Sued by Fund Liquidator Over Losses," Bloomberg News, July 7, 2010.

9. Edward Evans, "Carlyle Capital Nears Collapse as Rescue Talks Fail," Bloomberg News, March 13, 2008.

Chapter 3: The L Word

1. Miles Weiss, "Black's Apollo Strengthens Former Drexel Links with Push into Brokerage," Bloomberg News, April 12, 2011.
2. William D. Cohan, "Private Equity's Public Subsidy Is a Tragedy," Bloomberg View, January 22, 2012.
3. Cristina Alesci and Laura Marcinek, "Morgan Stanley Targets Mid-Market Private Equity to Boost Fees," Bloomberg News, March 18, 2011.
4. Peter Lattman and Jeffrey McCracken, "Equity Firms Cheer Return of 'Staple'; Critics Don't," Wall Street Journal, March 5, 2010.
5. Jason Kelly and Ian King, "Freescale Weighs IPO to Ease Chipmaker's $7.9 Billion in Debt," Bloomberg News, August 26, 2010.
6. Heino Meerkatt and Heinrich Liechtenstein, "Get Ready for the Private Equity Shakeout," The Boston Consulting Group and IESE Business School, Dec. 2008. www.iese.edu/en/files/PrivateEquityWhitePaper.pdf
7. Steven N. Kaplan and Per Stromberg, "Leveraged Buyouts and Private Equity," Journal of Economic Perspectives 22, no. 4 (Season 2008). http://faculty .chicagobooth.edu/steven.kaplan/research/ksjep.pdf
8. PitchBook Annual Private Equity Breakdown 2012. www.pitchbook.com/ component/option,com_performs/Itemid,179/formid,70/showthank,1/uid, g2fXicZXffYPSGNFaWcV

Chapter 4: "When Was the Last Time You Bought a Toilet Seat?"

1. Debbie Howell, "Dollar General's Cal Turner Sr. Dead at 85," DSN Retailing Today, December 11, 2000.
2. Steve Matthews and Rachel Katz, "Dollar General to Pay $10 Million to Settle SEC Probe," Bloomberg News, March 15, 2004.
3. Simon Clark and Randy Whitestone, "KKR Seeks Repeat of Past Supermarket Profits with Safeway Bid," Bloomberg News, January 19, 2003.
4. Dollar General Proxy Statement filed with the U.S. Securities and Exchange Commission, filed May 21, 2007. http://sec.gov/Archives/edgar/data/ 29534/000104746907004478/a2178068zdefm14a.htm
5. Dakin Campbell and Andrew Frye, "Buffett Says Buyout Funds 'Don't Love the Business,'" Bloomberg News, November 12, 2010.
6. Whitney Kisling and Joshua Fineman, "Ackman Buys Family Dollar Stake, Says It's an LBO Candidate," Bloomberg News, May 25, 2011.

Chapter 5: Modern Art

1. Bryan Burrough and John Helyar, Barbarians at the Gate: The Fall of RJR Nabisco (New York: Harper Perennial, 1990), 133.
2. Jason Kelly and Oliver Staley, "Kravis Pledges $100 Million for Columbia Business School Campus," Bloomberg News, October 5, 2010.

3. www.redf.org
4. Oregon Public Employees Retirement Fund Alternative Equity Portfolio. www.ost.state.or.us/FactsAndFigures/PERS/AlternativeEquity/FOIA%20Q3% 202011.pdf
5. Henny Sender, "KKR's Two Rising Stars Depart to Launch Fund," *Wall Street Journal*, September 14, 2005. http://webreprints.djreprints.com/ 1552540178006.pdf
6. Mary Childs and Julie Johnsson, "KKR's TXU Buyout Faces 91% Default Odds in Shale Boom: Corporate Finance," Bloomberg News, January 19, 2012.
7. Devin Banerjee, "KKR Hires RPM's Farley, Rockecharlie to Grow Oil and Gas Investments," Bloomberg News, November 1, 2011.

Chapter 6: Put on Your Boots

1. Jef Feeley, "J. Crew/s $16 Million Settlement over Buyout Approved," Bloomberg News, December 14, 2011.
2. Anne-Sylvaine Chassany, "Private Equity Has $937 Billion in 'Dry Powder,' Preqin Reports," Bloomberg News, October 17, 2011.
3. www.equityhealthcare.com/what_we_do/portfolio_companies.html

Chapter 7: Aura of Cool

1. Devin Banerjee and Cristina Alesci, "Rubenstein Says Carlyle IPO Benefit Is Freeing Up Money to Give to Charity," Bloomberg News, February 1, 2012.
2. Jason Kelly and Will McSheehy, "TPG Sees Itself on 'Tail End' of Buyout IPO Parade," Bloomberg News, December 11, 2007.
3. Jason Kelly, "Bonderman Says TPG Isn't Planning to Go Public Like Rivals," Bloomberg News, February 1, 2012.
4. Adam Bryant, "Deal Maker Takes Aim at Skies," *New York Times*, November 11, 1992. www.nytimes.com/1992/11/11/business/deal-maker-takes-aim-at- skies.html?pagewanted=all&src=pm

Chapter 8: Hundreds and Billions

1. www.pegcc.org/education/pe-by-the-numbers/
2. Jason Kelly and Laura Keeley, "Private Equity Seeks to Avoid Scrutiny as Washington Sets Rules," Bloomberg News, July 27, 2011.
3. "Private Equity Compensation Report Reveals More Good News." Private EquityCompensation.com press release. Distributed via PR Newswire, December 19, 2011.
4. Steven J. Davis et al., *Private Equity and Employment*, U.S. Census Bureau Center for Economic Studies, Paper No. CES-WP-08-07R, October 1, 2011.
5. Ibid.

6. Maeve Reston, "Gingrich, Romney Exchange Blows," *Los Angeles Times*, December 12, 2011.

7. Devin Dwyer, "Axelrod Jabs Gingrich: Higher a Monkey Climbs . . . More You Can See His Butt," Abcnews.com, December 13, 2011. http://abcnews.go.com/blogs/politics/2011/12/axelrod-jabs-gingrich-higher-a-monkey-climbs-more-you-can-see-his-butt/

8. Matthew Mosk and Brian Ross, "Fired Factory Worker Calls Mitt Romney a Job Killer," Abcnews.com, December 28, 2011. http://abcnews.go.com/Blotter/romney-critic-resurfaces/story?id=15244767

9. Peter Lattman, "Bain Defends Itself Amid Attacks on Romney," Nytimes.com, March 13, 2012. http://dealbook.nytimes.com/2012/03/13/bain-defends-itself-amid-attacks-on-romney/?scp=5&sq=bain%20capital&st=cse

10. National Venture Capital Association website. http://nvca.org/index.php?option=com_content&view=article&id=119&Itemid=621

11. Blackstone conference call, July 21, 2011.

12. Transcript, "Can America Get Its Entrepreneurial Groove Back?" Brookings Institution, November 15, 2011. www.brookings.edu/~/media/Files/events/2011/1115_private_capital/20111115_private_capital_panel2.pdf

13. James P. Hoffa, "Wrecking Healthy Companies and Killing Good Jobs Are Lousy Reasons to Get a Tax. Break," *Huffington Post*, April 16, 2010. www.huffingtonpost.com/james-p-hoffa/wrecking-healthy-companie_b_540371.html

14. Service Employees International Union, "Beyond the Buyouts." April 2007. http://gobnf.org/i/wog/behindthebuyouts.pdf

15. Service Employees International Union, "Who Owns Times Square?" Distributed by PR Newswire, July 18, 2007. www.prnewswire.com/news-releases/who-owns-times-square-52748002.html

16. SEIU Local 722, "A Stubborn Union Storms the Gates at Carlyle Group," February 18, 2008. www.seiu722.org/PressReleases/AStubbornUnion.html

17. Michael J. De la Merced, "Protesting a Private Equity Firm (With Piles of Money)," *New York Times Dealbook*. October 10, 2007. http://dealbook.nytimes.com/2007/10/10/protesting-private-equity-with-piles-of-money/

18. Andrew Ross Sorkin, "Is Private Equity Cheating?" Columbia Business School website, February 18, 2008. www4.gsb.columbia.edu/publicoffering/post/131034/Is+Private+Equity+Cheating%3F

19. Michelle Hillman, "Blackstone Group, Boston Janitors Reach Deal," *Boston Business Journal*, August 15, 2007. www.bizjournals.com/boston/stories/2007/08/13/daily27.html

20. Judy Woodruff, "Stern Says Obama Ultimately May Ease Tax Rule," Bloomberg Television, June 23, 2011. www.bloomberg.com/news/2011-06-23/stern-says-obama-ultimately-may-ease-tax-rule-transcript-.html

21. "Union Members Summary," Bureau of Labor Statistics, January 27, 2012. www.bls.gov/news.release/union2.nr0.htm

22. KKR Green Portfolio. http://green.kkr.com

Chapter 9: Take This Exit

1. Kevin Roose, "Decking the Halls, Carlyle Style," *New York Times Dealbook*, December 15, 2011. http://dealbook.nytimes.com/2011/12/15/decking-the-halls-carlyle-style/
2. "Private Equity Principles, Version 2.0," January 2011. http://ilpa.org/index.php?file=/wp-content/uploads/2011/01/ILPA-Private-Equity-Principles-version-2.pdf&ref=http://ilpa.org/principles-version-2-0/&t=1333650254
3. "Transaction and Monitoring Fees: On the Rebound?" Dechert LLP and Preqin, November 2011. www.preqin.com/docs/reports/Dechert_Preqin_Transaction_and_Monitoring_Fees.pdf
4. Ken Hackel, "How Dividends Can Destroy Value," Forbes.com, December 13, 2010. www.forbes.com/sites/kenhackel/2010/12/13/how-dividends-can-destroy-value/3/
5. Michael Barbaro, "After a Romney Deal, Profits and Then Layoffs," *New York Times*, November 12, 2011. www.nytimes.com/2011/11/13/us/politics/after-mitt-romney-deal-company-showed-profits-and-then-layoffs.html?_r=1&scp=1&sq=Dade%20Romney&st=cse
6. Andrew Ross Sorkin, "Romney's Run Puts a Spotlight on Private Equity," *New York Times*, December 12, 2011. http://dealbook.nytimes.com/2011/12/12/romneys-run-puts-spotlight-on-past-job-and-peers/
7. Dan Primack, "A Romney Talking Point That Should Stick," Fortune.com, December 13, 2011. http://finance.fortune.cnn.com/2011/12/13/a-romney-talking-point-that-should-stick/
8. Anne-Sylvaine Chassany, "LBO Firms Leave Backers in Lurch in Secondary Buyouts," Bloomberg News, October 5, 2010.
9. Ibid.
10. Jason Kelly and Jonathan Keehner, "Pension Plans' Private-Equity Cash Depleted as Profits Shrink," Bloomberg News, August 20, 2009.
11. Devin Banerjee, "Carlyle Said to Return Record $15 Billion Ahead of Going Public," Bloomberg News, December 27, 2011.
12. Jason Kelly and Jonathan Keehner, "Pension Plans' Private-Equity Cash Depleted as Profits Shrink."
13. Oliver Gottshalg, "Why More Than 25% of Funds Claim Top Quartile Performance," Buyout Research Program Research Brief, February 2, 2009.
14. Robert S. Harris, Tim Jenkinson, and Steven N. Kaplan, "Private Equity Performance: What Do We Know?" (February 10, 2012). Fama-Miller Working Paper; Chicago Booth Research Paper No. 11-44; Darden Business School Working Paper No. 1932316. Available at SSRN: http://ssrn.com/abstract=1932316 or http://dx.doi.org/10.2139/ssrn.1932316
15. "AIM Program Performance Overview," CalPERS website. www.calpers.ca.gov/index.jsp?bc=/investments/assets/equities/aim/private-equity-review/overview.xml

16. "Oregon Public Employees Retirement Fund Alternative Equity Portfolio." www.ost.state.or.us/FactsAndFigures/PERS/AlternativeEquity/FOIA%20Q3% 202011.pdf
17. Private Equity Growth Capital Council website. www.pegcc.org/education/ pe-by-the-numbers/
18. "Private Equity Glossary." Website of the Center for Private Equity and Entrepreneurship, Tuck School of Business at Dartmouth. http://mba.tuck .dartmouth.edu/pecenter/resources/glossary.html

Chapter 10: The Taxman Cometh

1. Andrew Ross Sorkin, "A Professor's Word on the Buyout Battle," *New York Times Dealbook*, October 3, 2007.
2. Lisa Lerer, "Professor's Proposal Angers Wall Street," *Politico*, October 30, 2007. www.politico.com/news/stories/1007/6594.html
3. Victor Fleischer, "Two and Twenty: Taxing Partnership Profits in Private Equity Funds," *New York University Law Review*, 2008; University of Colorado Law Legal Studies Research Paper No. 06-27; UCLA School of Law, Law-Econ Research Paper No. 06-11. Available at SSRN: http://ssrn.com/ abstract=892440
4. Cristina Alesci and Jason Kelly, "Romney Reports Income from Funds at Goldman Sachs, Golden Gate." Bloomberg News, January 25, 2012.
5. Howard Mustoe, "Don't Criticize Romney's Taxes, Carlyle Group's Rubenstein Says," Bloomberg News, January 25, 2012.
6. Michael Marois and Cristina Alesci, "CalPERS's Dear Calls Private Equity Tax Break 'Indefensible,'" Bloomberg News, February 14, 2012.

Chapter 11: It's a Steve, Steve, Steve World

1. David Carey and John Morris, *King of Capital* (New York: Crown Business, 2012).
2. Alex Pareene, "Billionaire Private Equity Mogul Will Get America Back to Work by Complaining about Government Spending," *Salon*, September 12, 2011. www.salon.com/2011/09/12/schwarzman_dimwit/
3. Matt Taibbi, "A Christmas Message from America's Rich," Rollingstone.com, December 22, 2011. www.rollingstone.com/politics/blogs/taibblog/a-christmas-message-from-americas-rich-20111222
4. Jonathan Alter, "A 'Fat Cat' Strikes Back," *Newsweek*, August 5, 2010. www .thedailybeast.com/newsweek/2010/08/15/schwarzman-it-s-a-war-between-obama-wall-st.html
5. James B. Stewart, "The Birthday Party," *New Yorker*, February 11, 2008.
6. Steve Schwarzman, "An Olive Branch to Obama: I Will Share the Pain," *Financial Times*, September 11, 2011. www.ft.com/cms/s/0/d5a798f8-db10-11e0-bbf4-00144feabdc0.html#axzz1rAzfYUue

7. James B. Stewart, "The Birthday Party."

8. Peter Lattman, "Birthdays Are Still Big in Buyout Land," *New York Times Dealbook*. August 18, 2011. http://dealbook.nytimes.com/2011/08/18/birthdays-are-still-big-in-buyout-land/

9. Craig Karmin, "Blackstone Raises $10 Billion," *Wall Street Journal*, February 24, 2012. http://online.wsj.com/article/SB10001424052970203960804577243352810410114.html

10. Kambiz Foroohar and Bhaktavatsalam, "BlackRock Is Go-To Firm to Divine Wall Street Assets," Bloomberg News, May 8, 2009.

Chapter 12: Not-So-Private Equity

1. Michael De la Merced and Peter Lattman, "Warburg Stays in the Fray, but off the Public Market," *New York Times Dealbook*, August 17, 2011. http://dealbook.nytimes.com/2011/08/17/warburg-stays-in-fray-but-off-public-market/?partner=Bloomberg

2. Nelson D. Schwartz, "Wall Street's Man of the Moment," *Fortune*, March 3, 2007. http://money.cnn.com/magazines/fortune/fortune_archive/2007/03/05/8401261/

Acknowledgments

The roots of this book extend back to February 2007, Groundhog Day to be exact, when the editors at Bloomberg News asked me to take a new assignment in New York. The intervening period was far from the same day over and over again, as that five-year stretch saw the crest of the biggest boom in leveraged buyouts and the biggest crash. It's an amazing beat to cover and I remain grateful for the opportunity.

The book wouldn't be possible without the vision of Evan Burton at John Wiley & Sons, who planted the seed and then helped me run with the idea. Emilie Herman kept me sane throughout the writing and editing process and Donna Martone shepherded it through production.

A huge number of people within Bloomberg News lent invaluable support and counsel, beginning with editor-in-chief, Matt Winkler. I'm grateful to Dan Doctoroff, Bloomberg LP's president and chief executive officer, for his encouragement. Reto Gregori believed in this project from the start, and encouraged me throughout, as did Dan Hertzberg, Rob Urban, Otis Bilodeau, Katherine Snyder, Cesca Antonelli, Karen Toulon, Jennifer Sondag, Tom Contiliano and Marybeth Sandell. Josh Tyrangiel, Bryant Urstadt, and Cynthia Hoffman were instrumental in a

2011 *Bloomberg Businessweek* story on TPG that helped lay the groundwork for the book.

Norm Pearlstine, Ben Cheever, Wendy Naugle, and Gwyneth Ketterer provided invaluable input throughout the writing process that made the final product better.

The U.S. Investing team, whose New York branch is known unofficially as "the Bayou," is a group whose talent and humanity run deep, and I'm especially indebted to Katherine Burton, Saijel Kishan, and Christian Baumgaertel. Larry Edelman, our managing editor, has looked out for me since my first day covering private equity. Cristina Alesci, who was there when the idea was born, has been a great partner on the beat. Devin Banerjee and Sabrina Willmer bravely stepped into the breach so I could pursue this project.

I drew journalistic and moral fortitude from many other colleagues, past and present, including Deirdre Bolton, Jeff McCracken, Mary Jane Credeur, Laura Marcinek, Allison Bennett, Jim Aley, Laura Chapman, Ian King, Beth Jinks, Sharon Lynch, Bob Ivry, Lisa Kassenaar, Robin Wood, David Scheer, Serena Saitto, Zach Mider, Adam Levy, Liz Hester, Jane Seagrave, Jonathan Keehner, Dick Keil, Nora Zimmett, Emma Moody, and Anne-Sylvaine Chassany.

I was granted generous access to firms described in this book, and there were a number of people who put up with a constant barrage of phone calls, e-mails, and visits: Kristi Huller, Peter Rose, Christine Anderson, Chris Ullman, Randy Whitestone, Adam Levine, Tom Franco, Brian Marchiony, Jennifer Zuccarelli, Mary Winn Gordon, Owen Blicksilver, Alex Stanton, Duncan King, Melissa Daly, Ellen Gonda, Suzanne Fleming, and Brooke Gordon. Marshall Mays, Kathy Daw, Lindsey Poff, and Aaron Nagler showed extraordinary patience with me in navigating schedules and locations.

For my personal sanity, I'm grateful to the running club that gathers weekly at Sleepy Hollow High School, especially to Beth Loffredo, who has logged hundreds of miles with me and my neuroses. Kendra and Billy Robins were gracious hosts during my travels west. And there were people and institutions that helped me unwittingly. The Ossining Public Library and the New York Public Library lent picturesque writing spots, while the Drive-by Truckers and R.E.M. provided a daily writing soundtrack.

I come from a sprawling Southern family that's a source of unwavering encouragement. My parents, Dennis and Debby Kelly, nurtured in me a curiosity about business and an appreciation for creativity that led me to become a financial journalist. My brothers Wynne and Sam are my sounding boards and role models, regardless of where in the world they happen to be. Alice and Jack Kane have a knack for knowing I need them, often before I do.

My sons Owen, William, and Henry, are my proudest accomplishments and constant sources of humor and perspective. My deepest gratitude is reserved for my wife, Jennifer. Her love, patience, and intelligence defy description.

J.K.

About the Author

Jason Kelly is a writer with Bloomberg News based in New York who covers the global private equity industry. During his 10 years with Bloomberg, he's also followed the technology industry and written about issues ranging from the aftermath of Hurricane Katrina to economic development during the war in Afghanistan. He's a frequent contributor to Bloomberg Television and *Bloomberg Businessweek*. Prior to joining Bloomberg, he was the editor-in-chief of *digitalsouth* magazine, a publication focused on technology and finance in the Southeast and Texas. Jason started his journalism career at the *Atlanta Journal-Constitution* and the *Atlanta Business Chronicle*. He earned a bachelor's degree from Georgetown University. Jason lives in Sleepy Hollow, New York, with his wife, Jennifer, and their three sons.

Index

Abu Dhabi fund, 16
Abu Dhabi Investment Authority
  (ADIA), 15–16, 36
"Academy companies," 101
Ackman, Bill, 68
ADIA. *See* Abu Dhabi Investment
  Authority (ADIA)
Advanced Micro Devices, 36
AFL-CIO, 124, 131
Agrawal, Raj, 58, 65
Air Partners, 119
Akerson, Daniel, 32–33
Alex. Brown, 24
Alfred E. Smith Foundation Dinner,
  170–173, 194
Alpha, 154
AlpInvest, 37
Altman, Roger, 183
Alvarez & Marsal, 182
American Pad and Paper, 126, 127

Apollo
  Abu Dhabi fund stake in, 16
  backing of Linens 'n' Things, 53
  fund raising prior to IPO, 114
  LeBlanc Teachers' money
    commitment to, 13
  Leon Black sixtieth birthday party,
    173
  on NYSE, 193
  as one of biggest private-equity
    managers, 44
  Teachers' Retirement System of
    Texas and, 153
Apollo Global Management, 44
Arcapita, 17
Ares, 6, 7
Arnold & Porter, 117
Arpey, Michael, 33
Assets under management (AUM)
  Bain & Co. and, 190

Assets under management (AUM)
(*continued*)
Blackstone hedge funds solutions
business, 167
Blackstone real estate business, 179
Carlyle and, 20, 37
Carlyle and Blackstone
engagement in, 195
companies with billions in, 153
Augusta Columbia Capital Group,
183
AUM. *See* Assets under management
(AUM)
Avenue Capital, 118
Axelrod, David, 127

BAAM. *See* Blackstone Alternative
Asset Management (BAAM)
Bae, Joseph, 81
Bain Capital. *See also* Bain & Co.
Mitt Romney as founder of, 126
Romney dispersion of ownership
of, 190
Bain & Co., 98
assets under management, 190
Capstone and, 60
on Dade International deal, 145
on Dollar General deal, 61
Domino's Pizza deal, 101–102
HCA and, 50, 109
jobs created through Domino and
Staples, 128
lineage of operations, 100
partnership with KKR, 50
Baker, James III, 34
Bank of America, 162, 171
Bank United, 162, 183
Barbarians at the Gate (Burrough and
Helyar), 12, 74, 89, 168
Barbaro, Michael, 145

Barrack, Tom, 114, 118, 154
Bass, Robert, 117–118, 119
Bass, Sid, 117, 118, 119
Baucus, Max, 159, 160
Bauer, Eddie, 161
BCE (Bell Canada Enterprises), 6– 7
BDM International, 24, 25
Bear Stearns, 81, 88
Beattie, Richard, 82–83
Beevers, Gary, 188–189
Bell Canada Enterprises (BCE). *See*
BCE (Bell Canada Enterprises)
Ben & Jerry's Ice Cream, 85
Bere, David, 58, 62
Berkshire Hathaway, 68, 108
Beyer, Rich, 52
"Beyond the Buyouts," 132
bin Laden family, 35
Black, Leon, 44, 173
BlackRock:
assets in September 2011, 183
Blackstone Group and, 182–183
BlackRockFink, Laurence, 182
Blackstone Alternative Asset
Management (BAAM), 181
"Blackstone bill," 159
Blackstone Group. *See also* Blackstone
Group acquisitions; James, Tony;
Peterson, Peter G.; Schwarzman,
Steve
advisory group, 181–182
Alternative Asset Management
Business, 181
annual dinner at Daniel, 165–166
diversification plan, 167
Dollar General deal and, 61
Financial Management Group
and, 183
fund raising prior to IPO, 114
going public, 190

headquarters of, 170
Hedge Fund Solutions, 180, 181
IPO of, 40, 159, 189, 190–192
on jobs, 130
New Jersey Investment Council
    deal with, 14–15
number of workers, 123
Oregon agreement with, 5
private equity and, 20, 167–168
real estate business, 177, 179
selling of Prime AmeriSuites
    Hotels, 178
S-1 filing with SEC, 191
takeover of Hilton Hotels, 166,
    175, 177, 178
TPG and, 109
turnover rate, 182
Blackstone Group acquisitions:
    of CNW, 43
    Equity Healthcare and, 109, 179
    of Equity Office Properties, 178,
        190
    of Freescale Semiconductor, 9,
        50–52
    of GSO Capital Partners, 113 , 175
    of Homestead Studio Suites, 177
    New Jersey deal, 184
    of Prime Hospitality, 178
    of UCAR International, 45
Blankfein, Lloyd, 191
Blitzer, David, 175, 176, 184
Bloomberg, Michael, 171
Bloomberg Businessweek, 96
Blue Wave, 39
Board of Overseers, 84
Bode, Clive, 118, 122
Bollenbach, Steve, 23
Bonderman, David, 98. *See also* TPG
    as active environmentalist,
        138–139

Barrack on, 114–115
    as co-founder of TPG, 16
    Continental and, 98, 119
    Coulter, Coslet, and, 112
    joining Robert Bass, 117–118
    qualities of, 122
    sixtieth birthday party, 173
    Teamsters members and, 137
    on TPG IPO issue, 113
Boston Consulting Group, 53, 60
Bower, Marvin, 29
Boyce, Dick, 98–99, 101, 112
Braniff Airlines bankruptcy, 117
Brimberg, Bob, 22
Brown Brothers Harriman, 113
Bruebaker, Gary, 148
Bruno's, 60
Buffett, Warren, 68
Bundy, Greg, 38
Burd, Steven, 104
Burger King, 23, 114
Burnham, Drexel, 44
Burrough, Bryan, 74
Bush, George H. W. (41st
    President), 34
Bush, George W. (43rd
    President), 139
The Business Council, 196

Calbert, Michael, 58, 59, 60–66
California Public Employees
    Retirement System
    (CalPERS), 13
    account arrangement, 184
    alternative investment program, 4
    Blackstone deal with, 15
    Carlyle Group and, 36–37
    commitment to private equity, 151
    Dear as CIO of, 8
    Freescale deal and, 9

CalPERS. *See* California Public
     Employees Retirement System
     (CalPERS)
Cambridge Associates, 150
Canada Pension Plan Investment
     Board (CPP), 8
Capmark, KKR's, 52−53
Capstone consulting firm, 106. *See
     also* Nelson, Dean
   Bain & Co. and, 60
   as division of KKR, 100
   Dollar General deal and, 68−69
   management of, 104
Carey, David, 166
Carlucci, Frank, 24, 34
Carlyle Blue Wave hedge fund, 38
Carlyle Capital Corp. (CCC), 38−39
Carlyle Global Market Strategies
     (Carlyle GMS), 39
Carlyle Group, 1, 100. *See also* Carlyle
     Group acquisitions; Conway,
     Bill; D'Aniello, Daniel;
     Rubenstein, David
   advisors of, 34
   building credit business, 37
   Carlyle Blue Wave hedge fund, 38
   chief officers of, 31
   expansion and broadening of
     adviser base, 35−36
   fund raising prior to IPO, 114
   government relations at, 92
   investors of, 35
   on IPO of, 40−41, 114, 192
   message to investors, 141−142
   Mubadala Development Company
     and, 16, 36−37
   as public company, 193, 195−196
   revisit by founders, 32
   role of Mathias in, 22−23
   roots in Washington, 25
   Service Employees International
     Union and, 133
   takeovers in 2006 and 2007, 29
   transition of responsibilities, 33
   2012 report on corporate
     responsibility, 138
Carlyle Group acquisitions:
   of BDM International, 24
   of Freescale Semiconductor, 9,
     50−52
   of Fresh Fields, 26−27
   of HD Supply, 29
   of Hertz, 107
Carper, Thomas, 188
Carry "Carried interest," 136, 157,
     192, 193
"Carry pool," KKR and, 89
CCC. *See* Carlyle Capital Corp.
     (CCC)
CCMP Capital, 128
CD & R. *See* Clayton Dubilier &
     Rice (CD & R)
Centerbridge Partners, 183
Cerberus, 60
Chambers, Raymond, 22
"Cheap debt," 48
Chemical Bank, 43
Cheyenne Capital, 14
China Investment Corp., 18
Chu, Chinh, 175
Citigroup, 7, 40, 62, 63, 191
Citigroup Deutsche Bank, 38
Clare, Pete, 26
Claremont McKenna, 83
Claren Road hedge fund, Carlyle
     Group and, 37
Clayton Dubilier & Rice (CD & R),
     41, 100, 106−108, 131

Clear Channel Communications, 128
CLOs. *See* Collateralized loan
    obligations (CLOs)
"Clubbing," 9
CNBC, 60
CNW, purchase of, 43
Cohan, William, 46
Coleman, Timothy, 182
Collateralized loan obligations
    (CLOs), 49
Colony Capital, 118, 120, 122, 154
Columbia Business School, 84
Combs, Chris, 188
Competition for deals, returns
    and, 152
Conglomerate, notion of the, 108
Conklin, Deb, 95–99, 109
Continental Airlines, 98, 116, 119
Conway, Bill. *See also* Carlyle Group
    about BDM, 24, 25
    as dealmaker, 26, 29
    educational background of, 26, 29
    Mathias and, 23, 24
    personal life of, 29
    qualities and focus of, 30
    Rubenstein *vs.*, 28–29
CoreTrust, 109
Coslet, Jonathan, 112, 115, 116, 122
Coulter, Jim, 2
    about, 111–112, 114, 115, 118
    Boyce and, 98
    changing his path, 120
    on J. Crew board, 99
    of TPG, 101
    TPG culture and, 121
    TPG's future and, 122
"Covenant lite" loans, 49
CPP. *See* Canada Pension Plan
    Investment Board (CPP)

Credit crisis, 5, 17, 50, 53
Credit-default swaps, 91
Credit Suisse, 40
Cuomo, Andrew, 171

Dade International, 126, 145
D'Aniello, Daniel. *See also* Carlyle
    Group
    about BDM, 24
    as administrator of Carlyle, 26,
      30, 31
    Bill Marriott, Sr. and, 23
    educational background of, 26
    One Carlyle program, 20, 30
Dasburg, John, 23
Davis, Kelvin, 118, 119
Davis, Steven J., 125
Dear, Joseph, 8, 161
Debt:
    during buyout boom, 50
    dividend recap and, 145
    private-equity money and, 45
    use in LBO, 47
Dechert, 143
Default:
    debt, 91
    by private-equity companies,
      52–53
"The Denver Group," 10, 11
Deutsche Bank, 7
DIFC. *See* Dubai International
    Financial Centre (DIFC)
Dimon, Jamie, 44, 109
Diversification, Blackstone Group
    and, 167
Divestitures, of Freescale, 50–52
Dividend recap, 144, 145–146
Dividends, 146
Dodd-Frank legislation, 162

Dolan, Timothy (Archbishop of New York), 172
Dollar General, 89. *See also* Dreiling, Rick
  Family Dollar and, 68
  headquarters of, 56
  100-day plan, 68
  initial public offering (IPO), 70–71
  KKR deal of, 60–63
  KKR theory after the IPO, 147
  recent history of, 57
  remerchandising plan, 69
  return to Big Board, 55
Domino's Pizza, 101–102, 128
Donaldson, Lufkin & Jenrette (DLJ), 174, 175
Doral, 86
Dreiling, Rick. *See also* Dollar General
  in 2009, 55
  accepting the offer of Dollar General, 66
  career of, 56
  insights of Dollar General, 67–68
  meeting Dollar General staff, 58
  offer of Dollar General, 66
  to run Dollar General, 64–65
Drexler, Mickey, 99
"Dry powder," 54
Duane Reade, 66
Dubai, Emirate of, 15
Dubai International Financial Centre (DIFC), 17
Dubilier, Martin, 107
Durant, Katherine, 3

"Easy credit," 48
Economic net income (ENI), 194
Eddie Bauer, 161
Endowments. *See* University endowments

Energy Future, 91, 92
ENI. *See* Economic net income (ENI)
"Enterprise tax," 160
Environmental, social and governance (ESG), 138
Environmental Defense Fund, 139
Equity funds size, 48–49
Equity Healthcare, 109
Equity Office Properties, Blackstone Group and, 60, 177, 178, 190
ESG. *See* Environmental, social and governance (ESG)
Evercore, 183
Exit, 141–154

Fahrenheit 9/11 (documentary), 35
Family Dollar, 68
Fanlo, Saturnino, 87
Farr, Craig, 62, 75, 88, 105
FBR, 83
Ferrell, Will, 28
Financial engineering, 97
Financial Management Group, 183. *See also* Blackstone Group
Financial Times, 169
First Data, 71, 89
First Interstate Bank, 24
First Reserve, 187
Fisher, Todd, 76, 80, 87
Fleischer, Victor, 157
Forbes.com, 144
Ford, 107
Formula One, 36
Forstmann Little, 107
Fortress Investment Group, 191
Fortune, 145, 183, 187, 190
Fred Meyer, 60
Freeman & Co., 48

Freescale Semiconductor, 9, 50–52
Fresh Fields, 27
Friedman, Adena, 31
Gallogly, Mark, 183
GCC. *See* Gulf Cooperation Council (GCC)
General Electric, 124
General Instrument, 33
General Motors, 32
General partners (GPs), 5
Gephardt, Richard, 93
Gerstner, Louis, 33, 35
Gibson Greetings, 21
Gilhuly, Edward "Ned," 87
Gingrich, Newt, 127
Giving Pledge, 27
Glucksman, Lew, 167
GNC, Ontario Teachers' Pension Plan and, 6
Gogel, Don, 107
Golden Gate Capital, 160
Goldman Sachs, 62, 92
    Blankfein to run, 191
    as private bank, 113
    private-equity fund, 162
    as provider of debt for LBO, 47, 63
    Romney funds management, 160
    Taibbi description of, 168
Goltz, Frederick, 77, 78–79, 80, 82
Goodman, Bennett, 175
Gottschalg, Oliver, 129–130, 148
GPs. *See* General partners (GPs)
Grady, Robert, 14
Grand Canyon Trust, 138, 139
Grand Central Terminal, 117
Grassley, Chuck, 159
Gray, Jonathan, 175, 176, 177, 178
Grayken, John, 118
Green Portfolio, 139

GRR. *See* Roberts, George
GSO Capital Partners
    Blackstone deal of, 113, 163, 179–180
    James proposal of acquisition of, 175
Gulf Cooperation Council (GCC), 15, 17

Hackel, Ken, 144
"Hall of Values," 56
Haltiwanger, John, 125
Hance, James, 35
Harper, Neil, 146
Harris, Britt, 10, 84
Harris, Joshua, 44
Harris, Robert, 150
HCA, 50, 59, 109
HD Supply, 29, 107
Hedge Fund Solutions (Tom Hill's group), 180
Helyar, John, 74
Henry R. Kravis Prize for Leadership, 83
Hertz, 107
High-yield debt market, 49
Hilex, 96, 97, 98
Hilex Poly, 96
Hill, J. Tomilson, 167
Hill, Tom:
    on Blackstone board, 175
    Hedge Fund Solutions, 180
    to run Alternative Asset Management business, 181
Hilton Hotels, 3
    Blackstone and, 23, 166, 175, 178
    deal, in mid-2007, 53
    Gray and deal of, 177
    Nassetta to run, 178–179
    outside the U.S. in 2012, 178
Hoffa, James, 132

Holt, Allan, 25
Home Depot, 148
Homestead Studio Suites, 177
Host Marriott, 179
Houlihan Lokey, 182
Howard, Bob, 163
HRK. *See* Kravis, Henry
Huffington Post, 132

IBM, 107
IHS Global Insight, 130
ILPA, 8, 11–12, 135, 138, 143
ILPA Private Equity Principles, 8
IndyMac, 162
Institutional Limited Partners
    Association (ILPA). *See* ILPA
Intel, 51
InterFinancial Ltd., 39
Internal Rate of Return (IRR),
    147–148
International Mining Machinery, 104
Intersil, 52
Investment banks, 49
IRR. *See* Internal Rate of Return
    (IRR)

J. Crew, 99, 109, 116
James, Tony, 15. *See also* Blackstone
    Group
  appointing Blitzer, 184
  cutting the deal with Oregon, 5
  hiring people from DLJ, 174–175
  on maturity of investments, 145
  meeting with Oregonians, 2–3
  proposal for acquisition of GSO,
    175
  on refinery reopening occasion,
    187–188
  role of, 169
  work habits and drive, 174

Jarmin, Ron S., 125
Jenkinson, Tim, 150
Jenrette, Richard, 174
Jeramaz-Larson, Kathy, 11
Job creation, 125
Job destruction/loss, 125–126
Johnson, Magic, 81
Johnson, Randy, 127, 128
Jordan, Jay, 102, 103–104, 152
The Jordan Company, 103
JPMorgan, 44, 47, 74, 117, 162
JPMorgan Chase, 40, 109
Juma Ventures, 85
Jumper, John, 36
Junk bond funds, 49

Kaplan, Steven, 149–150
Kaye, Charles, 190
KB Toys, 126, 128
KCM, 88
Kennedy, Edward, 127
KFN. *See* KKR Financial
Kiggen, Jamie, 183
King of Capital (Carey and Morris),
    166
KKR, 3, 4, 12, 13. *See also* Capstone
    consulting firm; Dollar General;
    KKR acquisitions; KKR
    takeovers; Kravis, Henry;
    Roberts, George; TXU
  annual revenues in 2010, 124
  Capmark, 52–53
  changes at, 87
  in Dubai, 17
  Farr and, 62
  filing S-1 on July 3, 192
  gaining and loosing money, 59–60
  Green Portfolio and, 139
  headquarters of, 74–75
  Hoffa on, 132

Knowlton advice about, 83
LeBlanc Teachers' money
  commitment to, 13
Menlo Park office, 84–85
Nelson at, 105
number of workers, 123
on NYSE, 193
private equity of, 20
Teachers' Retirement System of
  Texas and, 153
TPG and, 92
report on ESG issues, 138
KKR acquisitions:
  deals from 2005 to 2007, 89
  deals in 2006, 59
  Dollar General deal, 58, 59,
    60–63
  of HCA, 50, 59, 109
  Regal Cinemas deal, 105–106
  Safeway deal, 59
KKR Capital Markets, 70
KKR Financial, 87
KKR Millennium Fund, 152
KKR Private Equity Investors, 90
KKR takeovers:
  of RJR Nabisco, 50, 74, 76
  of Samson Investment Co., 53
Knowlton, David, 82
Kohlberg, Jerome (Jerry),
  73, 81, 107
Kohlberg Kravis Roberts & Co.
  See KKR
KPE. See KKR Private Equity
  Investors
Krause, William, 35
Kravis, Henry, 1, 12, 17. See also
  KKR
  business changes and
    opportunities, 87
  on culture of KKR, 88–89

elevation of Fisher, 80
interviews with KKR executives,
  81–82
Knowlton and, 82–83
last day at the firm, 81
meeting with Roberts, 86
multi-faceted approach,
  86–87
pension and, 4
philanthropy and, 83–84
relationship with Roberts,
  75–76, 77
selling shares in Europe, 90
startup of KKR, 73
vetting of Dreiling, 65–66
Kravis, Marie-Josée, 74, 83, 84

Labor unions, 131, 132
Lafley, A. G., 107
Lambert Inc., 44
Landy, Joseph, 190
Lasry, Marc, 118
Latham & Watkins, 79
Lazard Ltd., 61
LBO. See Leverage buyout (LBO)
Leahy, Terence, 107
Leary, Marty, 135–136
LeBlanc, Steve, 10–14, 157
Lee, Jimmy, 74, 167, 171
  at Chemical Bank, 44
  debt stack and, 47
  purchase of CNW, 43
  relationship with private
    equity, 45
Leech, Jim, 7, 8
Lehman Brothers, 17, 166, 167
Lenovo, 115
Lerner, Josh, 125, 131
Lerner, Stephen, 133
Leverage, 45

Leverage buyout (LBO), 6
  in 2007 and 2012, 53, 89
  boom of 2005 to 2007, 48
  debt committed to, 50
  default rates of, 53
  Equity Office Properties, 190
  global credit crisis and, 5
  HCA deal, 50
  job destruction and, 125−126
  providers of debts for, 47
  returns in 1990s, 6
Levin, Sander, 159, 160
Levine, Adam, 92
Levitt, Arthur, 35−36
Lewis, Kenneth, 134
Lexmark, 107
Liddy, Edward, 107
Light, Jay, 175
Limited Partners (LPs), 4, 5, 192−193
Linens 'n' Things, 53
Lipschultz, Marc, 81, 91
Lister, Thomas, 154
Loews Corporation, 108
Lone Star Capital, 118
Loral, 24
LPs. See Limited Partners (LPs)
LVMH Moet Hennessy Louis
    Vuitton, 83

Madison Dearborn, 7
Major, John, 34
Manor Care, 133
Marchick, David, 31, 32, 33, 92
Mark, Joncarlo, 12
Markell, Jack, 188
Marriott, Bill, Jr., 23
Marriott, Bill, Sr., 23
Mathias, Ed:
  Carlyle Group and, 22
  on Conway and D'Aniello, 30

Mayer, Michael, 52
McKillickan, Rebecca, 69
McKinsey & Co., 29, 60
Mehlman, Kenneth, 92, 139
Mergers and Acquisitions (M & A)
    activity, 48
Merrill Lynch, 7
Metropolitan Museum
    of Art, 84
Meyer, Andre, 24
Mezzanine loans, 175, 178
Michelson, Michael, 79
Milken, Michael, 44
Miller, Bill, 22
Miranda, Javier, 125
Moelis & Company, 182
MOIC. See Multiple of invested
    capital (MOIC)
Monaghan, Thomas, 101−102
Monitoring fees, 143
Moore, Michael, 35
Moran, Garrett, 174
Morelli, Vincenzo, 98
Morgan Stanley, 113 162, 146
Morris, John, 166
Motorola, 50−51
Mount Sinai Hospital, 84
Moynihan, Brian, 171
Mubadala Development Company,
    16, 36−37
Mulroney, Brian, 175
Multiple of invested capital (MOIC),
    151, 153, 176
Murray, Steve, 128

Nassetta, Chris, 178, 179
National Venture Capital
    Association, 130
Nature Conservancy, 138
Navab, Alexander, 79

Nelson, Dean:
  as head of Capstone, 69
  KKR recruitment of, 60,
    104–105
  Regal Cinemas deal, 105–106
New Jersey, commitment to
  Blackstone, 14
New Jersey Investment Council, 14
New Jersey pension plan, 184
Newman, Arthur, 182
Newman, Howard, 154
Newsweek, 168
New York City Investment Fund, 84
New Yorker, 172
New York's Museum of Modern
  Art, 84
New York Times, 128, 133, 145,
  157, 172
New York University Law Review, 157
Nexio, 138
Noninvestment-grade bonds (junk
  bonds), 44
Norris, Steven, 23
Norton, Ed, 138
Novy-Marx, Robert, 9
Nunnelly, Mark, 101–102, 190
Nuttall, Scott, 12, 77–78

Obama Administration, 130, 157
Occupy Wall Street movement, 47,
  132, 155, 172
OMG. *See* Operations Management
  Group (OMG)
Ontario Teachers Pension Plan:
  on BCE purchase, 6–7
  hybrid model of, 8
  private equity industry and, 6
Operations Management Group
  (OMG), 103
Ops function, 104

Oregon, state of:
  Blackstone and, 5
  KKR at, 151–152
  Pension fund investment, 2, 4
Oregon Treasurers office, 2
Ostrover, Doug, 175
"Out of the Storm but Not out of the
  Woods" (2012 conference), 41

Parrett, William, 175
Partnership for New York City, 84
PBF Energy, 187
PCRI. *See* Private Capital Research
  Institute (PCRI)
Peltz, Nelson, 68
Pension fund investment (Oregon), 2
Pensions, internal rate of return
  and, 148
Pensions, limited partners and, 4–5
Perdue, David, 61, 64
Permira, 9, 51, 154
Perry, Rick, 127
Peterson, Pete, 191
Peterson, Peter G., 174. *See also*
  Blackstone Group
  benefits of Blackstone IPO, 113
  as co-founder of Blackstone, 27
  positions at Lehman Brothers, 167
  retirement from Blackstone, 166
Petrick, Mitch, 31, 37, 38, 39–40
Petroff, Neil, 8
Pincus, Lionel, 190
Pine Brook Partners, 154
Pitchbook, 53
Plumeri, Joseph, 82
PNC Bank, 183
Portfolio Operations Group, 109
Premira, purchase of Freescale, 51
Preqin, 143, 148, 150
Pressler, Paul, 107

Price, Bill, 119
Primack, Dan, 35, 145, 146
Prime AmeriSuites hotels, 178
Prime Hospitality, 178
Private Capital Research Institute (PCRI), 131
Private-equity, 10, 142. *See also* Private-equity firms; Private-equity industry; Private-equity managers
  in 2006 and 2007, 59
  in 2010 and 2011, 52
  banks and, 47–48
  Blackstone and, 20, 167–168
  California Public Employees Retirement System commitment to, 151
  internal rate of return and, 147–148
  M & A deals and, 48
  protests and, 155–156
  in the public eye, 187–189
  Service Employees International Union criticism of, 132, 136–137
"Private Equity and Employment" (Davis, Haltiwanger, Jarmin, Lerner, and Miranda), 125
Private-equity backers, 148
Private Equity Council, 158, 159
Private-equity deals, 66
Private-equity executives, 124, 128, 130
Private-equity firms, 7, 9, 13, 108
  business of, 97
  defaults by, 52–53
  ESG and, 138
  on job creation, 128, 130
  number in 2011, 154

  number of employees in USA, 123
  performance of, 148
  publicly traded, 192
  purchase of companies and, 45–46
  recouping initial investment, 144
  returns and number of, 152
  selling to, 146
  Teamsters and, 132
  TPG as, 120–121
Private-equity funds, 142
  funds in, 144
  investors and, 148
Private Equity Growth Capital Council, 128, 153, 162
Private-equity industry, 16
  in 2009, 159–160
  debt and, 54
  early, 100
  jobs and, 126–130
  in Manhattan, 2
  Ontario Teachers Pension Plan and, 6
  Oregon and, 4
  Romney tax returns and, 160
  tax deductibility of debt, 46
  Washington and, 4, 157–158
Private-equity managers:
  Denver Group meeting and, 10
  on dividend recaps, 144–145, 146
  justification of fees, 142
  money flowing to, 143
  profits of, 4
  on tax treatment, 158
  use of leverage and, 45
  Warburg Pincus, 190
Private-equity money, 45
Private-equity tax, 156
Private-label project, Dollar General and, 69

"Proprietary deal," 100–101
Providence Equity, 7
Publicly traded partnership, 159
Public pensions, in United States, 8, 9
Public-to private deals, 126

Qualcomm, 51
Quellos, James, 109
Quinn, Thomas, 103

Raether, Paul, 78, 80
Rainwater, Richard, 118
Randalls, 59
Raptors, 6
Rauh, Joshua, 9
Ray, Wes, 107
REDF. See Roberts Enterprise
    Development Fund (REDF)
Regal Cinemas, 89, 105–106
Rice, Joseph, 41, 107, 131
Riverside Co., 183
RJR Nabisco, 50, 74, 76, 89, 168
R.L. Turner & Son Wholesale, 56, 59
Robert M. Bass Organization, 115,
    118, 119
Roberts, George, 12, 62. See also
    KKR
  on being in public eye, 92–93
  business changes and
    opportunities, 87
  as co-founder of KKR, 3–4, 73
  on culture of KKR, 88–89
  elevation of Fisher, 80
  Goltz and, 78
  interviews with KKR executives,
    81–82
  multi-faceted approach, 86–87
  personality of, 85
  philanthropy and, 85

relationship to Kravis, 75–76
Roberts Enterprise Development
    Fund, 85–86
  selling shares in Europe, 90
  vetting of Dreiling, 65, 66
Roberts Enterprise Development
    Fund (REDF), 85
Roehm, Carolyn, 83
Rolling Stone (Taibbi), 168
Romney, Mitt, 150
  Bain deals and candidacy of,
    126–129
  dispersion of Bain ownership, 190
  dividend recaps in 2011, 145
  on Domino's Pizza, 101
  tax as defining issue for, 156
  tax returns of, 160–161
Rowan, Marc, 44
Royal Ahold, 107
Rubenstein, David, 1. See also Carlyle
    Group
  Conway vs., 28
  as fund raiser, 26, 34–35
  on IPO, 113
  as keynote speaker at Columbia
    conference, 41–42
  on leaving Carlyle, 33–34
  Mathias and, 22
  mien and role in Carlyle Group,
    20–21, 26, 30
  on One Carlisle program, 20, 26
  personal disclosure and as
    philanthropist, 27–28
  purchase of Fresh Fields and, 27
  SEIU and, 133
  on speeches of, 19–20, 161
  staff recruitment, 39
  on Super Return Middle East,
    16–17

Safeway, 59, 89, 104
Salon (online magazine), 168
Samson Investment Co., 53
Samsonite, 6
Savings and loan crisis, 118
Schloss, Lawrence, 14
Schoar, Antoinette, 150
Schorr, Chip, 183
Schreiber, John, 176, 179
Schwarzman, Steve, 1, 90, 100, 155.
    See also Blackstone Group;
    Blackstone Group acquisitions
  at The Alfred E. Smith Foundation
    Dinner, 171–173
  appointing Blitzer, 184
  background and wealth, 169
  Blackstone shares and, 195
  deal with China, 18
  declaration of end of credit
    crisis, 17
  earning before Blackstone IPO, 41
  on hedge fund business, 181
  on IPO, 113
  James as successor of, 175
  M & A advice division, 163
  op-ed headline in Financial
    Times, 169
  participation in public calls, 92
  philanthropy of, 170, 171
  process of Oregon and, 5
  Salon magazine about, 168
SEIU. See Service Employees
    International Union (SEIU)
Senior debt, 47
September 11, 2001, 34, 35
Service Employees International
    Union (SEIU), 132–134,
    136–137
Shearson Lehman Holding
    Company, 180

Simon, William E., 21
Simpson Thacher, 82
Slavkin, Heather, 124, 131
Smith, Al, 171
Smith, Tripp, 175
Smith dinner, 171
Solotar, Joan, 174
Sonneborn, William, 77– 78, 79,
    82, 87
Sorkin, Andrew Ross, 134, 145
Sovereign wealth fund
    (SWF), 112
Spitzer, Eliot, 171
"Staple financing," 49
Staples, 128
Sterba, George, 137–138
Stern, Andy, 93, 132, 133,
    134–135, 139
Stewart, James B., 169, 172
Stop and Shop, 59
Stromberg, Per, 53
Stuart, Scott, 87
Studzinski, John (Studz), 181
Summit Properties, 10
SunGard Data Systems, 89
Super Return Middle East, 17
SWF. See Sovereign wealth fund
    (SWF)

T. Rowe, 24
Taibbi, Matt, 168
TCW, 78
Teachers' Retirement System of
    Texas, 10, 13, 153
Tehle, David, 58, 61, 70
Texas Instruments, 51
Texas Pacific Group. See TPG
Texas Teachers, 13, 157
The Texas Way, 12, 13
"The Birthday Party," 172

"The triumph of Blackstone on Wall
    Street" (Fortune), 183
Thomas H. Lee Partners, 128
Three Ocean Partners, 83
Tigard, 2, 4
Times, 145
Toronto-Dominion, 7
Toronto Maple Leafs, 6
Toys "R" Us, 60, 89, 132
TPG, 1, 7, 9, 16, 45, 90. *See also*
    Bonderman, David; Coulter, Jim
    Blackstone and, 109
    Boyce at, 98
    Burger King and, 23, 114
    Conklin at, 97
    Coulter and, 101, 111–112
    culture of, 114, 117, 121
    Freescale Semiconductor
        acquisition, 50–52
    J. Crew deal and, 99
    KKR and, 92
    KKR Dollar General deal and,
        61, 62
    Norton as senior adviser of, 139
    operations of, 100
    "ops" group, 96
    as private-equity firm, 120–121
    strategy prior to IPO, 114
    on succession, 121–122
    takeover of TXU, 116
TPG-Axon (hedge fund), 120
Transaction fees, 143
Turner, Cal Jr., 56, 57, 61
Turner, Cal Sr., 56, 57
Turner, R.L., 56
"2 and 20 structure," 156
TXU, 138
    buyout boom of 2007 and takeover
        of, 116
    natural gas prices and, 91

as record-setting LBO, 7, 45, 59,
    71, 90
regulatory approval and deal of, 92

U. S. Congress/Washington:
    "Blackstone bill," 159
    Private Equity Growth Capital
        Council and, 162
    private-equity industry and,
        157–158, 159
UCAR International, 45
United Nations Principles for
    Responsible Investing (UNPRI),
    138
United States, public pensions in, 8, 9
Unit Here, 135
University endowments, 4–5
Univision, 109
UNPRI. *See* United Nations
    Principles for Responsible
    Investing (UNPRI)
US Foods, 107, 131–132
US Food-service, 106

Valerus Compression, 97
Venture capital industry, 130
Venture Economics, 150
VentureXpert, 148
Vintage funds, 151
Vintage years, private-equity funds
    and, 149
Vogelstein, John, 190
Volcker, Paul, 162
Volcker Rule, 162
Vornado, 60

"Wall of debt," 50
Wall Street, 181
Wall Street Journal, 49
Wal-Mart, 123

WaMu. *See* Washington Mutual (WaMu)

Warburg Pincus, 154, 190

Washington Mutual (WaMu), 116– 117

Washington State Investment Board, 48

Watch Hill Partners, 83

Waxman, Alan, 122

Waxman joined, 122

Welch, Jack, 107

Wellington Capital Management, 62

WesRay, 21

White Rose Crafts & Nursery Sales, 6

Wilds, David, 61

Willis, 82

Wiseman, Mark, 8

Woody Allen approach, 20

Yellow Pages Group (Canada), 6

Youngkin, Glenn, 25
  on Bill Conway, 29–30
  focus and recommendations on Carlyle's issues, 31–32